BELIEVING

ALSO BY ANITA HILL

*Reimagining Equality: Stories of Gender,
Race, and Finding Home*

Speaking Truth to Power

BELIEVING

OUR THIRTY-YEAR JOURNEY TO
END GENDER VIOLENCE

ANITA HILL

VIKING

VIKING
An imprint of Penguin Random House LLC
penguinrandomhouse.com

Library of Congress Cataloging-in-Publication Data

Names: Hill, Anita, author.
Title: Believing : our thirty-year journey to end gender violence / Anita Hill.
Description: New York : Viking, [2021] |
Includes bibliographical references and index.
Identifiers: LCCN 2021024489 (print) | LCCN 2021024490 (ebook) |
ISBN 9780593298299 (hardcover) | ISBN 9780593298305 (ebook)
Subjects: LCSH: Sexual harassment of women—United States. |
Women—Violence against—United States. | Sexual abuse victims—
United States. | Abused women—United States. | Violence—United States. |
Women—United States—Social conditions.
Classification: LCC HQ1237.5.U6 H55 2021 (print) |
LCC HQ1237.5.U6 (ebook) | DDC 305.420973—dc23
LC record available at https://lccn.loc.gov/2021024489
LC ebook record available at https://lccn.loc.gov/2021024490

Printed in the United States of America
1   3   5   7   9   10   8   6   4   2

DESIGNED BY MEIGHAN CAVANAUGH

Believing is dedicated to my mentors and friends, Lillian Miles Lewis, Sydney Goldstein, Donald H. Green, A. Leon Higginbotham, Jr., and Ada Lois Sipuel Fisher and to the many pioneers in the struggle against gender violence.

CONTENTS

Preface		*xi*
INTRODUCTION: BOILING THE OCEAN		1
1.	OUR STATE OF DENIAL	15
2.	FROZEN	45
3.	A "RECURRENT FEATURE OF OUR SOCIAL EXPERIENCE"	63
4.	THE MYTH OF THE WOKE GENERATION	75
5.	INSTITUTIONAL NEGLECT	111
6.	THE MILLENNIAL WORKPLACE	141
7.	A WOMAN'S WORTH: REPRESENTATION, VIOLENCE, AND EQUALITY	165
8.	VICTIM SHAMING	213
9.	POLITICS: RAGE, COMPROMISES, AND BACKLASH	261
10.	ACCOUNTABILITY	291
	Acknowledgments	307
	Notes	311
	Index	325

PREFACE

finished the first chapter of *Believing* in 2020. But work on the book began years before.

Four months after I testified before Congress in October 1991, in what one commentator described as a wretched slanderous race and gender scandal, the Clarence Thomas confirmation hearing, I was at a crossroads. I had to decide whether to respond to appeals for clarity on the issue of sexual harassment or continue trying to take back my pre-hearing life as a law professor. From the time of my upbringing on a farm, work had played a large role in who I was. Though the civil rights movement had inspired me to get a law degree, I envisioned myself as an educator, not as a crusader. Neither charismatic nor a gifted speaker, I did not fit the stereotype of a movement leader. Two conversations that I had during a trip to Atlanta helped open my eyes to a new possibility.

That day in February 1992, in the house of the president of Spelman College, I had the privilege of meeting two civil rights veterans.

The first was Lillian Miles Lewis, a spirited intellectual and strategic thinker. Lewis was a university librarian whose interests were global. She was also married to Congressman John Lewis; she had helped to shape his political path and worked on civil rights issues in Atlanta. Over breakfast, Lillian convinced me of the importance of having a Black woman's voice in the public conversation about gender equality. This was my first conversation with her, but it would not be my last, as our friendship and her counsel continued until Lillian's death in 2012. With the morning's second visitor to President Johnnetta Betsch Cole's Spelman home, the conversation took a surprising turn. Andrew Young, former Atlanta mayor and UN ambassador, reminisced about the early days of the civil rights movement. He gave an account of Dr. King's decision to take on a leadership role "which was not of his choosing" but was one that was dictated by the urgency of the problems facing Blacks in the United States. Then, referring to his two daughters, Young shared his personal interest in ending harassment. His message went to the heart of my misgivings about taking an active role in the public conversation on sexual harassment. Nevertheless, Young, a minister, reminded me that the dilemma I faced was mine to pray about and resolve.

As I returned home to Oklahoma, the weight of the decision I needed to make was heavy. But the barrage of calls and letters I'd received and the conversations that continued for months convinced me that, as a victim and a teacher, I had a unique perspective to speak from. I would not dwell on being the perfect leader; my biggest challenge was getting the message about the harm of the behavior right. I made what I thought would be a two-year commitment to ending sexual harassment. While I hadn't chosen the topic, I chose the path I would take to pursue a solution to it.

All the answers weren't in my law books or in my job at the University of Oklahoma College of Law. As the first African American to be tenured at the state's only law school, I was a symbol of progress for the school's dean, David Swank, a staunch sponsor, as well as many colleagues, students, and alums. Yet my relationship with David Boren, the university president, was fraught even before he took the job in 1994. In 1991, when Boren was an Oklahoma senator, my senator, he voted to confirm Clarence Thomas. And by 1995, Boren's hesitation to meet with me about my future at the university convinced me that he would frown upon my taking a public stand against ending sexual harassment.

If leaving a tenured position felt like an enormous career risk, leaving Oklahoma and my family felt foolhardy. My parents and twelve siblings were the source of love and care that I could depend on in every aspect of my life, before, during, and after 1991. For ten years, I'd lived within a two-hour drive from my parents' home. Would the answers that I was looking for in my work be worth uprooting my entire life and risking the ties I had to the people I loved the most? Even asking the questions made me wonder if I was cut out to devote my life to such an immense calling.

However, I held on to the belief that change, monumental change, was called for and that I had a role to play in it. So despite my trepidation, I accepted an offer for a full-time position at Brandeis University and moved to Massachusetts in 1999. But I craved the familiar. Once I nested in my circa 1887 house with its creaky floors and horsehair plaster walls, I realized, without a doubt, that I wasn't in Oklahoma anymore. Nothing in New England says prairie, not the houses, the trees, the weather, or even the sky. I missed my family terribly—my parents were in their eighties by then. But I found a community that would help me grow my work. And best of all, I fell in love with a man who would come to support and share my passion for it. Though Chuck's pronounced Boston accent was not the familiar sound I longed for, the effort he made to connect with my family sealed our relationship.

By 2010, I had settled into my life in the Boston area. The Thomas hearing hadn't faded from my memory—it never will—but it had receded. Yet in the months leading up to the twentieth anniversary of my testimony, I found myself wondering whether it still mattered. Filmmaker Freida Mock convinced me that it did and that she was the person who could make a film that would show how it mattered. Mock began the production of *Anita: Speaking Truth to Power.* Her interviews helped me to focus on the hearing in ways that I had not done in years. Recalling the event was often painful but cathartic. Hindsight and years of perspective offered some clarity on the issues raised during and after my testimony. But an event at Hunter College on October 8, 2011, would show me the true legacy of that inquisition. As Freida was filming, a group of women were separately organizing a program that would commemorate the anniversary of the judiciary committee's hearing.

Law professor Patricia Williams and philanthropist and businesswoman Deborah Slaner Larkin, both of whom I'd known for decades, were joined by journalist Letty Cottin Pogrebin and civil rights attorney Kathleen Peratis in planning the daylong conference. With the help of Amy Richards and Cynthia Greenberg, all the details fell into place. When I entered the General Assembly Hall on the Hunter campus, I found myself surrounded by peers, including Charles Ogletree, Kimberlé Crenshaw, and Judith Resnick, and supporters of all ages. The age range of the people present was striking. Earlier, I had spoken at a program at Georgetown University Law Center, where the audience, mostly scholars and older students, looked back at the hearing.

My friends, Professors Emma Coleman Jordan and Beverly Guy-Sheftall had organized the event. It felt familiar. The diversity of the audience at Hunter was both affirming and daunting. Would my experience resonate with the people in the audience who were born after the hearing? The four organizers were members of a generation that had been second-wave feminism initiates, and who had helped give rise to the third and emerging fourth waves. For the second morning panel, these astute veteran feminists brought together activists, scholars, and artists who had launched their work in the twenty years since the hearing.

Rha Goddess, JoAnne Smith, Emily May, Ai-Jen Poo, and Melissa Harris-Perry were their generation's stars in the movement to end gender violence. They were working in ways that I had not imagined in 1991. As each panelist spoke about what the hearing had meant to them, I knew that I was witnessing the legacy of the hearing. Backlash against gender equity in the 1990s had disabused me of the idea that the race to equality was a sprint. So, over the years, I resigned myself to the idea that the struggle was more of a marathon. But this panel and the evening event, a stage performance produced by the inimitable V (formerly Eve Ensler), helped me to understand that the race—the struggle—is a relay. A new generation would come along and mine would pass the baton to them. To this day, I don't have the words to say how much the event at Hunter meant to me. The entire occasion was electric and sparked new energy for my teaching and my advocacy. Relay notwithstanding, there was no reason for me to relax. I hadn't finished my leg.

I sat in front of a computer in 2019 and began writing *Believing*. Months later, in February 2020, the world faced unfathomable prospects of morbidity from the coronavirus. In March, I traveled to Oklahoma for a sister's eightieth birthday. The day I returned, Massachusetts went into quarantine. At first, as we faced deaths as well as medical and food shortages, ending gender-based violence seemed ancillary.

As the pandemic became more ominous, the events that followed brought clarity to a number of issues. COVID-19's deep toll on the health of people and communities of color, the killings of Breonna Taylor and George Floyd, anti-Asian attacks, poor students' lack of access to technology for virtual learning, and the rapid drop in the number of women in the paid workforce alerted us to the urgency of addressing social injustices. With John Lewis's death in the middle of the pandemic, fear turned to despair. But with the massive anti-racism marches and protests of the summer came new calls for change and accountability for longstanding racial and gender inequities.

Soon the pandemic's relationship to gender violence began to show itself. The increased risk of violence when people are quarantined at home or in institutions fell most heavily on women and children, who are also more likely to be exposed to harm because of food shortages. Resources for mental health services, legal aid, and law enforcement to address it fell short. Shelters for victims and survivors could not keep up with the demand. These are the gender-violence consequences of the pandemic we know about, and we anticipate others will emerge. For example, pre-pandemic data shows a correlation between teens viewing pornography and dating violence. So we can expect that the pandemic surge in people of all ages watching violent pornography will increase the rate of dating violence among young people.

There are certainly enough "bad apples" deserving of accountability and full exposure for their abusive behavior. I commend the cascade of books and articles that have only begun to do this work. I hope support for these narratives continue. They inform us about the depth of the violence. In addition to sharing some of these stories, in *Believing*, I focus on gender-based violence as a systemic problem. Politicians, courts, schools, and private industry have acted in concert to undermine efforts to quell the varied and complex forms of gender violence. Cultural acceptance of misogyny, often in the form of entertainment, lulls us into believing that harm motivated by a victim's sex or gender expression is normal and inevitable. Historic and contemporary versions of racism, homophobia, and patriarchy offer the behavior refuge, just as misogyny harbors racism and homophobia. If we are to get to the bottom of this problem, we must let go of the familiar, often inconsistent ways we convince ourselves that the problem is individual, personal, not so bad, unsolvable, the fault of victims, or easily fixed if women come forward. We must acknowledge that gender violence is systemic and accept that the familiar solutions we've been offered to end the scourge are inadequate. Acutely embedded systemic cultural problems will not be cured by ad hoc, tepid solutions that, at best, only help a small percentage of victims. Comprehensive responses are required. And the powerful people in public and private leadership roles need to take responsibility for implementing those responses.

Though my parents and four brothers have passed since I moved away from Oklahoma, my surviving siblings and I, as we have aged, enjoy a closeness that defies physical distance and now the quarantine. As I write, my brothers, my sisters, and my ninety-six-year-old cousin forgive my lack of availability for long phone calls and frequent visits home. But we've figured out how to stay close to one another. And during the pandemic, my need for their support reached new levels. In April 2020, Chuck's doctor delivered a grim prognosis for the cancer he had battled for over a decade. Chuck faced his mortality with grace and courage. It was all I could bear to hear him ask the doctor what he should expect in his final days. When either of us was down, we talked it out. I tried to match his bravery.

As with everything that matters in my life, I called my family about the conversation Chuck and I had had with his doctor. My brothers and sisters were always there for me and for Chuck, to talk about the disease or to not talk about it, whichever seemed best in that moment. My sisters started a prayer chain. Their faith sustained when mine wavered.

I wanted to put the book aside, to be available no matter what, as his doctor proposed new therapies. But Chuck wouldn't have it. Even with his health challenges, Chuck's commitment to the book was beyond anything I might have dreamed. He sought out, read, curated, marked, reported on, and placed under my nose every news account of gender violence. Chuck began a new treatment. It did not improve his condition and neither did a second. But some months later, after a third treatment, the doctor revised his forecast. Instead of months, we again started to look forward to years together. We know how privileged we are. The pandemic taught us that. Chuck and I are forever grateful for the medical science that enabled his progress and our ability to access it. There aren't enough words to thank the loved ones who cared for and supported us through this period and made it possible to finish this book.

Believing could not have been written without including the stories I've heard and learned about over the years. In describing accounts of gender-based violence, I've attempted to be sensitive to and respectful of victims' and survivors' dignity. In a few cases, I've changed victims' names or used only first names. Some of the accounts are graphic and heartbreaking. Readers may find some content retraumatizing.

Boiling the Ocean

am by nature a very private person, raised by a mother who was extremely private. People meeting my mother for the first time usually mistook her quietness for arrogance. "They call me stuck-up," my mother would say. "But I'm not," she insisted. As an adult, I came to realize that this incredibly strong-willed mother of thirteen was shy. When she was sure of something, we all knew it and there was little chance of winning an argument with her. By "we," I mean my father, my twelve siblings, and me. She was barely five feet two inches, remaining slight even after she gained weight in her middle age, but she seemed to tower over us. Her position as the youngest daughter of her farming parents' fourteen children and the determined woman who, from the day she married my easygoing father at sixteen, farmed alongside him to support our large family seemed at odds with her shyness and her insistence on personal privacy. Life on a subsistence farm afforded little chance for solitude, let alone secrecy. But she claimed as

much of it as she could and encouraged me and my five sisters to follow suit.

I sometimes chalk up her wariness of exposure to the racialized
world in which she grew up. My uncle George, her brother, once told
me bluntly, "If you talk about harm done to you, those people will use
it against you." I understood that for their generation "those people"
were White folks. And though my mother was more subtle, I knew that
her advice—"Don't ever share your personal business. People will
judge you"—was rooted in a similar understanding.

Well, if you consider testifying about being sexually harassed in the
workplace in front of an all-White, male committee sharing your personal business, they were right about the outcome. For years, I had
followed their advice, keeping to myself that I had been harassed into
leaving my job as an adviser to the chair of the Equal Employment Opportunity Commission. I shared with only a few friends that Clarence
Thomas's behavior had been the main reason I'd left Washington and
returned to Oklahoma. When I did tell, testifying at Thomas's Supreme
Court confirmation hearing, people of all races judged me. In hate
mail sent to my office at the University of Oklahoma, on talk radio, in
magazines and books, face-to-face, and over the phone, they confronted
and condemned me.

I was still struggling to regain my sense of equilibrium after being
thrown into the public spotlight when a call came into my office one
afternoon. Without thinking or measuring the risk that it could be another threat or vitriolic rant, I picked up the receiver. In a deep, grainy
voice that seemed both hesitant and threatening, the caller warned me
that I "had opened up a whole can of worms." The caller never mentioned his name. Anticipating what I was sure would be a diatribe, I at
first wanted to hang up the phone. But instead, perhaps responding to

the hint of vulnerability in his voice, I listened as the caller recalled being molested by an uncle and what happened when he finally gathered the courage to tell his family. Rather than rallying to protect him, his parents had judged him and accused him of making up stories. The Senate Judiciary Committee members' questioning of me, he said, had reminded him of his family's dismissive reaction. The pain of the molestation and his relatives' condemnatory response, he said, "has stayed with me for years."

I mostly listened as he tried to make sense of his family's denials and their siding with his uncle. Surprisingly, though our experiences differed, the hearing had affirmed his understanding of his own painful situation. It counseled him not to blame himself, putting his family's reaction in the context of a larger systemic and societal denial and taking away the sting of a personal condemnation. To him, the "whole can of worms" that I had opened to the public was not limited to sexual harassment; it included incest, too. At the time, with my own pain still raw, I was guarded. Being open to hearing his story of survival was an act of courage on my part. No one had ever shared with me before that a family member had sexually violated them. The caller's story was hard for me to hear, but not nearly as hard as it was for him to tell. And over the years, thousands have shared their experiences of abuse with me. The incest survivor imagined that my testimony would trigger feelings for survivors of other forms of abuse and show that sexual harassment is not the only problem. And he was right.

Over the next months, letters describing behavior from workplace harassment to spousal abuse arrived every day alongside hate mail, and I had to muster even more commitment and emotional bravery. In one ear were the denials, warnings of the harm of accusations of sexual harassment, and challenges to the veracity of my claims. Some went as far as accusing me of inventing my entire testimony. In the other ear were the pleas for someone to see how society had abandoned victims of abuse. After a year of listening to countless stories of survival and attempts to survive, I became increasingly aware of the gravity of gender-based violence.

In 1991, before the hearing, sharing experiences of gender-based violence was taboo. Yes, a few exceptionally courageous and forward-looking women sued in courts to stop harassment, but often the court reports reflected only a few of the details of the behavior they endured. Testimony was usually very curtailed. People who wrote to me told me things that they had never shared with their family members. Some had held their secrets for decades. A woman whom I knew casually told me that she was harassed by her former high school principal when she worked in the school office during World War II. Until the hearing, she had kept the story from her husband, who had been fighting on the front lines in Europe while she was being harassed. These stories marked the beginning of my understanding of the issue of gender-based violence in all its complexities, at a time when the language and awareness around the issue were still developing. I heard from people all over the world. One woman, a sixty-eight-year-old band teacher from Oregon, predicted that there would be "waves of women" behind me. She was right. Sexual harassment claims went up, and stronger protections were created to prevent abuse in the workplace. Increasing public attention of sexual violence and spousal abuse put pressure on law enforcement to bring more rape and domestic violence charges. And in 1992, women ran for and won elections in record numbers, in a banner year called the "Year of the Woman." All this in defiance of pundits who declared that no women would come forward after witnessing my treatment by the Senate.

This seemingly rapid and seismic change gave me hope that a movement was stirring, and I started to envision my role in it as a law professor. I recruited an enthusiastic group of my students to help me scan the legal landscape for the increasing number of sexual harassment cases being brought to the courts. Our law school training had taught us that legal developments prompted social change. We wanted to show that survivors were victorious in the courts and that change in abusive behavior would ripple throughout workplaces if more women came forward.

But at the same time, a deluge of traumatic stories in letters and calls continued flooding my mailbox and telephone, filling file cabinet after file cabinet in my office. Some who contacted me sought legal representation, but most were just determined to tell somebody what had happened to them, many for the first time. As inspiring as they were, the mounting tales of abuse brought me a sense of dread. I hadn't calculated that the spattering of lawsuits and arrests were just a drop in the bucket. Court cases represented only a small portion of the issue, my correspondence a larger but still incomplete fragment. I realized that my students and I were just boiling the ocean. The few civil plaintiffs' successes we found and the paltry number of criminal sexual assault convictions were not enough to corral the staggering problem that was embedded in our culture and increasingly safeguarded by institutions more concerned with their own liability than about harm to victims. We actually had no idea how wide or deep the ocean of gender-based violence was. In what one writer dubbed the "naughty" 1990s, no one did. And what's worse, with no one asking, only a few were brave enough to tell.

Today, more survivors have found platforms to speak up, and what we've learned is how little progress has been made. Reading posts from the 2017 #MeToo movement was like revisiting 1991. More than a generation after I sat in my office wondering how many others were out there, millions of stories from around the globe affirmed and illuminated the thousands I had received. The chorus of stories from different voices and in different languages revealed the depressing tale of gender-based violence and the desire to reach out to others who had suffered, and the connections were obvious: relatively minor aggressions were too often a prelude to violent abuse, and occasional abusive behavior usually became more frequent. What we once thought was an individual behavioral problem suffered by a few was revealed as cultural and endemic.

When we gather the emotional courage to ask the right questions, listen for the answers, and believe survivors, we learn that gender-based violence happens to our acquaintances, colleagues, friends, and, yes, family members. It occurs at our workplaces, on the streets, in our homes, and in the military. One in four women in the United States experience intimate partner violence, including sexual abuse. One in three say they've been harassed at work, but few report these incidents because they're afraid of retaliation. Women of color experience sexual harassment at higher rates than White women, and sexual harassment often includes racist as well as sexual language and behaviors and innuendo. Seventy-three percent of LGBTQ+ college students experience sexual harassment or abuse. Street harassment, as we know, is ubiquitous and can escalate into violence, and transgender and nonbinary people are particularly vulnerable to abuses. In 2020 in this country alone, at least twenty-six trans individuals were killed under circumstances that suggest that they were targeted because of their gender identity, and most of them were Black, suggesting that race was also a factor in their deaths. Men experience abuse, too, of course; one in six men are victims of sexual violence. But women and nonbinary people disproportionately bear the brunt of these abuses, so gender-based violence can be understood as primarily being perpetuated by men against women. Even when men are the victims, the abuse or harassment often reflects attitudes or behaviors aligned with and supportive of strict societal gender mores, standards that rely on the rejection or subjugation of women, such as when men are bullied for displaying qualities generally associated with femininity. Gender, specifically gender discrimination, is a root cause across the spectrum of abuse.

Gender-based violence always causes injury, whether it's physical, verbal, or a combination of the two. It exists everywhere, yet in the 1990s, other than victims, few were seeing the whole of the problem: the pipeline of bad, often legally actionable, behavior that follows individuals from home to school to work and back home. Today, the harm of gender-based violence has reached a public crisis level on many fronts, including health, basic safety, and economics, threatening education, work, and housing options. Domestic violence is the leading cause of homelessness for women. According to one study, "Survivors have reported that if a domestic violence shelter did not exist, the consequences for them would be dire: homelessness, serious losses including loss of their children, actions taken in desperation, or continued abuse or death."[1] Yet because of overburdened systems and limited resources, on any given day more than seventy-five hundred survivors who request housing assistance are turned down.

Women with a history of sexual assault are more likely to have higher rates of attempted suicide and post-traumatic stress symptoms. Evidence mounts of the disturbingly high correlation between a history of sexual assault and the incarceration of LGBTQ+ individuals and women of color. Sexual harassment also costs employers. Businesses face costs both tangible and intangible, like legal fees or settlement amounts, as well as high turnover rates and decreased productivity. And a 2018 Marketplace poll found that nearly 50 percent of women who have been harassed leave their jobs or switch careers because of it. The author and businesswoman Nilofer Merchant warns that sexual harassment can have an "insidious economic impact" not only on the individual but on the entire economy.

A range of violent and coercive behaviors, including various forms of physical, psychological, and financial abuse, constitutes the web of abuse that I call gender-based violence. *Believing* tells stories of people who have experienced incest, intimate partner violence, harassment, rape, and assault. And though the abusive acts differ, they evoke similar emotional responses. Fear, anger, sadness, and despair accompany the bruises, broken bones, black eyes, torn muscles, cuts, burns, emotional abuse, and extortion. These violent behaviors have another commonality: their perpetuation of a gender hierarchy that values men over women, leaving the latter vulnerable, often to life-altering effect.

Through the years and more than a few disappointments, trials, and errors, I have come to see gender-based violence as the literal and figurative foot on women's necks. It impacts nearly every aspect of our lives, including our physical and mental health, housing stability, and financial security. We are beginning to understand it as the bane of our society, not just something borne by survivors and their families. If all of our opportunities to be in the schools, workplaces, and homes of our choices can be defeated by an act of brutality, we are unlikely to have any real chance of sustaining social, economic, and political equality. We have yet to reckon with the full impact of the ocean of violations victims and survivors experience routinely. Far too many still cling to the familiar notions that women are at fault for their own brutalization and that gender-based violence impacts only "others," not them or their loved ones or their communities, and certainly not the nation.

Gender-based violence is understood to be a form of misogyny. But it's also a conduit through which biases based on race, sexual orientation, and class get channeled and heaped on women and girls. Think about the role that sexual abuse has taken in armed conflict throughout the world, including the rape of Native women during colonization. Think about how White men in this country have claimed ownership of White women's bodies to support lynching and political disenfranchisement of Native and Black people. We need to acknowledge that gender-based violence is in place to preserve leadership, hierarchies, and control.

The enormity of gender-based violence is only one reason for its broad impact. Society's reaction to gender-based violence also makes it a tangled morass of a problem to solve. We respond to obvious and ubiquitous abuses by pretending they don't exist. Outright denial is only one response. Minimizing the problem through the language we use to describe abuses and their impact is just as widespread as our denials. We favor piecemeal solutions directed at intimations of gender-based violence—like telling women not to drink to excess or dress in sexually suggestive clothing—so we can ignore the many cultural and social factors that suborn it and the way it inhabits our systems. And the ocean of gender-based offenses continues to grow and get passed on from generation to generation. Because the impact of abuse varies over time and from individual to individual, I use the term "victims and survivors" to talk about people who have experienced gender violence.

My goals for this book are as enormous as the problem itself. The issue, the problem, is nothing short of a national crisis. In seeking to change the way we think and talk about gender violence, I run the risk of biting off more than I can chew, but my goal only matches the size of the crisis. Add actually changing what we *do* about gender-based violence, and I'm sure to be labeled as too ambitious—the bane of working women no matter their job or occupation. I'm willing to take that risk.

When I first spoke publicly about my experience of being sexually harassed, at thirty-five years old, I was young and patient. Thirty years later, I make no claim to youth. And when it comes to ending violence and the inequality that it spawns, I am no longer patient. According to the authors David Benjamin and David Komlos, business specialists who consult with companies at an inflection point, solving "interconnected, dynamically changing, non-deterministic" complex business problems demands that we "boil the ocean." They contrast complex problems with what they call complicated problems, which, though vexing, can be readily solved by someone with the right technical skills.

The challenge of addressing gender-based violence is that the problem is complex and any solutions will require more than technical skills. Gender-based violence is a global phenomenon. According to the United Nations' secretary-general's report on violence against women, gender-based violence takes many forms—physical, sexual, psychological, and economic—that are interrelated and affect women from before birth to old age. And over time, like viruses, patterns of violence evolve and new forms emerge. It "drains resources from public services and employers, and reduces human capital formation,"[2] making it a business problem as well as a social problem. It can ravage survivors' health as well as thrust them into poverty. It has infiltrated politics and disrupted workforces, schools and universities, and communities all at once.

Individuals, schools, businesses, and government have relied on a range of legal responses, civil and criminal, to address the problem. The procedures that are in place today have done little to reduce routine bad behavior that can add up to create a hostile environment. Instances of egregious serial violations, like the Catholic church sexual abuse cases and the charges the Manhattan district attorney filed against Jeffrey Epstein for alleged sex trafficking, go unaddressed for years. Clearly our current legal approaches to ending both everyday and extraordinary abuse are inadequate, showing that legal systems alone are not the whole of the solution. Gender violence will continue to exist until we change the culture that supports it and the structures that enshrine it.

After thirty years, I see that the only way to address the troubling and persistent issue of gender violence and abuse is to take it apart and look at it step-by-step—where it comes from, how it builds—and thus understand how it's perpetuated within our culture and existing systems, or even in the language we use for it. We take too much of it for granted ("that's just the way men are," for example). And we also need to see how identity factors, including race, class, and sexual identity, can influence folks' experience with it.

To reveal the vast scale of the "ocean" of gender violence, in chapters 1 through 6, I examine the enormity and deep entrenchment of the problem in our culture and in our systems. Its resolute presence in our political arenas is matched by its persistence in our schools and workplaces, which means that some survivors live with one form of abuse or another throughout their lives. Yet despite its omnipresence as an undeclared element of our everyday interactions, judges limit the protections against it, ignoring the intent of civil rights laws and basic safety requirements.

In chapters 7 and 8, I describe how the economic, political, and social value we have ascribed to women throughout history continues to restrict our ability to enact protective legislation to address such a complex problem. Though we often label intimate partner violence as a "personal problem," I share stories to show the damage that intimate partner violence and other forms of gender-based violence cost individuals, our local communities, and our nation. And I interrogate gender violence through the lens of ethnic, racial, and gender identity to demonstrate how each exacerbates abuse and to show the misogyny, racism, and homophobia at the heart of gender abuse and aggression.

Together, the first eight chapters of *Believing* show the deep and troubling ways in which gender-based violence lives in our society, why its rates continue to climb, and how new forms develop to counteract gender gains. Gender-based violence is an ongoing catastrophe. In chapters 9 and 10, I scrutinize the politicization of the violence, looking at both organized campaigns to end it and the backlash against those efforts. I take up the question of how to make nonviolence the norm. Though ending gender-based violence requires each of us to be socially and emotionally courageous enough to acknowledge our own responsibility in supporting it, we need leadership to openly and intentionally commit to stemming the tide of abuses suffered because of one's gender. Chapter 10 is a call for leadership and accountability. As demands for a reckoning for violence in the name of gender increase, commitment and immediate action from the top are imperative. This concluding chapter sets the framework for the role the president of the United States must play in eliminating the problem that Axel van Trotsenburg, the World Bank managing director of operations, called the "invisible pandemic."

I know that convincing people that gender violence should be one of the highest priorities of our country won't be easy. I believe that if enough of us come to see the devastating consequences of this scourge, we will commit to breaking the cruel cycle of passing the problem on through multiple generations. My willingness to commit my life to this work comes from my family history. I am the descendant of slaves. And from one generation to the next we survived by believing that we deserved better than discrimination and oppression. I measure progress based not on my own lifetime but on my grandparents' and my mother's. My maternal grandfather was born into slavery, while my maternal grandmother was never allowed an education and could not read or write. My mother, the shy, private person who intuitively kept secret both her triumphs and her heartaches, did everything in her power to make sure her children had a better life than hers. She was born in 1911 in the Jim Crow South, in a country that did not recognize her right to vote. Yet, in insisting that her children get an education that far exceeded the opportunities available to them at the time, she showed her belief that the world would change for the better and that her children would be prepared to enjoy the benefits. And it did change. Her life was fundamentally different in the end from when it began ninety-one years before her death in 2002. Throughout it, my mother, with my father's blessings and sometimes without them, cobbled together the resources needed for her children's own advancement. My parents believed that their children deserved a better world than the one they were born into.

Such a legacy brings with it a responsibility to the next generation. My mother never had a platform like mine, but she taught me that no goal was too big to aim for and that each of us has a duty to use the tools at our disposal to improve the world in our lifetime. We've come far in two generations. We got here because many people were willing to tackle abuses that were seemingly too large to correct. We are not home free, but I believe that we are now on the verge of monumental change once again.

ONE

Our State of Denial

F ar too many claims of gender-based violence, whether sexual assault, workplace harassment, or intimate partner abuse, are closed without a meaningful search for the truth. Often, when we do investigate, we ignore facts that are inconvenient, dismissing them as insignificant. Both failing to probe and ignoring the findings reflect a shared state of denial about the pervasive role of gender-based violence in society. And denial is more than an oversight. It is a strategy that employers, politicians, and judges employ to escape assigning accountability for addressing the problem.

Here's an example of how denial works in terms of women's health. Imagine waking up one morning with pain in your neck, jaw, back, and arms, as well as nausea, sweating, shortness of breath, and light-headedness. You call your doctor hoping to get an appointment right away, but instead he suggests that you may be suffering from anxiety. He recommends that you take an over-the-counter drug like Tums or

Prilosec for the stomach problem or Tylenol for your neck and jaw pain. He insists that what you describe "doesn't appear to be too bad—nothing that a few days of rest shouldn't take care of." Your doctor is missing the symptoms of a possible heart attack. I hope you've never encountered this kind of treatment, but unfortunately others have. In the first decade of the twenty-first century, researchers discovered that women were at high risk for misdiagnosed, mistreated, or untreated cardiac arrests, in part because doctors were looking for symptoms that were more common to men—chest pain and pain in the left arm. But another element was the assumption that women were overreacting to their health concerns. As a result of social and medical biases, tests that could have revealed women's heart ailments were never prescribed. Instead, women's cardiac arrests were dismissed as heartburn or a panic attack. Women weren't getting the same quality of treatment as men, the treatment they deserved. The gender gap in treating heart disease is not new. And more than a decade after it was discovered, the gap continues to exist. As a result, women are dying or suffering from life-threatening conditions because they didn't get the proper diagnosis and treatment.

The gender gap in taking women's health concerns seriously isn't limited to heart conditions, as shown in an episode that took place at the Indiana University Health North Hospital. In 2020, in a video posted on Facebook, a Black woman physician, Dr. Susan Moore, complained that a White doctor who was treating her for COVID-19 denied her request for pain medication. Not taking Moore's word about the level of pain she suffered, he challenged her to prove that she was in as much distress as she claimed. And instead of the treatment she asked for, he recommended she be sent home. Moore eventually was treated for pain, but not as she had requested. About two weeks later, Moore died from complications of the coronavirus infection.[1] Following a preliminary review of the case, the hospital's CEO expressed his full confidence in the "technical aspects of the delivery of Dr. Moore's care." However, he called for an external review and expressed concern that the medical team "may not have shown the level of compassion and respect we strive for in understanding what matters most to patients."[2] So would an external review tell us why Dr. Moore didn't receive the "compassion and respect" she believed she deserved? Perhaps. Moore had attributed the rebuff to racism. But the brush-off she got could have stemmed from sexism or from racism and sexism combined. A similar disregard occurs when women complain about workplace sexual harassment and assault. And most organizations review their complaint-handling processes internally, even when there are multiple accusations against an individual. As with health issues, sexism, organizational loyalty, and a host of other biases lead some internal investigators to disrespect women who complain. Far too often, concerns go uninvestigated or are shoddily probed and dismissed as insignificant. And as with prejudging women's ability to communicate their medical conditions, when we discount women's credibility to describe gender violence, the outcomes are the same. Women suffer—regardless of whether the prejudice is overt or implicit.

"BUT I DON'T KNOW THE FACTS"

The very first national attempt to get the facts about sexual harassment in the workplace did not come from federal agencies. In 1976, after hearing about readers' experiences, the popular women's magazine *Redbook* conducted a survey of nine thousand women, the first of its kind to explore the reality of women's workplace experiences. The magazine's report on the findings was called "What Men Do to Women on the Job." *Redbook* called the findings "eye-opening." Between ads for Dynamo and Ivory detergents and Arthur Murray dance lessons were accounts of sexual comments, groping, leering, extortion, and more. More than eight thousand of the women who responded said they had experienced at least one form of sexual harassment. Claire Safran, the article's author, concluded that the problem was "a pandemic—an everyday, everywhere occurrence."[3]

Five years after hearing from women employees, *Redbook* teamed up with the *Harvard Business Review* to collect business executives' views on sexual harassment in American workplaces. The following are three telling responses from the two thousand men and women who participated in the follow-up study.

"In my own circumstances, sexual harassment included jokes about my anatomy, off-color remarks, sly innuendo in front of customers—in short, turning everything and anything into a sexual reference was an almost daily occurrence," said a thirty-four-year-old first-level female manager in environmental engineering for a large producer of industrial goods. "I have just left this company [a big chemical manufacturer] partially for this reason," she added.

Another person, a fifty-three-year-old man who was a vice president at a medium-sized financial firm, said he was skeptical about sexual harassment existing within his company. "I used to believe it was a subject that was being exaggerated by paranoid women and sensational journalists," he said. "Now I think the problem is real but somewhat overdrawn. My impression is that my own company is relatively free of sexual harassment. But I don't know the facts."

"This entire subject is a perfect example of a minor special interest group's ability to blow up any 'issue' to a level of importance which in no way relates to the reality of the world in which we live and work," said another man, a thirty-eight-year-old plant manager for a large manufacturer of industrial goods.[4]

In the 1981 survey, 88 percent said that sexual relations, even consensual ones, had "no business in the business world," and 78 percent called propositions to swap sex for good performance reviews sexual harassment.[5] The three statements above offer just a glimpse of what the business world thought of harassing behavior. Each sentence describes either a firsthand experience with harassment, reactions to harassing behavior, questions about its significance, or denials of its existence. Which of these perceptions accurately reflect reality in 1981? The truth is that they all do, and the comments can serve as a starting point for determining where we are today.

Why begin this book with a *Redbook* poll? Because many of the same experiences and attitudes expressed in the 1981 poll sponsored by *Redbook* and the *Harvard Business Review* still exist. Also, it's telling that before *Redbook*, a women's magazine, conducted its initial survey in 1976, no other broad inquiry into sexual harassment existed. And the survey had its limitations. The majority of the women who responded to the poll held white-collar jobs. There was limited information collected on the experiences of those working in private households, food service, agriculture, or other low-wage positions. The federal government only began to collect data in 1981, when Congress asked the U.S. Merit Systems Protection Board to conduct two surveys. By then, the Equal Employment Opportunity Commission was beginning to develop policies to eliminate the problem. Two studies conducted by the MSPB in the 1980s found that workers in federal offices and installations widely perceived sexual harassment to be a problem. Far too often investigations were inadequate, and nothing was being done to fix their shortcomings.

Getting a clear picture of sexual harassment and how effective prohibitions might have been requires us, at the very least, to see it from the point of view of each participant: the female supervisor, the male company vice president, and the middle manager, generally also a man. Who is most likely to have experienced harassment? Who is likely to have committed it? Who is most likely to be held accountable for a company's failure to stop it? Whose job is most likely to be on the line if they are found to have committed harassment or reported it? The bottom line is that without more information we couldn't be entirely sure of our answers. That's why the vice president who said, "I don't know the facts," but was still willing to reach a conclusion is in my opinion the most troubling respondent. Not knowing the answer to the question of whether sexual harassment exists doesn't necessarily disqualify him from leading a modern workplace, where rules to end harassment are starting to be enforced, but not using his status to find the answer does. His is a classic denial. His motives seem clear. His apparent interest is in protecting his company rather than learning what goes on inside it and addressing it. It's a familiar stance.

MAKING HARASSMENT ILLEGAL

Early sexual harassment cases show that the manager's and the vice president's views of the problem of sexual harassment were typical. And the female manager's decision to leave was also predictable. In the decades before the Thomas hearing, courts routinely rejected the idea that women had any right to complain about the sexual comments, groping, leering, extortion, and exploitation that *Redbook* uncovered. Some courts excused the behavior as natural and expected:

The abuse of authority by supervisors of either sex for personal purposes is an unhappy and recurrent feature of our social experience.... It is not, however, sex discrimination within the meaning of Title VII, even when the purpose is sexual.

—FEDERAL JUDGE HERBERT JAY STERN, *TOMKINS V. PUBLIC SERVICE ELECTRIC AND GAS COMPANY* (1976)

Before working on the landmark *Alexander v. Yale University* case in 1980, which argued that sexual harassment violated students' rights under Title IX, Catharine MacKinnon, a student at Yale Law School, was already at work developing her theory explaining why the sexual harassment facing women in the workplace was a form of sex discrimination that violated Title VII of the Civil Rights Act of 1964. Lawsuits filed in the 1970s showed her that getting courts to rule that harassment was a violation of the law would be a laborious undertaking. Yet the decade saw other activism around the issue of sexual harassment. Eleanor Holmes Norton, head of the New York City Commission on Human Rights, convened the first government hearings on the behavior in 1975. Carmita Wood, an administrative assistant at Cornell University who had filed a claim against her employer, testified before the commission's hearings on women and work. Lin Farley, who was supporting Wood and others who had harassment claims, also testified. Farley is credited for coining the term "sexual harassment" for behavior that results in women losing their jobs for saying no to "sexual byplay."

At the same time, in Boston, the business consultant Freada Kapor Klein started her early work on what she termed "sexual extortion." Klein's expertise was her pioneering prevention efforts, working with businesses to detect and address factors before violations occurred.

Despite this growing awareness of the problem and attempts to elevate it to both social and legal consciousness, harassment went largely unchecked. Between 1986 and 1989, a number of state task force surveys questioned women in the legal profession about their experiences with harassment. Professor Marina Angel, who analyzed the surveys, found that women lawyers in several states had witnessed judges soliciting "sexual favors from [women who came before the courts, including] criminal defendants, civil litigants, lawyers (including prosecutors, public defenders, and private counsel), law clerks, law students, court employees, job applicants, probation officers, juvenile court wards, and jurors."[6] Yet rarely was the conduct found to have violated state codes of judicial conduct.[7]

Under the Civil Rights Act of 1964 and its 1972 amendments, sexual harassment is defined as persistent or severe, unwelcome or unwanted sexual behavior. By the late 1970s, MacKinnon had framed the legal concept to enshrine two new categories of behavior. They are quid pro quo, sex in exchange for employment, pay raises, promotions, and so on, and what would be called "hostile environment sexual harassment," which refers to persistent and pervasive harassment, such that the workplace becomes tainted and negatively impacts a worker's ability to do their job.

But MacKinnon's successful attempt to advance these concepts into law was fraught. Some courts rejected the idea outright. This is not surprising. There was considerable evidence that some male judges' perspectives cause them to view women's experiences very differently than women might.

If any theory were going to test male judges' bias inside the judicial process, the legal validity of sexual harassment was it. In the 1970s, when MacKinnon was arguing for courts to recognize this new idea that sexual harassment constituted discrimination, judges routinely rejected her position. A slew of decisions by male judges demonstrated a deep, culturally loaded resistance to acknowledging the cause of action. They denied that the facts parties alleged amounted to a legal violation no matter how vivid and horrific or accurately they described reality in the complainants' workplaces.

To justify turning away complaints, judges would either characterize sexual exploitation as "normal" or too common for the law to curtail, or they'd argue that such behavior is a result of biology and cultural inevitability (that is, boys will be boys). These personal assessments of the behavior clouded judges' abilities to imagine the legal harm it caused to the women who suffered from it.

Take, for example, one of the earliest decisions in this vein, that of Judge William C. Frey in the 1975 case *Corne v. Bausch and Lomb.* Judge Frey was in the U.S. Army as a major during World War II. He left the military, went to law school, and practiced law in a private firm before serving as an assistant Arizona state attorney general. While Frey was serving as a county superior court judge, President Richard Nixon nominated him for a position on the federal bench. Six years later he wrote the opinion in the *Corne* decision, the first sexual harassment case to reach a federal court. Jane Corne and Geneva DeVane, two administrative assistants at Bausch and Lomb, an eye product company based in Canada, brought the suit, charging that their supervisor, a man named Leon Price, repeatedly took unsolicited and unwelcome sexual liberties with them and other female employees. The advances were verbal as well as physical and eventually escalated to a level that both Corne and DeVane found intolerable. They left Bausch and Lomb and sued their supervisor and the company. A Nixon appointee, Judge Frey was well liked across ideological lines. He was friends with the

Arizona Democratic senator Dennis DeConcini and Representative Morris K. Udall, a Democrat from Arizona. And "despite political differences," in a memorial to Judge Frey upon his death a few years after the *Corne* decision, Udall applauded the jurist's "mastery of the art of judging" for his handling of a highly "emotional Arizona busing case."[8]

The exact facts of the *Corne* case were obscured, but the opinion's blanket description of Price's behavior as persistent verbal and physical advances is telling. And though Judge Frey openly acknowledged that the facts were as Corne and DeVane had alleged, he was brazenly skeptical about the validity of the legal claims they brought, at one point in his opinion calling it "ludicrous." Frey's opinion minimized Price's behavior, characterizing it as "nothing more than a personal proclivity, peculiarity, or mannerism. Mr. Price was satisfying a personal urge." His chosen language not only denied the significance of the claim of a civil rights violation but also insulated Bausch and Lomb from accountability for stopping what the court acknowledged as Price's sexual extortion.

At one point, Judge Frey seemed to portray the company as the real victim of Price's verbal and physical abuse. "It is obvious [Bausch and Lomb] can only be damaged by the very nature of the acts complained of," he said. Invoking the biological inevitability of sexual harassment, Frey concluded, "The only sure way an employer could avoid such charges would be to have employees who were asexual." And so went the first sexual harassment claim, setting the stage for those that followed. When it was all said and done, neither Price nor Bausch and Lomb bore any accountability for Corne and DeVane's being pushed out of their jobs because of harassment.

The few details that emerged in Judge Spencer Williams's 1976 opinion in *Miller v. Bank of America* showed what women were putting up with from employers. Margaret Miller, a Black woman, worked as a cashier for Bank of America. In her affidavit, which Judge Williams accepted as uncontroverted, meaning the bank had not challenged it, Miller alleged that her supervisor, "Mr. Taufer," a White man, promised her a better job if she would be sexually "cooperative"—the very definition of a quid quo pro as introduced by MacKinnon. One other aspect of the opinion stands out. Apparently, Miller's boss had wondered out loud, what would sex with a "black chick"—his words—be like? He approached her as an object of both racial and sexual curiosity. When Miller declined his advances, Taufer fired her. Judge Williams, who heard the case, was a Californian who, like Frey, was a Nixon appointee to the federal bench. Williams's tenure began in 1971, following stints in the U.S. Naval Reserves and the Santa Clara County government and as secretary of the California State Human Relations Agency. By the time he was assigned the *Miller* case, Judge Williams had been on the bench for five years.

Despite Taufer's clear racial language, Judge Williams noted specifically that Miller's case was "not a race discrimination case" and should instead "stand or fall on the issue of sex discrimination." Yet even though the bank had a policy discouraging sexual advances and disciplining employees who violated them, the judge rejected Miller's claim. Instead, he relied on his own view of biology and nature to excuse Taufer's apparent race- and gender-motivated behavior. "The attraction of males to females and females to males is a natural sex phenomenon," said the judge, "and it is probable that this attraction plays at least a subtle part in most personnel decisions." By explaining away Taufer's behavior and going so far as to excuse the "subtle" consideration of attraction in hiring decisions, Judge Williams denied any violation of Miller's civil rights, even though the facts showed that Miller lost her job because she failed to comply with her supervisor's boorish request for sex.

After the *Corne* decision, opinions written by Nixon appointees (all White men) put on the bench in the early 1970s continued to deny women's right to work in places free from sexual harassment. It wasn't that these judges didn't believe the women who brought their claims to the courts. This set of judges just didn't believe that what happened to the plaintiffs mattered in any legal sense. Yet such decisions and other evidence of male bias do not necessarily establish sweeping gender differences in judging. In fact, considerable evidence suggests that other factors, such as background and ideology with regards to the protection of civil rights, are better predictors than sex in accounting for judicial decisions.

Early harassment decisions pointed squarely to the need for a different kind of judge and approach to judging if the concept of sexual harassment was ever to be seen as a violation of an individual's civil rights. That judge would turn out to be Spottswood Robinson III.

Judge Robinson's road to the bench differed significantly from Frey's and Williams's. Frey and Williams were White. Robinson was Black. He had experienced racism firsthand growing up under Jim Crow laws in Virginia. He attended two historically Black universities, Virginia Union and Howard University. He got his law degree from the Howard University School of Law in 1939, where he studied under Charles Hamilton Houston, the legal expert who served as the mastermind behind the theory leading to the landmark case *Brown v. Board of Education.* Houston planted the seed for Robinson's career as a civil rights attorney. When he graduated from Howard, Robinson and a partner opened a practice representing clients who were challenging segregation in Virginia. As a young lawyer he litigated race discrimination cases and saw racism through the eyes of his clients, some of whom, unlike Robinson, were poor and illiterate. In that role, Robinson had heard opposing counsels argue that segregation and other forms of racism were "not so bad" or were natural and in the best interests of both races. In 1951, he was the attorney for Black families challenging school segregation, arguing before the Supreme Court as it considered the *Brown v. Board* case. In 1954 the Court decided the *Brown* case and declared that separating by race in public education was a denial of equal protection under the law. The *Brown* case was one of many desegregation cases Robinson argued during the 1940s and 1950s before returning to Howard Law School to become a professor and the dean in 1961.

In 1964, President Lyndon B. Johnson nominated Robinson to the United States District Court for the District of Columbia while the Senate was in recess—called a recess appointment—which allowed him to bypass Senate approval. Just shy of three years later, Johnson nominated Robinson for a post on the highly influential U.S. Court of Appeals for the District of Columbia. Along with his experience as a litigator, Robinson brought to the bench what was described as a professorial understanding of civil rights history. Robinson's race distinguished him from his judicial counterparts who heard the early sexual harassment cases. However, it was not his race alone, but Robinson's experiences as a student, a teacher, and a lawyer for clients challenging discrimination that shaped his understanding of civil rights law. In 1949, Jack Greenberg, who was White, joined the team led by Thurgood Marshall (a graduate of Howard Law School and student of Houston) at the NAACP Legal Defense Fund. Greenberg, who argued the *Brown* case along with Robinson, was drawn to civil rights work in part because he saw a resemblance between the anti-Semitism his family struggled against and Black oppression in the United States. His thinking about the law was equally steeped in antidiscrimination reasoning. So much so that in 1961 he succeeded Marshall as the LDF's director-counsel. Robinson and Greenberg both pursued the law as a tool for expanding the protections offered under the Constitution and emerging civil rights legislation. Once on the court, Robinson worked with White judges who, like Greenberg, had the capacity to see the law's potential to protect against sexual harassment, but they lacked Robinson's belief that the law was meant to discredit false ideas that normalized, excused, and denied bias.

Though race alone doesn't explain the difference between Robinson's decision and the conclusions reached by Frey and Williams, race writ large played a role in Robinson's acceptance of sexual harassment as a civil rights violation. Early race decisions gave Robinson a basis for framing his decision. Robinson's experience as both a lawyer and a judge convinced him that the sexual extortion that Paulette Barnes complained about in the case of *Barnes v. Costle* ran counter to the protections of the law. And in evaluating Barnes's sexual-harassment Title VII complaint, Robinson applied the same thinking to gender bias as he applied to racial bias.

Judge Robinson looked at the statute's language and noted that it protected race and sex similarly. What led to his decision in four pivotal sexual harassment claims brought before the D.C. court during his tenure in the 1970s and 1980s was his belief that civil rights protections should be progressive, forward looking. The judges who were determined to prevent women from using the law to fight harassment largely based their reasoning on what they presumed were natural inequalities—men naturally demanding sex and women having to comply or move on to other jobs.

Robinson's history of litigating race discrimination cases and promoting the idea of a broad interpretation of civil rights protections, to cover a range of exclusionary practices that racial minorities experience, led him to the conclusion that sex discrimination should also be broadly protected. And that meant that to protect women, the law was obligated to put aside culturally based presumptions about male entitlements, in the same way that protections against racial discrimination meant denying White racial privileges. Robinson cited the legislative history of the Civil Rights Act, which he said assured that sex discrimination "is no less serious than other forms of prohibited employment practices and is to be accorded the same degree of social concern given to any type of unlawful discrimination." Judge Robinson was known for his attention to detail, legalities as well as relevant historical particulars. He would have known that several of the women in prior sexual harassment cases were Black and that they, because of their race, would likely have a peculiar vulnerability to sexual misconduct owing to both race and gender. So when Barnes appealed the dismissal of her complaint that the Environmental Protection Agency abolished her job because she rejected her male superior's sexual advances, she could not have had a better judge than Robinson.

Judge Robinson's *Barnes v. Costle* opinion is notable, first, for capturing the workplace power dynamics that culminated in the suit. The story begins when Barnes interviewed with the EPA's director of equal employment opportunity for a position as his administrative assistant. The job interview went well and, according to Barnes, the director (whose name is not mentioned in the case report) promised that if she took the job, he would promote her within ninety days of her start date. Barnes agreed and began working at the lower rank. Soon, the director started making repeated sexual advances—soliciting Barnes to join him for social activities after office hours, directing sexual comments to her, and suggesting she would get her promotion if she had sex with him. All the while, Barnes said she rejected his overtures and made it clear that she wanted a strictly "professional relationship." In time, the director began to belittle her, stripped her of her job duties, and finally fired her, in essence, by eliminating her job. For the record, Judge Robinson made note of the fact that both Barnes and the equal opportunity director were Black.

Unlike some of the cases by other judges, Judge Robinson took care to provide details of the offensive behavior in his written opinion. And in breaking a line of reasoning that stood in the way of women's claims for protection—that sexual harassment was a personal, not a civil rights, violation—Judge Robinson strategically laid the grounds for his court's decision. He did so by noting the close correlation and similar characteristics between discrimination based on sex and discrimination based on race. By tying the relatively new claim of sexual harassment to race discrimination, Judge Robinson grounded sexual harassment complaints in what was becoming settled law. He couched the legitimacy of Barnes's complaint in simple language: "She became the target of her superior's sexual desires because she was a woman, and was asked to bow to his demands as the price for holding her job." The court decision for *Barnes* is a landmark decision in the legal history of sexual harassment.

Nearly a decade after the *Barnes* decision, Robinson wrote an opinion in favor of the plaintiff Mechelle Vinson in *Meritor Savings Bank v. Vinson*. In 1986, a year after Robinson's appellate opinion, *Vinson* became the first sexual harassment case decided by the Supreme Court. Once again, Robinson's reasoning prevailed, the Court acknowledged hostile environment sexual harassment as a violation of Title VII, and

Vinson won her case. In no small way, he paved the course for recognition of future harassment claims. But some courts still seek to invalidate women's perspectives about the abuses they continue to face. Professor Shirley Wiegand, a professor emerita of law at Marquette University whose work centers on legal procedure, has chronicled numerous examples that demonstrate a judge's apparently limited vision. One of Wiegand's examples comes from the case that served as the basis for the 2005 movie *North Country*, a grim and painful, if sometimes fictionalized, account of sexual harassment at a mine in Minnesota. The fictionalized version was apparently no more grim and painful than the real experience the women in the suit faced in the mine or the hostility they faced during the case, which was first filed in 1991. According to Wiegand,

> The Special Master's report (adopted fully by the federal district judge) revealed that he could not understand why one woman was fearful when a man who she said had exposed himself to her several years earlier began driving his truck in circles, over and over, around her work area. "This court has difficulty understanding why the appearance of a suspected flasher outside the building in which she was working ... would cause great fear—of something—in a reasonable woman."
>
> The judge also could not understand why a woman would fear rape simply because "a man who had repeatedly and crudely propositioned her suddenly lunged at her one night at work with his arms spread, only stopping when she began screaming."
>
> (It is worth noting that the trial judge who adopted the above language was overturned on appeal some eleven years later.)[9]

MacKinnon's concept of sexual harassment and discrimination gained traction in the courts, but the general public routinely questioned why women didn't report violations or just leave toxic workplaces. Few asked why men didn't just leave work situations they detested. It took a while for people to empathize with losing one's livelihood or facing retaliation, both of which kept women and others in places where they no longer wanted to be. The public underestimated the fear or the social and cultural structures that compelled victims to suffer in silence. Some asked questions not out of genuine curiosity but to politely (or rudely) confirm a conclusion they had already reached: that staying meant there was no problem. Their reaction is one facet of our collective denial of the reality of women's experiences with abuse. Psychology tells us that denial is a defense mechanism that serves as ego protection. It's a concept that was introduced by Anna Freud, Sigmund Freud's daughter. Her theory is simple: people refuse to accept the truth or reality of a fact or experience that they cannot address or change. To alleviate their discomfort, they blame victims. According to Anna Freud in her book *The Ego and the Mechanisms of Defense*, the ego "refuses to become aware of some disagreeable reality" or "unwelcome facts." Survivors insulate themselves with their own form of denial, by adamantly rejecting the notion that they are vulnerable. They "develop a thick skin" to defend themselves against being labeled as "snowflakes," not tough enough, "oversensitive." And in some cases that means denying that their own pain exists or that it matters.

It's ironic that Anna Freud put so much stock in denial as a form of ego protection, as her father developed an entire psychoanalysis for denying his patients' claims of sexual abuse. Ultimately, he concluded, the women's abuse claims were played out from sexual fantasies they had as children. Sigmund Freud's theory, itself a rarefied way for some abusers to avoid accountability or for parents to excuse their failure to protect their children, has been challenged if not entirely debunked. But because taking responsibility for ending problems so deeply ingrained in our culture is hard, public willingness to tackle the task lagged behind legal recognition of the right to work free from workplace abuses. And so did the Senate Judiciary Committee when I testified in 1991 at the Thomas hearing.

THE POWER TO DENY

Once the committee reopened the hearing to consider my testimony, the members' first responsibility was to discover the facts behind my complaint. As Spottswood Robinson made clear, facts matter. Whether in a court of law or congressional hearing, getting to the facts is critical to deciding what to do with credible claims of harassment, assault, and other forms of gender-based violence. But political hearings are not like courts of law. And members of the Senate Judiciary Committee could ignore legal precedent and make their own rules for evaluating candidates' fitness for the Supreme Court. Congressional rules are shrouded, obscure, and often archaic. They are designed to achieve political ends and give members the power to control the information the public receives, making it easier to evade or deny the reality of women's experiences. In October 1991, the public would learn that controlling the facts would mean blocking chances to get to the truth. By refusing to call upon experts on sexual harassment and fellow employees whose experiences with Thomas were similar to mine, the committee failed its obligation to the public. We would also learn how the senators who controlled the facts determined the outcome and shaped the stories that emerged from the proceeding.

"THIS IS NOT TOO BAD"

In addition to limiting the findings of fact, another form of denial was happening during the Thomas confirmation hearing. Like the snapshot of Judges Frey and Williams and executives' thinking about sexual harassment in 1981, statements from Thomas's Senate confirmation hearing sheds light on how the depth of politicians' denial of the problem of sexual harassment put the integrity of the Supreme Court at risk. In 1991, flawed thinking about whether gender-based violence even mattered was evident in politicians' comments. And attitudes from decades past held sway. In the days prior to the hearing, Senator Arlen Specter, a former prosecutor, declared that he had done his duty to find the facts when he looked Judge Thomas in the eye and Thomas denied the harassment. It wasn't Specter's cursory investigation alone that troubled me. His dismissal of my experience as unimportant because I didn't claim that Thomas touched me stood out as particularly noxious. Specter was in effect saying that sexual assault was the only behavior that called for judicial disqualification, no matter that the law prohibiting sexual harassment includes verbal, emotional, and physical harassment. In essence Specter was saying that a Supreme Court justice is exempt from accountability for some legal violations. But in retrospect, his assertion that Thomas's behavior wasn't "too bad" was nothing new. Except for Spottswood Robinson's reasoning, Frey's conclusion that persistent physical and verbal harassment was bad enough to violate Title VII might still be the law. And outside of the courtrooms, victims and survivors have heard their experiences discounted throughout their lives. Statements like "You're making too much of this," "You're overreacting," "That's nothing to complain about," "Why are you the only one complaining?" and their equivalents are ubiquitous and intended to silence and shame victims. The low bar that Specter set for qualifying Thomas to sit on the Court was an insult to survivors as well as to the Court itself. But Specter's posturing is best understood as political theater—more showmanship than substance—with little connection to providing a process for victims to raise complaints about sexual harassment or maintaining public trust in the nation's highest court.

On October 11, 1991, at 11:31 a.m., I sat alone at a long table in room 325 of the Russell Senate Office Building and began my statement in Clarence Thomas's confirmation hearing. I spent the first fifty minutes of my testimony that day chronicling Thomas's discussions of sex and pornography in the workplace. At 12:15, the Senate Judiciary Committee chair, Joe Biden, asked, "Can you tell the committee what was the most embarrassing of all the incidents that you have alleged?"

I told him that what was most embarrassing was Thomas's discussion of pornography involving "women with large breasts and engaged in a variety of sex with different people, or animals." But in truth, I had no real idea how to determine what was the most embarrassing of the crude and obscene comments I had to put up with. Nor did I fully realize how my answer would be used against me.

Within an hour of giving my answer to Biden, Specter, the Kansas-born senator from Pennsylvania, took his turn questioning me. He started by saying, "Professor Hill, . . . [y]ou testified this morning, in response to Senator Biden, that the most embarrassing question involved—this is not too bad—women's large breasts." He misstated both Biden's question and my response. "That is a word we use all the time. That was the most embarrassing aspect of what Judge Thomas had said to you," he continued, disparagingly belittling me for being upset that Thomas wanted to discuss pornography in the office.

It wasn't just the mention of women's breasts that made me uncomfortable, but rather Thomas's vivid descriptions of the women's sexual acts in pornography videos. But it didn't matter. Specter had made his point, signaling his empathy—or *him*pathy—for Thomas. He said "breasts" was a word "we" use all the time. But who was Specter's "we"? Who were the "we" that talked about women's large breasts in the workplace all the time? By repeating the phrase but omitting the pornographic context, Specter had achieved his goal of minimizing "Thomas's talk about [sex] in the workplace, arguing they were commonly used words and 'not so bad,'" as the columnist Winnie Brandfield-Harvey wrote in *The Daily Princetonian*. Specter reduced Thomas's offense to being merely descriptive. At the same time, the senator evoked the prude trope frequently hurled at women who resist their work colleagues' attempts to engage them in sexual banter.

The following day, after having testified for seven hours the day before, I was back in my hotel away from the Russell Senate Office Building when Specter seized upon my absence to accuse me of "flat-out perjury" and demolish my credibility in front of the press.

Other than our participation in the confirmation hearing, Specter and I had, by fate, three things in common: We were both born and raised in farming communities, me in Oklahoma, him in the neighboring state of Kansas. We went to the same law school, Yale. And he had spent his first year of college at the University of Oklahoma, where I taught during the 1980s and 1990s. The OU connection led to a chance encounter with Specter in 1997, years after the Thomas hearing. We were both at the Will Rogers World Airport, getting ready to board the same plane from Oklahoma City en route to Houston.

Specter recalled the encounter in his book *Passion for Truth: From Finding JFK's Single Bullet to Questioning Anita Hill to Impeaching Clinton*. "In

October 1997, in the Oklahoma City airport, [Specter's wife] Joan's luggage cart became entangled with another woman's purse strap as we were preparing to board a flight to Houston. Untangling the bags, I looked up and saw Anita Hill," he wrote. "Quite surprised, I said, 'Hello, Professor Hill.' Hill looked at me and said, 'Senator, Senator,' either not remembering my name, which I doubt, or not wanting to utter it."

I was gobsmacked to see him. Before the plane took off, we chatted casually. He mentioned something about exploring a gender equity project that "we could work together on." I interpreted it as a shiny political bauble dangled in front of me, perhaps his version of an olive branch. I knew it wasn't genuine. He told me to give his office a call to set up an appointment. When the plane took off, I felt as though I were being held captive at twenty-five thousand feet midair between Oklahoma City and Houston.

I told the *Washington Post* reporter who got wind of the encounter that my conversation was sort of chitchat. Upon reflection, I'd call it bizarre. At first, I was shocked, and I thought, "Am I mistaken, or aren't you the person who accused me of flat-out perjury?" I realized then that to him the hearing was "just politics." For me it was about my life. I never made the call. My passion for advancing gender equality was tempered by my memory of his using my words as ammunition against me. I didn't want to give him the opportunity to say that all was forgotten or that I had called his office looking for the chance to work with him. He had done nothing to earn my trust.

Seventeen years after the Thomas hearing, Senator Specter had an exchange with a member of the audience at a Hudson Union Society event. "Senator, you've told us today about many of your learning experiences," said the audience member. "When you look back, in your questioning of Anita Hill, do you come back with any learning experiences?" It was clear Specter was caught off guard, because his answer did not reflect the customary certainty of a prosecutor or a politician. "Hardly a week goes by that I don't get a question about Anita Hill," he said. (As I watched the tape, it occurred to me that every week he got to shape my story to suit his ambitions, because that is what happens when he controlled the facts.) "What I learned was a very sensitive subject is involved on the subject of sexual harassment. People heard me questioning Professor Hill and felt that they were being challenged." He added, returning to his 1991 self, "I believe that I asked the questions in a very professional, low-key way." A member of the audience let out an unrestrained *harrumph*, to which Specter shrugged and glibly retorted, "You may disagree with me. That's America."

Specter had not learned that many survivors keep in touch with their harassers, their assailants, and even their rapists. We remain civil because we know that the powerful ones often hold our future in their hands and can be vindictive if we don't. Regaining his polemical posture, misstating some of the facts, and omitting others, he went on to outline what he saw as the weaknesses in my testimony. "Telephone records show that she had contact with Thomas" after leaving Washington, including "inviting Thomas to speak at Oral Roberts University" law school and driving Thomas to the airport after his talk, he said. Yes, I contacted Thomas for a reference, and there was a little back-and-forth before I realized that I couldn't trust him to give me a good reference. But the invitation to Thomas to speak came from my dean at Oral Roberts, who was a Thomas fan, not me. Relieved when the whole visit was over, I rushed at the chance to get him on a plane to wherever he was heading. The year was 1984. Thomas was no longer a factor in my life. "Bye, Felicia."

"Not that bad" reflects the attitude that survivors often internalize; that our abusers' behaviors "were not the worst thing that ever happened to us" serves as a coping mechanism that is problematic. In her anthology *Not That Bad: Dispatches from Rape Culture*, the writer, public intellectual, and cultural critic Roxane Gay writes with painful eloquence about how for a long time she minimized the gang rape she survived as a teenager. And the heartrending stories in her book from other women who experienced gender-based violence include scores who remained friendly or intimate with harassers and abusers. *Not That Bad* poignantly reminds us of the way we deny our pain to keep living. Convincing herself that her experience was not as bad as others' was Gay's way of managing her trauma "instead of allowing the magnitude of it to destroy" her. But as Gay points out, this defense mechanism comes at a cost. In her case, as with countless other victims, it numbed her to the pain of her other bad experiences, as well as the trauma others suffered. "The surface of my empathy became callous," she writes.[10]

Looking back at how the Senate exchange went, I wonder, was Specter gaslighting me and the public, or was he mansplaining? I've concluded that he was doing both. If gaslighting was his intent, he was manipulating me (and the public) into questioning the reality and my perception of my own experiences. Given his condescending tone, Specter was also mansplaining—trying to convince us all that he knows better than me how a woman experiences sexual harassment. Mansplaining was the technique, and gaslighting was the goal. Both are forms of denial employed to discount claims of abuse, and they deserve to be called out because they prevent women from being heard and believed when they testify about abuse. Both tactics foster self-doubt, coaxing victims into thinking that coming forward is pointless, that no one will care.

I chuckle when I think about that experience in these modern terms. But even thirty years later, I remember Specter's tittering tone, his smirk, and his pronouncement that my experience and others like it were "not too bad." The senator questioned both the importance of what I went through and my veracity. Many of his colleagues contributed to the wholesale dismissal of the idea of sexual harassment; at the hearing, the Wyoming senator Alan Simpson described my account as "sexual harassment crap." Specter's and Simpson's disdain resonated with women painfully because it echoed messages they had heard throughout their lives. And when senators express their contempt for the very idea that sexual harassment is a serious concern, women around the country get the message that the judiciary committee does not care about sexual harassment.

How do three simple words, "not that bad," become so powerful? They gain steam when they are absorbed in all of our social systems, permeating survivors' minds. The hold that those three little words have comes from hearing them repeated multiple times over the course of a lifetime. The exact language may change, as do the circumstances, but the message that your hurt is of no consequence, so back off, remains the same. Schools deny and neglect gender violence, undermining survivors' confidence and secure identity even as small children. The same attitude exists in the workplace, which can lead survivors to feel self-doubt. Individual denial breeds institutional denial, and survivors pay the price. Specter's words were aimed at persuading me to doubt my significance. His strategy was to convince other potential witnesses and the American public that the stories survivors seek to share and the people who want to hear them are of no importance. Specter's belittlement of my pain had one clear beneficiary, Clarence Thomas. To abusers, harassers, and rapists, "not so bad" is an absolution and, in Thomas's case, an assurance that the Senate confirmation process would protect him. To survivors, these words are like a dagger.

When individuals deny reality, they turn to tropes or stories others are likely to believe even when the facts don't match their situation. Thomas's "high-tech lynching" metaphor, for example, invoked our country's dark racial history. His supporters seemed oblivious to the fact that in reality the history didn't fit his circumstances. He was not being wrongly accused by powerful forces. Like most accusers of powerful men, I had no political connections that I had enlisted to threaten his appointments. His protectors included the president, White House and Senate staffers, and the FBI. And no member of the committee challenged Thomas's characterization of the hearing. Four months later, the insincerity of Thomas's portrayal of himself as a victim of racism was made even clearer. Thomas used his first written opinion as a Supreme Court justice to deny a handcuffed and shackled Black inmate, Keith Hudson, the right to be protected from being beaten by prison guards. In his *Hudson v. McMillian* dissent, Thomas argued that the Constitution's protection against cruel and unusual punishment didn't forbid the pounding—swollen mouth, cracked dental plate, and loosened teeth— leveled against the subdued prisoner as a prison supervisor looked on, warning guards only against "having too much fun." Hudson's experience with the criminal justice system reflected the well-known history of abuse of Black Americans from slavery to this day. The symbolism of the shackles and cuffs and the suggestion that violence was permitted in the name of "fun" cried out for a reference to our violent, racist past. Thomas, who just months before during his confirmation hearing had evoked the specter of racial violence, offered not even a mention that race might have played a role in how Hudson was treated.

Institutional denial, as shown by the refusal to acknowledge the truth about harassment in the Senate and the courts, was dangerously evident in 1991. In the fifteen years after that *Redbook* survey, data had emerged establishing the regularity of harassment in various fields—including the judiciary and the courts. The state task force surveys of women professionals conducted in the 1980s documented the extent of harassment by judges, legal clients, and other participants in the judicial system.[11] Senate Judiciary Committee members would have been completely negligent to ignore that data—especially when considering a high-profile case of harassment before them. But some members stated that they were completely unaware of the problem of sexual harassment. This is how institutional denial works: individuals, representatives of an institution (in this case the Senate) whose job it is to know, claim ignorance on behalf of the institution.

Structural denial relies on rules and systems to mask the truth. To shape the narrative coming out of the Thomas hearing, the Judiciary Committee relied on Senate procedures to deny the public a chance to hear corroborating witnesses and experts with experience in how harassment works in real life. Instead, the committee chose to have the four women's statements about experiencing or witnessing similar treatment by Thomas included in the written record, which only a fraction of the public would ever see. As late as 2016, people were surprised to hear that there were four independently corroborating witnesses ready to testify but who were never called. More recently, the committee chair, Biden, used this systemic failing as a shield, attributing any failure on his part to conduct a fair and open hearing to the committee rules. "I did everything in my power to do what I thought was within the rules," Biden said in 2019.[12] But he didn't explain whether the rules were fair or acknowledge that the "rules" he relied on impeded getting all the facts.

The 1991 Senate Judiciary Committee ducked its responsibility to the public by reverting to theories spun out of nothing that were repeated by committee members as explanations for sexual harassment. One baseless conjecture was that my testimony was part of a political conspiracy to derail Thomas's nomination. Another was that I was suffering from erotomania (a delusional belief that Thomas was in love with me) and had imagined the behavior. What was at stake was our commitment to basic fairness and safety in our workplaces and respect for all victims of sexual harassment. In the public eye, women accusers were cast as spurned, prigs with vendettas, incompetent dupes manipulated by others, martyrs for some political cause, or gold diggers seeking attention. Pick one or two or all of the above. What was also at stake was our belief in the integrity of the court and the processes by which judges are selected. And many of us wondered if the power to deny would hold sway, causing another shameful public debacle. The answer came twenty-seven years later.

Frozen

Denial was a constant theme in Thomas's confirmation hearing. It would continue in Brett Kavanaugh's Supreme Court confirmation hearing as reactionary comments and pretense made in 1991 were reprised and repurposed in 2018. Victim blaming, flat-out denials, mansplaining, and gaslighting were plentiful. What was missing was accountability—individual, institutional, or structural—for the hearings' failures. Here are a few telling examples.

Senate Judiciary Committee Members' Reactions to Sexual Harassment During the Clarence Thomas Confirmation Hearings, October 1991

DENNIS DECONCINI: If you're sexually harassed, you ought to get mad about it, and you ought to do something about it and you ought to complain, instead of hanging around a long time and then all of a sudden calling up and say, "Oh, I want to complain." I mean, where's the gumption?

ALAN SIMPSON: She will be injured and destroyed and belittled and hounded and harassed, real harassment, different from the sexual kind, just plain old Washington-variety harassment.

ORRIN HATCH: Her story's too contrived. It's so slick it doesn't compute.

STROM THURMOND: The good name of a good man has been tarnished.

CHARLES GRASSLEY: He was miraculous in how he handled it. He handled it in a way that looked responsible. . . . I hope he stays on there till he's 95 years old.

CHARLES GRASSLEY: I am going to work towards ensuring that this never happens again. . . . I would like to work . . . to establish a new ground rule. . . . When the FBI has completed its work, every committee member should be notified and have access to that report. And a determination by the committee should be made as to how we need to proceed with any allegations. A rule like this should ensure, once and for all, that even an 11th hour charge, like yours, has been fully considered.

On September 27, 1991, the Judiciary Committee voted to send the Thomas nomination to the full Senate, which confirmed his appointment by a vote of 52–48 a few weeks later.

Senate Judiciary Committee Members' Reactions to Sexual Assault During the Brett Kavanaugh Confirmation Hearings, September 2018

CHARLES GRASSLEY (CHAIR): We've offered Dr. Ford the opportunity to share her story with the committee, as her attorney said yesterday she was willing to do. We offered her a public or a private hearing as well as staff-led interviews, whichever makes her most comfortable. Dr. Ford's testimony would reflect her personal knowledge and memory of events. Nothing the FBI or any other investigator does would have any bearing on what Dr. Ford tells the committee, so there is no reason for any further delay.

SUSAN COLLINS: Chairman Grassley, along with his excellent staff, treated Professor Ford with compassion and respect throughout the entire process. And that is the way the Senator from Iowa has conducted himself throughout a lifetime dedicated to public service.

ORRIN HATCH: I don't think she's uncredible. I think she [*sic*] an attractive, good witness. . . . In other words, she's pleasing.

SUSAN COLLINS: We've heard a lot of charges and counter charges about Judge Kavanaugh. But as those who have known him best have attested, he has been an exemplary public servant, judge, teacher, coach, husband, and father.

THE KAVANAUGH DEBACLE

On September 27, 2018, there was a chill in the air in the cloudless sky over Salt Lake City. Gradually, the temperature rose. The sun's warmth offered the comfort I needed that morning. Christine Blasey Ford was about to testify before the Senate Judiciary Committee that, when she was a teenager, a boy she barely knew sexually assaulted her. The boy, Brett Kavanaugh, was now a federal judge and a nominee for a position on the Supreme Court. From my own experience in 1991, I knew that from the minute she began her testimony, her life would never be the same.

On that fall day, my schedule was quite full. It started with a women's studies class and a visit with the course instructor at the University of Utah. Then I had a quick bite to eat before doing a virtual panel discussion with a group of tech industry diversity and inclusion specialists. Following the panel, I would be off to the airport for my afternoon flight to Houston, where the next morning I was giving a keynote talk at the annual Grace Hopper Celebration of Women in Computing hosted by AnitaB.org, an organization centered on supporting women in tech. I was excited about every event, because each reminded me to be forward thinking. Like teaching, the ability to look beyond immediate conflict has sustained me whenever I was in doubt about the present. I've been on college campuses for most of my adult life—over four decades, counting my time in college and law school and my years teaching at three universities. I feel at home in just about any classroom. Yet the morning of the Kavanaugh hearing was not like every other. And this particular classroom at the University of Utah would be filled with people who had attended my lecture the night before. In that talk, I had assured them that the past thirty years had set the stage for change and that the #MeToo movement of the year before was the spark that would ignite the flame to end sexual harassment and other forms of gender abuse. But once again, the public was about to witness a test of the strength of our democracy. Would our political processes allow an individual citizen with relevant and critical information about the qualifications of a Supreme Court nominee to be heard?

Dr. Ford's testimony was the first thing on my mind when I woke up. I was grateful that the two-hour time difference between Salt Lake City, where I was, and Washington, D.C., would allow me to view this historic moment. Some parts of my heart, stomach, and head were with Christine Blasey Ford as she testified in the Hart Senate Office Building, though I was two thousand miles away. I hadn't planned it that way. The talk at the University of Utah on September 26 had been on my calendar since April, months before Donald Trump chose Brett Kavanaugh to replace Justice Anthony Kennedy on the Supreme Court. But on the morning of September 27, 2018, I, like so many people, held my breath in anticipation of Dr. Ford's testimony. In theory, what she was about to testify could determine whether Judge Brett Kavanaugh would be given a lifetime appointment to the Supreme Court. But I was filled with doubt about whether anything Dr. Ford said would make a difference. For Kavanaugh, there was a lot at stake. He had been chosen and groomed for the position by a powerful conservative group, the Federalist Society. I was certain of Dr. Ford's ability to tell her story and the truth of it. But I had no confidence in the Senate Judiciary Committee Republicans being willing to hold a hearing aimed at getting to the truth. I hoped to be proven wrong, and I wanted to pass that hope on to the students waiting for me on the University of Utah campus. And for myself, I wanted to believe that a witness who had a credible claim about a judicial nominee's alleged assault would have the opportunity to present all of the facts.

I had never spoken to Dr. Ford directly, but once the Judiciary Committee chair, Charles Grassley, who also heard my testimony, announced that she would testify, email flooded my in-box. Some suggested politely, "I would like to see you sitting behind Dr. Ford as she testifies on Thursday." Others argued that my presence "would certainly send a message to those, dare I say, incorrigible, ignorant men who did not listen to your honest pleas to be heard those many years ago." My instinct told me that those "ignorant men" and many others would make political hay out of any gesture I made to show my support for Dr. Ford. I recalled the claims from 1991 that left-wing, pro-choice feminists had duped me into testifying about Thomas's behavior. I was certain that Ford was hearing something of the same.

My biggest hope for the day was that it would be a completely different experience for her than it had been for me. That a lot of hard work by activists, researchers, lawyers, and others raising claims and demanding change in their workplaces in the twenty-seven years since I had faced that same Senate committee had resulted in the evolution of a new awareness of gender violence. But with some of the same members as the 1991 Senate Judiciary Committee and the Republican Grassley in charge, I could not bring myself to be optimistic that the entire committee had evolved. The 1991 committee was made up of all White men, and men in the Senate outnumbered women ninety-eight to two. That the 2018 Senate Judiciary Committee included women, one of whom was African American, and an African American man gave me hope for a greater understanding of gender and power, as did the fact that twenty-three women were Senate members. My hope was that, between 1991 and 2018, enough senators had read the Department of Justice or Centers for Disease Control and Prevention reports about the prevalence and health consequences of sexual violence to counter the committee's naysayers.

In 1991, one public showing of solidarity stands out as having put me on the path of making sense of my experience. A group called African American Women in Defense of Ourselves, led by three feminist scholars, Elsa Barkley Brown, Deborah King, and Barbara Ransby, placed an ad in *The New York Times*. Without the benefit of social media, the effort came together quickly and seamlessly; sixteen hundred Black women rallied, collecting $50,000 to buy a full page. They joined to "bring to light the history of Black women's unacknowledged abuse, and to decry many of the senators' fierce rejections of [my] right to speak." Their words and their act of broadcasting them publicly helped me understand the importance of my coming forward and left me feeling less isolated. Being made to feel alone is an oft-used tactic victims face when they choose to testify about gender-based violence. Like outright denials, it causes witnesses to doubt themselves and their importance despite their truthfulness. The ad stopped short of declaring that Thomas relied on racist and sexist myths embedded in our culture and distrust of women, particularly of a Black woman, to make his case. But as important, the ad's writers expressed outrage, something neither I nor Ford, nearly thirty years later, could do without destroying any chance that we would be taken seriously.

Despite the support of her family, lawyers, and others surrounding her, I knew that Ford would feel isolated and, perhaps, outraged. The morning of her testimony, an ad fashioned after the Black feminists' ad appeared in *The New York Times*. This time Meena Harris, founder of the Phenomenal Woman Action Campaign and niece of the then-senator Kamala Harris, and Alicia Garza, cofounder of the Black Lives

Matter Global Network Foundation, started the initiative titled "1,600 Men for Anita Hill & Christine Blasey Ford." The signers to the ad agreed to do their part to end gender-based violence and urged the Senate to provide a "just process, and for the rights of women like Dr. Blasey Ford to be heard fully, fairly, and with respect." As I opened the paper to the page in the *Times*, I felt a sensational rush of affirmation for myself and for the impact that Brown, King, and Ransby were still having. I prayed that it gave Ford a sense of assurance that she was not alone and that what she was about to do mattered. The 2018 ad boosted my spirits even with no way of knowing for sure how Ford felt about it.

Women, especially sexual violence victims and survivors, wanted to hear her voice—waited for her chance to tell what happened to the sixteen-year-old who had gone to what she thought was a typical teen party, but that ended with a life-changing event. Many of us were closely monitoring the hearing from our homes and workplaces. We were millions of "hearing watchers," alert to any signs of prejudice against Ford, outright intimidation, or behind-the-scenes dealmaking, and ready to call them out. She was poised to exercise her right to be heard—our collective right to be heard.

From the time Ford took her seat in front of the Senate Judiciary Committee and read her opening statement, I was engrossed. Ford's statement opened with biographical details, including her impressive academic career, her fifteen-year marriage and two children, her childhood in the D.C. area and enrollment in a private high school. Then she got to the point: "This is how I met Brett Kavanaugh, the boy who sexually assaulted me."

I admired her composure. Ford acknowledged that she was nervous. Over the years, people have said that they don't know how I was able to stay so calm and cool under all that glare and scrutiny. Yes, there were cameras shoved in my face and people agitating in ways that made it unclear if they were for me or against me. In retrospect, the whole spectacle was terrifying. Still, once you raise your hand and swear on a Bible, your focus becomes laser clear: to tell the truth. What I heard in Ford's voice and choice of words was a commitment to tell the truth. What I also heard was a resolve to make the committee and the public understand her experience.

Republican senators hired the Arizona prosecutor Rachel Mitchell to question Dr. Ford, another signal that Grassley had no intention of giving Ford a fair hearing. Like Specter, Mitchell was a prosecutor, and she questioned Ford as if Ford were on trial. Despite Ford's admitted nervousness, she was clear about what she experienced and equally clear when she didn't recall something. I watched Mitchell try to discredit a credible witness and poke holes in solid testimony, looking for inconsistencies—some minor—like how loud the music was at the party and whether there was a TV. I wondered if the former sex-crimes prosecutor would regret accepting the role of being Ford's inquisitor. Was this really what she wanted her legacy to be?

Then I turned the TV off, not because it was painful (although it was) and not because the hearing was a sham (although it was), because watching the first few minutes had given me confidence that Ford was up to the task of convincing a majority of the committee that she had been sexually assaulted as a teenager and that Kavanaugh had been the assailant. For the time being, the classroom of students at the University of Utah had to be my priority no matter how the hearings unfolded. What was about to occur in the form of the only fully public portion of the procedure used to determine Kavanaugh's fitness for the country's highest court would force us to call into question what we value as a nation. I wanted to help the students make sense of this and perhaps to prepare them for the disconnect between what they were about to witness and what they had been raised to believe about progress in this country.

Wanting to give the students some hope, I put my own cynicism on hold. They shared their stories about why they majored in gender and sexuality studies and what their courses had taught them. We talked about shared aspirations for gender equality. Yes, they were concerned, but they appeared to be sanguine about the process. They were a generation that had grown up with the belief that sexual assault and harassment victims and survivors were taken seriously and that abusers would be held accountable. The compelling stories of the #MeToo movement were fresh in their minds. By the end of our session, they were focusing on their own ambitions and how what they had learned in the gender studies classes had prepared them to understand what was unfolding in Washington. I left the class feeling less anxious than when I had arrived but was unconvinced that they were ready to deal with the dejection of another process that might very well minimize the behavior that they or their friends likely had suffered. Perhaps my own experience with testifying at the Thomas hearing was causing me to overreact. Not so.

I would learn from friends that the hearing was not going well for Ford. Though Ford, the psychologist, eloquently explained her memory lapses in scientific terms, the Republicans seemed indifferent. She told how since the alleged assault, Kavanaugh's and his friend's uproarious laughter was indelible in her hippocampus. She risked being caricatured as too smart and thus unintentionally undermining her claim. Would Republican senators argue she was too intelligent to be a victim of sexual assault? Ford acknowledged that the pain she felt at the time of the traumatic experience and in the years since was locked in her brain. Would they say that she was too emotional in explaining her experience? Throughout Ford's testimony, Senator Grassley had tried to put on a facade of impartiality, but it was clear that the Republicans on the committee were not moved by what she had shared with them. I also learned that Mitchell had a strategy. At one point in questioning Ford, Mitchell appeared to imply that the anxiety and fear of flying that Ford attributed to her assault were "not so bad." Mitchell noted that Ford had taken vacations to Hawaii and Costa Rica, traveling to each location by plane. As though the mere suggestion that Ford wasn't really afraid to fly showed she couldn't have been assaulted by Kavanaugh.

Back in my room to pack before heading to the airport, I turned the TV back on. Thankfully, my spouse, Chuck, was with me in Utah to watch Kavanaugh's response. And I became hopeful that the committee would see that Kavanaugh's anger and veiled threats against senators who rejected his nomination were disqualifying. But when Grassley abruptly cut off Mitchell's questioning of Kavanaugh before she was able to grill him about his activities at the time Ford says he assaulted her, the pretense of fairness completely vanished.

Later that afternoon during the three-hour flight to Houston, I tried to keep calm. But I was anxious about my Grace Hopper talk. Brenda Darden Wilkerson, a former computer programmer and an inspired leader in the movement for diversity and inclusion in tech, had invited me to speak. Twenty thousand attendees had landed in Texas for the convention. As a girl, I dreamed of a career in STEM, and I didn't want to let Brenda or the crowd of tech and science professionals who had achieved that goal down. How could I infuse my talk with hope at this critical and concerning juncture?

By the time I arrived in Houston, the hearing was over. Denial—

individual, institutional, and structural—had a two-pronged effect, disparaging Christine Blasey Ford's credibility and undermining the gravity of the behavior she described. Elected officials who are meant to serve the people used political procedures, a shoddy investigation, and a perplexing hearing as a pretext for a fact-finding process. The power these individuals hold makes structural denial the most destructive form.

President Donald Trump caved to public demands that the FBI investigate Christine Blasey Ford's claims. But in the same request to the FBI, he limited the investigation to interviews with Ford and Kavanaugh. No other information about the context and circumstances of the events from that era was brought to bear. As a result, the process devolved to a perfunctory "she said, he said" matter. And thus, Ford's word was pitted against the word of the president's nominee for the Supreme Court and all his endorsers, including the president himself.

On September 28, when the Judiciary Committee voted to move Kavanaugh's nomination to the Senate, I sat before the crowd at the Grace Hopper Celebration. This time the audience was older than in the gender and women's studies class, mostly women and nonbinary individuals working in the tech industry. And I was well aware that some of the people looking back at me had joined the Women's March in January 2017 to protest the very dismissal of women's voices that we had witnessed the day before in the Kavanaugh hearing. For many, Donald Trump's election and inauguration were ominous signs of our acceptance of misogyny. His bragging of entitlement to his own predatory behavior—grabbing "women by the pussy"—was despicable. And Trump's ludicrous characterization of the comment as "locker room talk" only angered us more. The "locker room talk" defense was the presidential candidate's version of "not so bad." And professional athletes who had spent more time in locker rooms than Trump found his justification for the vile remark offensive. Though the intense stage lighting kept me from seeing many of the faces in the crowd, I could tell that the mood was somber. I implored them, reminding them that though we seemed to have little influence over the way the Kavanaugh hearing transpired, what comes next was yet up to us. I assured them that they still had the power to act, whether in their own workplaces or through civic engagement. Though I would learn that many in the audience were crying, the event turned out to be affirming for me and the audience. It felt good to be together in this moment of uncertainty about the upcoming vote on Kavanaugh's nomination and whether our experiences mattered to our government.

If Grassley had learned any lessons from 1991, he could have warded off these perceptions as chair of the 2018 hearings. If Grassley had believed that women's claims of sexual assault matter in choosing who gets to sit on the country's highest court and believed in women's right to be heard, he would have demanded a thorough investigation with all relevant witnesses testifying. He would have demanded that Deborah Ramirez and her corroborating witnesses testify about Kavanaugh's drunken behavior—including an alleged sexual assault—that occurred when Ramirez and Kavanaugh were in college at Yale. Grassley would have brought in experts on sexual assault and trauma to talk about its effects on victims' reactions to and their recollections of their assaults. At the very least, given emerging information documenting the prevalence of sexual harassment and assault, Grassley would have kept his promise to provide a process for receiving and vetting claims that accuse a nominee of gender-based discrimination and violent behavior. But the limited investigation, and Collins's suggestion that a criminal standard of "innocent until proven guilty" was applicable (as if it could possibly be fulfilled in a single-day political process without calling other witnesses), all but assured Kavanaugh's position on the Supreme Court. On October 2, Rachel Mitchell declared that there was not sufficient evidence to support Ford's claim without so much as mentioning that evidence had been suppressed by the narrow investigation. That same day, Trump went so far as to mock Ford's testimony at a rally in Mississipi and warned that "young men in America" were in danger of false accusations. At the same time, the president extolled Kavanaugh as "one of the finest people" he knew. That Trump had called Ford a credible witness a few days earlier no longer mattered. The power imbalance created by the president's endorsement of Kavanaugh made it nearly impossible for Ford to be taken seriously in a battle over credibility. In the end, it didn't matter that the 2018 Senate Judiciary Committee had more gender and racial diversity. It didn't matter that Senator Amy Klobuchar forcefully challenged Kavanaugh's recollection about some of the events that Ford testified to. And although Senator Cory Booker gave an impassioned plea for the committee to dispense with its denials and fulfill its obligation to listen to survivors of sexual assault, the rush to approve the nominee continued without pause. In twenty-seven years, the committee makeup had changed, but the rules that allowed for relevant facts to be excluded remained the same.

On October 6, along party lines, the Senate confirmed Kavanaugh's appointment by a vote of 50–48. After the vote, politicians and Kavanaugh supporters in the press put their own spin on Ford's narrative. Some of the accusations were ludicrous conspiracy theories. Senator Tom Cotton opined to the press that Senate minority leader "Chuck Schumer's political operation knew about Ms. Ford's allegations as far back as July and manipulated the process all along to include taking advantage of Ms. Ford's confidences and directing her towards left-wing lawyers."[1] One claim was bizarre: the Republican commentators Mollie Hemingway and Carrie Severino put forth the idea that Democratic senators had praised Dr. Ford's blue suit and referenced Coca-Cola to suggest parallels to my testimony at the Thomas hearing.[2]

RESOLVE

My first face-to-face meeting with Christine Blasey Ford came just over a year after her testimony. She movingly introduced a lecture I gave at the University of Washington in Seattle. When I met her, I noticed the same genuineness that I saw in her testimony—the same seriousness and clarity—and a warmth that was hidden by the glare of the hearing. We've kept in touch, and on one occasion I asked her if she thought the committee could have done something differently in her case.

Though Ford and her family were the targets of death threats, she was resolved to make sense of her experience. And a year after the Senate dismissed her testimony, Ford was determined to improve the way the Senate Judiciary Committee handled complaints of gender violence. She wanted the public to understand that the Supreme Court should play a critical role in addressing the problem of gender-based violence and therefore should be beyond reproach. I was struck by how hopeful Ford remained that the Senate would somehow step up to create a system for handling sexual misconduct complaints. Dr. Ford suggested that future complaints could be collected in an office set aside for that purpose, and make the public aware of its procedures and provide whistleblower-type protections for people who came forward. This, she believed, would help both witnesses and the public's perception of a fair process. Ford was also clear that the process shouldn't end when the hearing closes. Help afterward with attaining closure, she said, would include having the opportunity to share any documents or relevant materials with the public to maintain a historical, accurate record. Hers was a plea for inclusion of survivors' experiences and accountability in a process that by a number of measures appeared to lack both.

And the results of the next election, just weeks after Kavanaugh's confirmation, indicated that voters were interested in accountability and more diverse representation. As in 1992, women headed to the polls in record numbers for a midterm election. *The New York Times* reported that "117 women were elected on Tuesday; 100 Democrats and 17 Republicans." The 2018 midterm races made history with forty-two winners who were women of color and at least three LGBTQ+ individuals elected to office. When the ballots were finally counted, there were a total of twenty-four women elected to the U.S. Senate.

That's why 2018 came to be called a "second year of the woman." But even this development was bittersweet. The millions of marchers who had gathered the day after Trump's inauguration, as well as the 2018 election results, gave me hope, but as the civil and women's rights activist Pauli Murray wrote in her poem "Dark Testament," "Hope is a song in a weary throat." In the face of such disappointment over the Kavanaugh hearings and what was to many a repeat of 1991, it felt as if we were always defending our political disenfranchisement and claim to equality but not building on it.

So what is our resolve to make sure that what happened in 1991 and 2018 doesn't happen again? Though news outlets recognized the election as a "historic moment" in gender representation, Rutgers University's respected Center for American Women and Politics was more cautious. "We've seen important breakthroughs, particularly in the U.S. House," said the center's director, Debbie Walsh, "but deepening disparities between the parties in women's representation will continue to hobble us on the path to parity. We need women elected on both sides of the aisle." But would more Republican women in office have changed the Kavanaugh hearing? Or would the gravitational pull of partisan politics prove so strong that even claims of sexual harassment and abuse might be discounted? The words of Hatch and Grassley demonstrate their disregard for the seriousness of the charges against two individuals being considered for lifetime appointments to the country's highest court.

The damage done to the reputation of the Supreme Court by the hearings of 1991 and 2018 remains. Those who supported the nominees believe that Democrats on the Senate Judiciary Committee have debased the judicial selection process by conducting witch hunts based on unfounded accusations. On the other side, the polls suggest that at least half of the population believe that two out of the nine judges currently on the Court have engaged in sexual misconduct. And though the 1991 and 2018 hearings were indeed political theater, they also shed light on where the country stands on gender violence. The senators' regressive positioning on sexual misconduct is now reflected in the country's legal system. Our civic participation, which includes our right to bring claims of sexual misconduct to confirmation processes, something basic to our citizenship, was disregarded in 1991 and in 2018.

And more than the Supreme Court was at stake. Damage was done to survivors and all women who understand their risk for being a victim of violence. The idea that sexual violence is "not so bad" carried the day. The credibility of women survivors in workplaces, reporting to police and appearing in courts, was put on trial in a process that was deeply flawed. It was, to quote Dahlia Lithwick, "the very opposite of truth-seeking, the opposite of justice."[3] We may feel less safe today because the Senate Judiciary Committee's model of a "neutral fact finding process" is one that might well be justified as the model for other hearings. It's left to us to repair the broken system that yielded the Thomas and Kavanaugh hearings and that continues to imperil hard-won legal battles. When we look closely at the state of our response to sexual violence today, we can't help but see how fragile our right to be free from gender violence truly is.

THREE

A "Recurrent Feature of Our Social Experience"

O ur tendency to deny well-documented abuse is one of the most vexing aspects of the fight against gender violence. Today, denial of women's claims still shows up in questions survivors and victims face. And though many deniers actually want solutions, they, like some of our leaders and the public at large, cling to this defense mechanism, hampering efforts to change the systems and cultures that enable gender violence. We can't fix what we refuse to acknowledge. For all the attention sexual harassment received after the Thomas confirmation hearing, the number of sexual harassment cases filed in court still doesn't match the frequency of the problem. Some estimates are that 25 percent of working women face sexual harassment; others are as high as 85 percent. And lawsuits are not easy to file. First, small businesses are exempt. Title VII, the federal law prohibiting sexual harassment, does not cover a business with fewer than fifteen employees. That means workers in small towns, where there are relatively fewer large operations, are unable to file complaints with the federal government. The same is true for independent contractors no matter the size of the business. Title VII covers only employee protections, which means there are no protections for contractors and many of today's gig workers. Second, lawsuits are costly, which leaves out low-income workers. And the short statute of limitations, the 180-day (or 300-day, depending on the jurisdiction) window during which victims must file their claim or lose the option to do so, doesn't give victims much time to come up with the funds it takes to hire a lawyer. Just a few years ago, I heard from one woman whose mother took out a second mortgage on her home to pay for her daughter's lawsuit. In the end, they lost both the suit and the home.

In addition to the statutory and economic barriers to filing sexual harassment claims, court decisions from the mid-1990s and first decade of the twenty-first century imposed other limitations. In 2020, the U.S. Commission on Civil Rights reported that a "judicial test for actionable sexual harassment which requires that it rise to the level of being 'severe or pervasive'" has drawn criticism because its ambiguity invites inconsistent results.[1] In a 2018 article in the *Stanford Law Review*, the former federal judge Nancy Gertner highlighted cases in which judges dismissed vulgar antiwoman comments and acts as not severe or pervasive ("not so bad") enough to be harassment. Evidence in the decisions Gertner cited included the following: the statement "fucking women, I hate having fucking women in the office" made by a defendant; a defendant who leaned over and "kissed [the plaintiff's] right buttock"; and testimony that a supervisor referred to a plaintiff as a "dumb shit," "whore," "stupid bitch," and "hooker." In cases from the 1990s and first decade of the twenty-first century, the above behaviors were dismissed as "stray remarks" or "general vulgarity that [the law] does not regulate."[2]

Title VII allows for suits against employers, not individual managers. In order to recover damages, a claimant must show that the employer was aware of the behavior or that the individual harasser was a supervisor. In the case of *Vance v. Ball State University*, a racial harassment case, Maetta Vance complained that a university employee, Saundra Davis, slapped Vance, directed racial slurs at her, and stood by as others taunted her with violence from the Ku Klux Klan. When Vance complained, Davis reduced her working hours. The plaintiff showed that Davis had the power to control Vance's day-to-day schedules and assignments. But the Supreme Court concluded that despite the harsh treatment, to be considered a supervisor for the purposes of workplace employer liability, Davis had to have the power to hire, fire, fail to promote, reassign to a task with significantly different duties, or cause a significant change in benefits available to the victim.

Thomas, now acknowledged as one of the Court's more conservative thinkers, agreed that the ruling established the "narrowest and most workable rule" for determining an employer's liability for harassment. But the former chairman of the EEOC, whose agenda entailed enforcing Title VII's protections, joined the majority—despite supervisors' power to make work lives unbearable even if they can't hire or fire an employee. What is even more disturbing is that Davis's unchecked authority to engage in blatantly racist and hostile behavior showed just how much power she wielded in the office. In her dissent, Justice Ruth Bader Ginsburg called out the majority for not understanding how modern workplaces work. Ginsburg cited sexual harassment cases where supervisors had made life for women miserable, including one in which a supervisor pledged to make an employee's life a "living hell." In another case the supervisor "commented frequently on [a female worker's] 'fantastic ass,' 'luscious lips,' and 'beautiful eyes,' and, using deplorable racial epithets, opined that minorities and women did not 'belong in the business.' Once, he pulled her on his lap, touched her buttocks, and tried to kiss her while others looked on." The other cases Ginsburg brought up involved verbal assaults, sexual slurs, posting pornographic images, sexual references to women workers' anatomies and genitalia, and sexual extortion. But under the Supreme Court's definition of "supervisor," none of the employers would be accountable for the supervising employees' behavior. Ginsburg warned that the grudging definition of "supervisor" did a disservice to "the objective of Title VII to prevent discrimination from infecting the Nation's workplaces." She went even further, accusing the majority of "constructing artificial" barriers for complainants as a step in what she described as her colleagues' "unrestrained course to corral Title VII." Ginsburg ended her dissent with a plea to Congress to correct the Court's weakening of Title VII and to restore the "robust protections" Title VII was intended to offer.[3] To date, Congress has taken no action to restore the law's safeguards.

In addition to shining a light on the way the Senate treats sexual harassment and assault, the 1991 and 2018 hearings show how harassment and assault claims are treated outside the political process. Whether the complaints arise from behavior in workplaces, in homes, or on the street, officials may forgo full investigations and/or dismiss the conduct as harmless. And despite credible evidence confirming an accuser's claim, accountability may still be lacking.

Today, sexual assault claims are more frequent in court than in the past. But the hurdles to prevailing in assault and rape suits are still extremely high. First, local law enforcement assesses their ability to get a conviction. Law enforcement's search for the perfect victim—a flawless straight, young, and, typically, White (a factor, but by no means dispositive) woman who behaves after the rape in a way that is mythologized as appropriate—leads to victims never reporting or getting to have their day in court. In her book *Is Rape a Crime? A Memoir, an Investigation, and a Manifesto*, Michelle Bowdler tells the chilling story of her brutal rape and her harrowing decades-long search for justice. In asking us whether rape is a crime, Bowdler reminds us that it is the least reported criminal offense and that less than 1 percent of rapes are likely to result in a conviction. In her case, police identified a suspect, a potential serial rapist, but no conviction followed. And yet thousands of rape kits are stored in warehouses across the country never to be processed or even labeled. In some locations, police misclassify rape and sexual assault to tamp down the rate of violent crimes under their watch.[4] Chanel Miller was unconscious when she was sexually assaulted outdoors on the campus of Stanford University. Miller's haunting memoir *Know My Name* details the difficulties she encountered navigating the criminal justice system even though two witnesses to the attack testified on her behalf. Miller's experience of assault and the trial of her accused assailant expose both the public's and the legal system's bias against sexual assault victims. She was one of the 0.5 percent whose assailants were convicted for sexual assault. But despite the witnesses and an impact statement that vividly displayed Miller's trauma, in 2016 the judge in her case sentenced Brock Turner, the accused whom a jury found guilty, to six months in prison, of which he served three. We can begin to break the cycle of aggressive and violent behavior by acknowledging the price we pay for gender violence.

THE COST OF OUR DENIAL

Facts matter. And money matters. We know that harassment and assault are costly. They are a financial and reputational drain on institutions, public and private. And the societal toll paid cannot be measured in monetary terms alone. The costs to victims and survivors are enormous and increasingly documented by researchers and chronicled by survivors themselves. Miller's and Bowdler's memoirs compel us to recognize the physical and emotional price that sexual assault and rape victims pay. Harassment victims can suffer dire mental and physical health issues as well. One study of more than twelve thousand soldiers found that those who experienced sexual harassment were five times more likely to commit suicide.[5] And victims can suffer serious financial costs as well. In the civilian workforce, the economic costs of workplace harassment can add to victims' and survivors' emotional trauma. A 2018 Marketplace poll found that nearly 50 percent of women who have been harassed leave their current job or switch careers because of it.[6] Author and businesswoman Nilofer Merchant warns that sexual harassment can have insidious economic effects not only on the individual but on the entire economy. And, as with sexual assault and rape, not all of the costs owing to sexual harassment are economic. It has also been linked to increased incidents of illness, injury, or assault.

But in truth, no one has calculated the full price of sexual harassment or assault. The U.S. senators Dianne Feinstein, Kirsten Gillibrand, Patty Murray, and Elizabeth Warren have pushed the Government Accountability Office to get actual figures on the price businesses pay. "While employers tend to focus on direct costs to a business, such as legal fees or settlement amounts, the true cost of sexual harassment includes indirect costs such as decreased productivity, increased turnover, and reputational harm," they wrote in a letter to the GAO. "All of this is an impediment to employee performance and employers' bottom-lines."[7]

Over the past thirty years, I've encountered an open refusal to accept the "disagreeable reality," as Anna Freud termed it, and unwelcome facts of gender-based violence, words that imply that this abuse is nearly a societal pill we have to swallow. For whatever reason, it has been difficult for us to even do that, to see clearly what is in plain view. It's selective vision. It's a refusal to see reality as it exists to millions of survivors, in which pain keeps touching the people we know and love. Yet though acknowledgment of the problem and the need for change is the most elemental step to recovering our society, many outright refuse to do that work.

I May Destroy You, the HBO show that premiered in the United States in June 2020, follows Arabella, a young Black woman who is sexually assaulted one night in London. It's a piercing, darkly comic show about how the experience makes her manic, anxious, and depressed, and how she tries to get out of it. Her best friend, Terry, is her partner on this journey. In one scene, warning an unsupportive friend to stay away from Arabella, Terry says, about recovering from sexual violence, "Self-care is important in the first two stages," before adding, "The only thing more important is to avoid friends who don't affirm or comfort." Imagine, then, an entire society, an entire world even, that for some reason does not believe, affirm, or comfort you. Instead, what we have is a world where one is more likely to be faced with doubt than support.

The Senate confirmation hearings for Thomas and Kavanaugh show the dire consequences when we put up roadblocks to understanding the truth of women's experiences. Both hearings functioned as a reality check of where our political leadership stood on sexual harassment and assault at two points in our history. In both instances, government leaders disappointed the public. And the Senate Judiciary Committee, however powerful, is not the only place where disregard for our lived experiences occurs. Historically, we've denied the problem in nearly all aspects of our lives, and past courts showed open disdain for sexual harassment and assault claims. Today, such a reaction may be more subtle, but nonetheless remains apparent in many cases, as will be clear in the chapters to follow. Yet we still ask domestic violence sufferers why they "didn't just leave." We don't ask abusers why they stay and beat their partners. Routinely, survivors face questions that ignore the psychological and physiological effects of sexual violence, and we require them to give us explanations that we refuse to accept. Why do we require multiple victims and survivors to come forward before we believe a single one? Whether in the political sphere, in workplaces, in our justice system, or in the court of public opinion, this dismissive attitude diminishes our political and legal protections. Denying accountability for the behavior makes us *all* less safe.

Cardiologists have begun to address the gender heart health gap written about in chapter 1. Some efforts have been successful. And as in health care, how successful we are in addressing sexual harassment turns on who we believe is accountable. Think back on the quotations from the *Redbook* survey in chapter 1. The thirty-four-year-old first-level female manager who left her job because she was harassed could have reported the behavior. But it's unlikely that there was a safe procedure for her to report into or that her harassment would have been seen as important enough to bother with. The thirty-eight-year-old plant manager (who believed that the issue was overblown) might have been in a position to witness behavior and even participate in it. But given his resistance to the notion that harassment exists, his concept of what is unfair behavior is unlikely to be the same as his female employees'. And according to the *Vance* decision and other legal barriers, unless he had the power to hire and fire, he and his company may be let off the hook for allowing it to continue. The skeptical fifty-three-year-old male vice president, as a corporate leader, might be able to insist that his company put in place the procedures needed and demand that all employees be treated with respect and dignity. But the *Vance* case and other cases discussed in later chapters do away with some of the incentive for corporations to get the facts about what's happening under their auspices and take proactive stands against the problems they identify.

There is no easy fix to the problem of sexual harassment in the workplace or the other forms of gender-based violence. Responses coming out of the courts are not keeping up with the reality and severity of the problem. Many current approaches shift responsibility for ending the problem away from leaders. They don't work. For example, insisting that survivors and victims can control bad behavior by standing up to their abusers, telling them that their problems will be solved if they report into processes that are stacked against them, and pledging to get rid of a few bad apples are all forms of denial, none of which have been effective solutions.

We cannot risk the damage that can be done by another public debacle that questions the damage of gender violence. But leadership at the top establishing a tone of respect is the best first step to changing culture and behavior. Leaders' responses that match the significance and harm of the problem of gender violence are key to eliminating it. As of the printing of this book, the Senate Judiciary Committee had not announced any new procedures for hearing complaints about alleged abuses by nominees. The Congressional Accountability Act of 1995 overburdened accusers with waiting periods and mandated counseling before they could report. The act also shielded offenders from exposure and paid for the settlements to victims and survivors out of Treasury funds. In 2018, following a public uproar about the act's lack of protections for survivors and victims, Congress passed the Congressional Accountability Act of 1995 Reform Act. The new procedures provide employees with a four-step process for filing harassment and discrimination complaints, eliminate the wait and counseling requirements, and require offenders to foot their own settlement costs. In September 2020, Eleanor Holmes Norton, a pioneer in recognizing the harm of sexual harassment, a former head of the EEOC, and now a congresswoman representing the District of Columbia, saw the need for more reform. She proposed the Congress Leads by Example Act of 2020 to respond to ongoing reports of workplace abuses in the legislative branch. Norton's proposal would appear to be uncontroversial. She called for Congress to lead by example by adhering to the same laws that the rest of America abides by. This example of leadership acting to set the tone is a move in the right direction toward accountability and ending structural and institutional denials.

Yet the denials and myths that tell us sexual harassment, extortion, and assaults don't exist or alternatively are harmless and therefore don't matter continue to silence witnesses and victims and control the narrative of harassment and assault claims. They are the foundation on which many of our policies that purport to be antiviolence are built. Yes, aggressive and violent behavior motivated by gender seems to be a recurrent feature of our social experience. But it's high time we reject the idea that it will always be so. Knowing how deeply entrenched gender violence is in society is the start of knowing how to root it out. I see guidance for how we can change courses in Ginsburg's dissent in *Vance* as well as in pop culture's rejection of the inevitability of abuse.

What if we truly believed that we could put an end to gender-based violence? Where would we start? I would start by attending to the routine gender violence children experience as victims and observers. We are just beginning to understand the price we pay for clinging to a notion that abuse is foreordained and/or natural. None of these unfounded ideas are more dangerous and in urgent need of debunking than those that imperil children—for whom we've only begun to calculate the harm.

FOUR

The Myth of the Woke Generation

n October 2017, sitting at my desk reading through some of the many stories being shared under the banner of #MeToo, I felt a sense of déjà vu. A similar groundswell of outrage and activism had followed the Clarence Thomas hearings in 1991, and many believed it would be a turning point, that sexual harassment and assault would finally be taken seriously by society and the courts.

We all hoped that the reports of long-standing abuses in Hollywood and other industries, and the flood of stories they unleashed, would usher in a period of reckoning. All seemed to agree: time was up—*needed* to be up—for sexism and its insidious choke hold on everyone's lives. Yet despite the progress made over the past few years, it's become apparent that the reckoning that has materialized has in no way matched the volume of complaints. And disappointment is mounting in those who expected #MeToo to be the wake-up call our government needed to address gender-based violence. The truth is, I am not surprised. History has taught me that it will take more than mere testimony to solve the deeply embedded problem of this form of violence.

The #MeToo movement did accomplish something that did not exist before 2017. It broke open a public conversation about the harsh reality and pervasive nature of gender-based violence. People around the globe, aided by social media and a broadened media landscape, shared stories of sexual harassment and assault that were horrific and familiar. It also prompted a more nuanced conversation about all that falls under the gender-based violence umbrella and how it creeps into our lives at an early age and follows us from place to place. No longer could one credibly claim that the abuses a few had stepped up to complain about in courts were fictitious or overblown.

One of the most troubling #MeToo revelations was how often and regularly young people experience gender violence. Survivors and victims of all genders described abuse that began when they were children and continued on a daily basis in our elementary, middle, and high schools, generational wave after wave.

With participants of all ages, the movement made clear that gender-based violence has existed for generations in precisely the same forms as it exists today. And that will continue to be the case until we let go of a persistent myth: that one day a generation will come along that will no longer tolerate it. It won't magically disappear any more than pollution or poverty or racism or hunger or any of the other evils that are recurring features of our human experience.

I remember when it was thought that the baby boomer generation would be the one that would put bias aside, along with the violence prompted by prejudice and animus. We were the generation that criticized our parents for segregating housing, schools, and workplaces, and for tolerating glass ceilings and pregnancy or parental discrimination that blocked women's success. But though boomers preached love and peace, they largely ignored intimate partner violence in our homes, sexual extortion on work sites, and sexual assault in our schools. It's no surprise that we have now seen prominent baby boomers, including actors, politicians, and journalists, exiting the scene in shame.

It is true that Gen Zers and millennials are more accepting of LGBTQ+ people, less tolerant of racism, and more likely to say that sexual harassment is a problem, according to public opinion polls. And optimists, me included, would like to believe that a new generation's thinking about differences will lead to a natural evolution of ideas and conduct in our colleges and universities, as well as in our workplaces, homes, and streets. We cite promising surveys providing proof that a higher percentage of Gen Zers and millennials think same-sex marriage is good for society, that people ought to avoid offending people from different backgrounds, and that online profiles that ask about a person's gender should include options other than "man" or "woman."[1] We take comfort in statistics verifying that 91 percent of Gen Zers believe that everyone is equal and should be treated equally.[2] We read articles declaring that because of these progressive attitudes, the youngest generation won't tolerate sexual harassment in our workplaces.[3] And thus, they represent our hope for ending gender-based abuses. So we tell ourselves that we need only wait for them to come of age or for a change of the guard—the tipping point when they will hold most government and workplace positions and can implement policies that reflect their progressive values. We also ignore the culture that the twenty- and thirty-year-olds of today grew up in and how it has shaped their thinking and behavior. Many millennials and Gen Zers may lean toward liberal policies and ideas, but a significant portion of them do not. A 2018 Pew poll showed that roughly 30 percent of both groups approved of Trump's job performance and nearly 40 percent were not convinced that racial and ethnic diversity in the United States is a good thing. Big questions are yet to be answered. What political and social events will shape their thinking in the future? And will progressive ideas inspire action against gender violence, or will younger generations prioritize other causes?

More than polls, online activities of teens and tweens offer us a glimpse of how much we can count on a younger generation to evolve us into a society of egalitarianism. In the first decade of the twenty-first century, online chat rooms emerged as a new go-to way for young people to express themselves. With the growth of the internet has come the growth of the culture of gender violence. Chat rooms and other social media can offer young people a way to connect, find communities of peers with whom they identify, and even heal from school pressures and other challenges that teens and tweens face. However, these chat rooms also sometimes breed bad behavior of all sorts, including gender-based violence. Chat rooms have been used for bullying, spreading rumors, harassment, and "flaming" (posting profane or bigoted insults and name-calling). Young girls have been targeted by older men pretending to be their peers. And as newer forums like Facebook and Instagram developed, cyberbullying became a staple of tween and teen life. Ready accessibility to technology made it a popular tool for spreading sexist and violent messages. *The Tab*, an online media outlet covering youth culture, calls itself "the voice of students." In this case the subjects are college students. *The Tab*'s reporters follow and write about group sexist and homophobic posts. The chat group topics include homophobia, rape jokes, contests about sleeping with the "poorest girls," and rape threats.

But the most striking feature of online abuse is its prevalence among tweens. Tweens are not the only youths using social media for harmful purposes, but their age makes them more socially and emotionally vulnerable and more likely to be bullied. Disturbingly, according to Common Sense Media, more than a third say they have been cyberbullied, compared with 5 percent of young people who are self-confident, feel accepted by their peers, and are generally happy. The Cyberbullying Research Center's 2020 survey of nine- to twelve-year-old middle school students across the United States found that one in five tweens has been cyberbullied.[4] When cyberbullying is piled on top of in-school bullying, victims are five times more likely to consider or plan suicide and eleven times more likely to attempt suicide than those who are not bullied.[5] And adolescents' exposure to offensive messages is on the rise. "Nearly two-thirds (64 percent) of teen social media users in 2018 say they 'often' or 'sometimes' come across racist, sexist, homophobic, or religious-based hate content in social media"; one in five say they "often" do so.[6] From 2012 to 2018, young people's exposure to hate content rose from 8 to 12 percent. Online experiences of hate and harassment are growing, and the rules for how to police this toxic behavior, which often happens outside school, are just beginning to catch up. Whether cyberbullying and social media harassment are protected by the First Amendment will likely only be resolved by the Supreme Court. But no legal decision can delete the cultural influence of social media and other online activities. And when online toxicity combines with in-person violence, the mix can be lethal.

Millennials and Gen Zers did not invent the myth of the woke generation. Each generation before them has employed some version of it.

Passing off the culture of gender-based violence that Gen Xers and boomers inherited to younger generations only delays progress. And relying on Gen Zers and millennials to reform society in the future does not relieve older generations of our responsibility to end the abuse happening in elementary and secondary schools throughout the country today.

GENERATIONS SCHOOLED IN GENDER HIERARCHY

Based on its ubiquity and tenacity, it's fair to say that gender-based violence is a systemic problem. What makes a problem systemic is that it becomes entrenched in our institutions and protected by our processes. For example, in chapter 1, we learned that training physicians to follow the same protocol for diagnosing heart conditions in men when examining women is one way to systematize health outcome disparities. If we want to begin to eliminate the disparities, we can start at medical schools, with training on how to conduct proper examinations and how to identify the underlying biases that support the ineffective procedures. If we want to understand how gender violence gets perpetuated from generation to generation, we should look at elementary school, an institution where it is practiced in various forms with a range of consequences, some of which are deadly.

Jo, May 1, 2008

I went to Catholic grammar school in Boston area in the 80s. We wore uniforms. We had nuns and laypersons for teachers.

Discipline was strict. and almost every girl in my class was subjected to physical sexual harassment in the 4th and 5th grade by the boys. Those boys that did not participate were bullied and labeled homosexual. I remember it clearly and I have discussed it with other now adults classmates who also remember this.

The teachers did nothing either because they were embarrassed or because they thought it was just what kids did.

School Sexual harassment is nothing new, has nothing to do with uniform vs no uniforms, and has nothing to do with "nowadays vs the good old days." At least now it is publicized and getting some recognition.[7]

This reader comment from Jo, a millennial, on the *New York Times* reporter Tara Parker-Pope's May 2008 *Well* blog entry on sexual harassment in schools is a great place to start to think about how routine happenings in our schools mark the beginning of gendered, aggressive behavior that will continue to happen in the future. It is a harbinger of what will happen in their workplaces or in their own homes as schoolchildren become adults.

Gender-based violence, sexism, and misogyny are abhorrent ideas that we baby boomers inherited and passed on to our children, just as our parents passed them to us. Placing responsibility on young people to correct abuse and violence handed down through the ages spares us the unsavory task of challenging the thinking and the systems that tolerate and perpetuate gender-based violence. Change can be achieved only through intentional implementation of dynamic, new solutions. Our own denial and our reliance on young people's idealism amount to complicity in the abuse. We must lift that veil if we want any chance of revealing it.

While each generation has offered its own responses to the problem, including stricter discipline, lenient discipline, and, as Jo noted, requiring students to wear uniforms, they haven't solved the problem. Telling evidence of our failure is found in examining stories from the past along with what really goes on in elementary schools these days. Throughout the country, abusive behavior that mirrors adult gender-based violence is routine. Children from prekindergarten through twelfth grade sexually harass, bully, and rape classmates at alarming rates; most (though not all) of the targets are girls or gender nonconforming. If we are to intervene effectively, we must acknowledge the problem's roots in school culture—in our elementary, middle, and high schools.

It helps to think first about what is driving kids to act out in vicious ways. Let's not fall back on the false and dangerous notion that some children are just "bad seeds"—predisposed to violence and naturally predacious. We've covered up the situation with euphemisms that disguise the toxic atmosphere that often drives this threatening behavior. We should be asking ourselves what it is about school culture and structure that reinforces and then excuses intolerance and cruelty. The innocuous words "clique" and "popular" might have easily been invented to describe what drives much behavior at schools. School culture is often anchored by the ranking and sorting of students. A 2018 study published in the *Journal of Adolescent Research* identified twelve peer groups, with populars, jocks, floaters, and good-ats in the top tier of cool kids, and loners, emo/goths, and anime fans ranking at the bottom. Stoners, nerds, fine arts kids, and so-called normals ranked in the middle. The study, conducted by researchers from the University of Illinois at Chicago and the University of Texas at Austin, also showed that Black and Latinx students often sorted themselves into ethnic cliques that served as their "home base," even though they associated with other cliques.[8] This hierarchy typically placed White straight men at the top, with others sorted according to their ability to conform to popularity standards often based on gender and racial expectations.

Cliques can help students navigate school culture and find people who share their interests and perspectives. But they often serve a more nefarious purpose: to separate students into insiders or outsiders, which then creates a perfect template for bullying and harassment. Kids who don't fit into stereotypical gender roles more often than not fall into the outsider category, and they suffer greatly for it.

If you weren't targeted by bullies (or were the bully), you may not even be aware that harassing was going on around you, as early as elementary school. But ask a contemporary, a gay, lesbian, trans, or nonbinary friend, and it's very likely they have a story to tell that may embarrass you because "it never occurred to you" that they would have been targeted for their gender or sexual identity. Incidents that are painful to others and leave lifetime scars often don't register as significant to those who weren't a target of the abuse or those who were the perpetrators of it.

Until Donald Trump's *Access Hollywood* tape put the whole question smack in the middle of the 2016 campaign, a presidential election was an unlikely place for a conversation about bullying or sexual harassment. But recall that the presidential candidate Mitt Romney found himself in the middle of a similar discussion courtesy of a story reported by *The Washington Post* in 2012. According to five of Romney's Cranbrook prep school classmates, Romney, as a senior, had bullied a younger student, John Lauber, who was presumed to be gay. Classmates of the future Massachusetts governor and U.S. senator told the *Post* that after spring break one year, Romney noticed that Lauber had returned to school with "bleached-blond hair that draped over one eye." Romney was clear in expressing his disapproval, allegedly saying, "He can't look like that. That's wrong. Just look at him!" A few days later, Mitt marched "out of his own room ahead of a prep school posse shouting about their plan to cut Lauber's hair."[9]

Phillip Maxwell, now a lawyer in Michigan, had participated in the event and recalled it in an interview with *The New York Times*. "It started out as ribbing, sort of a pointed ribbing about his hair, but it very quickly became an assault, and he was taken down to the ground, pinned," Maxwell said. "It all happened very quickly—it was like a pack of dogs." When questioned by the press about the episode, a spokesperson for Romney's campaign told the *Post*, "The stories of fifty years ago seem exaggerated and off base and Governor Romney has no memory of participating in these incidents." In an interview with Fox News, Romney later softened his response: "I did some dumb things, and if anybody was hurt by that or offended, obviously, I apologize for that. . . . You know, I don't, I don't remember that particular incident [laughs]. . . . I participated in a lot of hijinks and pranks during high school, and some might have gone too far, and for that I apologize."[10]

In the days that followed, the press coverage of Romney's part in the attack garnered a significant amount of public attention. Questions about the story and Romney's role in it typically fell along two lines. Did he not remember, or was he covering up for his behavior? And was the behavior severe or incidental to high school settings—just "what you'd expect that boys in prep school do"? One of Romney's classmates had called the attack on Lauber "vicious," but media characterizations seemed to support the view of the behavior as mostly harmless. Maggie Haberman, now a reporter for *The New York Times*, wrote an article for *Politico* with the headline "A 'Vicious' Romney Prank?" An ABC online story politicized the matter, publishing a story titled "Democrats Pounce on Story of 'Vicious' Young Romney Bullying Student." Many readers, often divided along political lines, took issue with the description of the event as a prank. They saw him as an insensitive bully who had committed a hate crime and lied about it. But others said it was "grossly unfair," "inane and ridiculous," to go back and criticize a presidential candidate for something he had done as a teenager.

The politicization of the incident prevented real conversation about what the behavior really meant and represented. How could Romney call this a forgotten "prank"? The way he remembered his own behavior is likely quite different from the way John Lauber, the target of the attack, recalled what happened to him. The dynamics of a popular student, the son of a governor, who held enough sway over his classmates to get them to go after a fellow student for his appearance might in fact be what boys in prep school do, but that does not make it anything less than harassment, bullying, or assault. Lauber was a soft-spoken younger student who "was perpetually teased for his nonconformity and presumed homosexuality," according to the *Post* account. And he was forced to wear the hack job done to his hair like a dunce cap. He left school for days after the incident before returning with a haircut and his hair its natural color. Still, it seemed Lauber would never fit in at Cranbrook. One Saturday, a classmate spotted him behind some hedges in a quiet area of the campus smoking a cigarette. The classmate reported the school policy violation to the headmaster, who expelled Lauber from Cranbrook. The same headmaster had failed to act when the group ganged up on Lauber. The group of students who bullied Lauber graduated from Cranbrook and went on to become schoolteachers, lawyers, and senators.

I am convinced that Romney's confrontation of Lauber was a vicious assault, aimed at him because he was not in the popular group. This was no prank. Romney might well have remembered what he did to Lauber, and he should have. But I am willing to accept that he didn't, because to bullies and harassers the actions may be so insignificant as to be forgettable.

According to David Seed, another Cranbrook student and participant, Lauber remembered. To borrow terminology Christine Blasey Ford used in her Kavanaugh hearing testimony, it's likely that the assault—a trauma experience—was coded into Lauber's hippocampus and locked there. Seed and Maxwell remembered also because trauma experiences happen not only to the direct victims but also to those who are present and feel shamefully complicit or vulnerable and helpless to stop an assault. Bessel van der Kolk, psychiatrist, trauma specialist, and author, writes, "Trauma affects not only those who are directly exposed to it, but also those around them."[11] Seed graduated from the prep school and went on to become a high school teacher and principal. In a chance encounter with Lauber at a bar in the Chicago O'Hare airport years after their school days, Seed had an opportunity to apologize for his role. Lauber expressed to Seed that he had found the incident horrible and frightening, something that he not only remembered but also thought about often.

It's not entirely unreasonable to think that it's all a blur to Romney fifty years later, but like Lauber, most students who are the targets of abuse recall very accurately how it felt to be victimized by one's peers even when they don't recall the exact details of who, what, or where it happened. Some bullied students survive and remain in school; others withdraw physically or psychologically, causing grades to drop, depression, or both. Some contemplate taking their lives to escape bullying and harassment, and others, tragically, act on the impulse.

The latest available data from the Department of Education's Office for Civil Rights reports roughly 9,700 yearly claims of sexual assault, rape, and attempted rape in K–12 schools throughout the country. Given that the department surveys 96,300 schools, its figures amount to 1 claim for every 100 schools. But these figures do not square with findings by the Centers for Disease Control and Prevention, which are much more troubling. In 2013, the CDC found that 1 in every 5 female high school students has experienced some form of dating violence in the past year. Just how many of those complaints involved peer-on-peer behavior is unclear. And research led by Dorothy Espelage shows that bullying, like sexual harassment, is rampant in middle schools. Boys are more likely to bully than girls. And bullying can be tinged with sexual aggression and may be a precursor to sexual harassment or assault. According to a 2016 study, 35 percent of middle and high school girls report experiencing sexual harassment in a given year. It peaks between sixth and eighth grades, increasing significantly until age fourteen, and takes forms both verbal and physical. It happens in hallways, classrooms, gym class, and locker rooms, during lunch or after school. As an American Association of University Women study put it, middle school sexual harassment is "just part of the school day." Middle school students report that the most upsetting behavior they experienced included homophobic language, sexual commentary and sexual rumor spreading, unwanted physical touching, pulling down pants, being sexually assaulted, and dismissiveness of victimization.[12] An NBC News count of court records discovered as many as 330 K–12 suits filed between January 2018 and May 2020.

Even this number is nowhere near the number of sexual harassment incidents that are likely taking place in schools. And none of these calculations take into account those around the direct victims who

Van der Kolk notes are exposed to and affected by the traumatic experiences of their peers. Schools are social settings where adolescents identify with classmates and friends and aim to fit in. As mentioned, cliques can offer students a sense of belonging and emotional support in what for many kids is an emotionally challenging time. Belonging to an affinity group results in emotional attachments, including internalizing their peers' trauma. And there are all sorts of reasons that students, victims and witnesses, don't report bad experiences even when reporting may offer relief. A student's desire to be one of the crowd, along with fear of disapproval or being seen as weak and too dependent on adults in the system, might override the desire for the abuse to stop. Reporting can be risky, and retaliation is real; reporting has been known to trigger additional abuse. Telling a teacher or counselor might seem like a good response, but to the student it feels like a scary proposition. "Snitching" might lead to something adolescents dread most: being treated like an outsider. Millions of girls attend middle and high school in the United States. Only a fraction of the students who reported experiencing sexual assault to Espelage will report their experiences to the Department of Education. And fewer still end up in a court of law.

It's no wonder that advocates believe that the Office for Civil Rights undercounts the behavior. And remember, these young people are ten, twelve, fourteen years old. We don't like to think of them as having sexual identities, much less being harassed for their sex or gender. While college campus sexual harassment has gotten lots of media attention, little is given to the climate in elementary and secondary schools. The difference might be attributed to student advocacy on college campuses. Bullying gets press when a terrible incident occurs—a suicide—but for the most part we don't take it seriously enough. Attention to peer abuse of younger children is inconsistent and unreliable.

In many cases, schools have been found to be deliberately indifferent to claims of harassment by students. Jaden, an eighth-grade girl in an Alabama middle school, reported repeated harassment by an older boy in the school. The male student kept asking the fourteen-year-old Jaden to have sex with him in a school bathroom. She declined and complained to a teacher's aide, June Ann Simpson, in hopes that Simpson would put an end to the harassment. Instead, Simpson suggested the girl act as bait, arranging to meet the boy in the school bathroom, where Simpson would "catch him in the act." Jaden hesitated, but Simpson urged her to go through with the scheme, saying, "Just get him to meet you, and we'll catch him." Before any staff arrived in the bathroom, the boy had raped her. A federal district court dismissed Jaden's father's claim against the school on behalf of his daughter in what became known as the "rape bait" case. But a court of appeals found that the school had shown deliberate indifference to Jaden's claim in part by requiring that her assailant had to be caught in the act for the school to take responsibility. And though the court of appeals reached what I believe is the correct legal outcome, some of the language in the opinion is cause for alarm. The judge wrote in the case of *Hill v. Cundiff* that "some risk of sexual harassment is inherent to the enterprise of public education, in particular, because public schools must educate even the most troublesome and defiant students."[13]

It's this kind of thinking that troubles Catherine Lhamon, who was the assistant secretary for civil rights at the Department of Education when the decision was announced. According to Lhamon, the fact that "the school administration and its lawyers took the position that the school bore no liability for that conduct," that the district court dismissed the student's claim, and that the appellate court showed a willingness to tolerate a certain amount of abusive behavior is indicative of our dangerous denial of sexual harassment and assault of children. It's her assessment that "this country still operates as if sexual harassment does not take place for students younger than the age of majority." What's more, educators have used language suggesting that some amount of violence was acceptable, depending on the victims. Noting barely coded racist language used by some educators, Lhamon brought my attention to a case she resolved in which school officials told OCR investigators that "the rampant sexual harassment they both witnessed and heard reported from students merely represented the middle school students' 'urban culture,' which the educators used to excuse themselves from responsibility to act to protect students from discrimination."[14]

Sarah McBride, a spokesperson for the Human Rights Campaign, which bills itself as the "largest national lesbian, gay, bisexual, transgender and queer civil rights organization," said young members of the LGBTQ+ community, especially those of color, are more likely to die by suicide linked to social stigmas, family rejection, bullying, harassment, or abuse. And while some research shows that adolescents rate homophobic slurs as less serious than racial slurs, the combination of racism and homophobia can be devastating.

"There's not enough data out there for a clear picture of the full scope of the challenges they face, but from what we know, both anecdotally and from the data we have already, this is a significant crisis," McBride said. Therein lies the problem with data on the confluent impact of race and gender on bullying and sexual harassment: we don't collect it. And the same inattention is paid to the problem of bullying, sexual harassment, and assault of students with disabilities. Does the behavior toward victims with disabilities differ? Are the consequences and our responses to the behavior the same for students with disabilities as they are for students without disabilities?

In her memoir, *Nobody's Victim: Fighting Psychos, Stalkers, Pervs, and Trolls*, the attorney Carrie Goldberg writes about the Black girls she represented in school cases. "It's impossible not to be aware of the impact of race on who gets considered an 'innocent victim' and where we place our compassion and concern. Every day, I see the disparity play out in the way my clients and others are treated by law enforcement, school officials, the public, and the press."[15] The chapter is appropriately titled "Girls' Lives Matter."

Lhamon is resolute, insisting that "no child deserves the harm perpetrated on the child . . . and no quantum of sexual harassment is acceptable. . . . Failing to uphold in the lives of students in school the decades-old nondiscrimination promises from Congress and our courts perpetuates an ugly message, inculcated in school and lived in the bodies of young people who grow into adults throughout our country, that some among us are expendable, and available for the mistouch and misuse of others among us. Our children and our communities deserve better."[16]

POLICING IDENTITY

Bullying and harassment enforce conformity. And in schools, conformity can mean anything from wearing the "right clothes" to expressing sexual or gender identity in stereotypical ways. Whether the source is television, gaming, or social media, kids get the message that physical and sexual aggression is the way to show strength. By the same token, a girl's value is measured by her submissiveness to sex with boys. She learns that to conform, she shouldn't be too bossy or too smart "for her own good." In schools, these ideas get played out in relatively benign ways as well as through aggressive behaviors.

And tragedy can occur when aggressive bullying and harassment are left unchecked. Nigel Shelby was a fifteen-year-old Black boy from Alabama who loved theater and music and often promised his mom that he would someday "be a star." Nigel's mother, Camika, always assured him he could have whatever he wanted in life and affirmed his sexual identity: "Who you choose to love has nothing to do with the person that you are." But his schoolmates' bullying drowned out Camika's voice. In April 2019, Nigel died by suicide.

For the middle school student Seth Walsh, who was White, the federal authorities' investigation into his sexual harassment experience came too late. Like the telegrams delivered to families of fallen soldiers, the U.S. Justice Department's press release only began to capture the tragedy of Seth's experience:

> In September 2010, Jacobsen Middle School student Seth Walsh committed suicide at the age of 13. In October 2010, the Department of Education received a complaint alleging that Walsh had been the victim of severe and persistent peer-on-peer sex-based harassment while he was a student at Jacobsen Middle School. After receiving the complaint, the Department of Education . . . worked collaboratively with the school district to resolve the violations.

It took an investigation and a consent decree issued jointly by the attorneys Zachary Pelchat and Anurima Bhargava of the U.S. Departments of Education and Justice, respectively, to begin to explain how the "intrinsically happy," "kind-hearted, social boy with a gentle disposition" came to take his own life. Both Pelchat and Bhargava were veteran civil rights attorneys, and for the most part the decree was written in language aimed at making the government's case for intervention. But before turning to a career as a civil rights attorney, Pelchat had taught fifth grade. Perhaps it was the experience of teaching kids around Seth's age that compelled him to include the voices of Seth's many friends, most of whom were girls. They revealed the tragedy of what happened to Seth and kids like him and to their friends. Dr. van der Kolk's work reminds us that it takes a tremendous amount of energy to carry "the memory of terror, and the shame of utter weakness and vulnerability." And Seth's friends were left to bear witness to Seth's as well as their own feelings of being helpless to stop the violence they collectively experienced.[17] They spoke about his gentle nature, his caring and compassion. Some were taken in by his sense of style. He frequently changed the color and style of his hair. He preferred skinny jeans, scarves, and fitted V-neck T-shirts to the hoodies and flannel shirts his classmates wore. But what endeared Seth to those who admired and loved him, his openness in expressing his true self, made him a target. Seth's friends were clear in describing a day in his life, his daily struggle to find spaces in his school where he felt safe to be himself. Through his friends' recollections and a few words of his own scribbled on a note in his last desperate days, Seth's torment came to life.

The taunting started almost immediately after he entered Jacobsen Middle School, in Tehachapi, California, a town just over a hundred miles north of Los Angeles. When he arrived as a sixth grader in 2008, Seth might have easily gotten lost among Jacobsen's thousand students. But he had the misfortune of drawing the attention of a group of eighth-grade boys who set out daily to make Seth's school life miserable. They succeeded. Their behavior began with name-calling, terms meant to demean Seth because of his sexual orientation—"sissy," "girl"—and vulgar references to female anatomy. By seventh grade, antigay slurs and epithets, meant to insult Seth's masculinity, made his life "unbearable," according to the government decree.

In November of his second year at Jacobsen, having tolerated as much as he could, Seth asked to be put on an independent study program. He would take his courses at home, avoiding the regular interaction with his abusers. On one occasion Seth came on campus, and the vice principal heard another student yell "queer" at Seth from inside a classroom. In response, she wrote an article in the November 19, 2009, parent newsletter that read, in part,

> The student body is not only diversified by gender, race, and ethnicity, but also by dress style, hair style, likes, dislikes, maturity, and ambition. Some are tolerant of this diversity, others are not. . . . A few make life miserable for those that appear different than "normal" even though these students don't bother them. . . . Please discuss with your child that while they may find some students different and "odd," everyone deserves the right to receive an education without being harassed or bullied because of their hairstyle or fashion sense or their mannerisms or their weight or their . . . you get the picture. While we aren't going to hold hands in a giant circle and sing "Kumbaya," we do need to respect each other and even celebrate our uniqueness.

The vice principal's message appeared to place the responsibility for keeping Seth safe on the parents and suggested that children were targeted because they were somehow peculiar. Her choice of words suggests that singling out "others" for abuse is natural—a level of tolerance that could easily be read as victim blaming. And though the school official spoke of the "need to respect each other," she did not say what the consequences were when students failed to respect their fellow students.

While independent study was keeping Seth safe, the isolation of learning at home was weighing on him. Like any outgoing kid, the twelve-year-old missed his friends. He craved being back in a regular routine, even if it meant returning to Jacobsen, so after a few weeks at home, he started going to school regularly again. Pretty soon, the verbal assaults resumed, including derogatory remarks about sex between men, crude questions about sexual acts, and suggestions that Seth had engaged in them.

Seth's desperation was palpable by the time he reached eighth grade. "I want to live elsewhere. . . . I feel like [an] utter failure. School, I'm terrified to go to," Seth wrote in a note to his friend. The verbal assaults and rumors escalated into physical harassment, like being shoved or cornered in the hallways or having food or other items knocked out of his hands in the cafeteria. Seth's friends witnessed his tormentors throwing food, water bottles, pencils, and erasers at him and subjecting him to unwanted sexual contact. "On one occasion, a student attempted to shove a pencil up the seat of the Student's pants," read the attorneys' report. For Seth, each school experience—sitting in his classes or the cafeteria, walking down the hallways, or lingering after school—could become a terrorizing episode. The locker room experience was perhaps the worst. After one student threatened to rape him, Seth refused to change clothes for PE class. Inevitably, his grades dropped from As and Bs his first year at Jacobsen to Ds and Fs by 2010, his second year of middle school.

At the beginning of what would have been his final semester at Jacobsen Middle School, Seth hanged himself. He died a week later after days on life support. A year later, the federal government mandated that the Tehachapi School District reform its system for addressing sexual harassment and assault. The government's consent letter clearly indicated that Jacobsen had failed Seth at nearly every turn. The school should have "conduct[ed] a prompt, thorough, and impartial inquiry designed to reliably determine what occurred." Given the evidence of harassment, school personnel should have taken "reasonable, timely, age-appropriate, and effective corrective action, including steps tailored to the specific situation." Measures "sufficient to stop the harassment, to prevent its recurrence, or to eliminate the hostile environment" should have been taken. Finally, the government's decree suggested that actions to repair the educational environment at the Tehachapi School District "may also be necessary." Those actions included new policies, dissemination of information, special training, and messaging that indicated the school district had zero tolerance for harassment.

What was missing from the report was any information about the group of boys who tormented Seth. We know only that Seth and his friend thought they were eighth graders and that one had curly hair. In the absence of any indication in the official report about who in the school threatened and harassed Seth, one could conclude that the school never bothered to identify them. But without that information, we can't say exactly what provoked the behavior. We see a school system that appears to have placed an inordinate portion of the burden to end the behavior on Seth's willingness and ability to identify and point the finger at his schoolmates. In a school the size of Jacobsen, Seth might not have known the boys who made his life miserable. We don't know whether the group that bullied Seth was small or whether the bullying involved numerous boys. There was also little if any information about the school culture, a critical element in determining the risk of abusive behavior. We don't know if there were cliques or clubs, or whether others might have been victimized, too. A thorough understanding of how to prevent what happened to Seth and to change the behavior of those who were responsible requires us to understand how the school culture supported his torment. Stopping vicious behavior in schools ultimately depends on school administrators taking full responsibility for failure to end the behavior.

In 2019, nine years after Seth's death, the U.S. Departments of Education and Justice ceased monitoring the Tehachapi School District to make sure students were safe from harassment. The agreement releasing school officials stated that the school system had met the federal government's recommendations.

While middle school students who identify as nonbinary or male are more likely to be harassed and bullied than those who identify as females, girls are similarly castigated by their peers for not meeting the expectations assigned to their genders. A case filed in Minnesota in 2012 on behalf of five students outlines how both boys and girls were pummeled with homophobic slurs. The boys in the suit were called "gay boy," "homo," and "fag." Classmates called a girl who, according to the suit, "chose not to dress in a 'girly' way, had a low voice, and liked playing video games, which her peers have called a 'boy's activity,'" "guy," "manly," and "transvestite." One student told her that she should "go kill herself." Another classmate tripped her in the hallway twice, pushed her into the lockers multiple times, and pushed her into a trash can once. Another girl was called "gay," "faggot," and "dyke" nearly every day in the hallway, in her math class, in the locker room, and when she was on the bus.[18]

Not all attempts to police sexual identity or gender expression are as relentless and aggressive as the behavior in the Minnesota case. But even less persistent attempts to limit ways of expressing identity can be harmful when understood in the context of the environment in which they took place. The first time that I recall hearing a homophobic slur, it was aimed at me. Throughout my middle school and high school days in Morris, Oklahoma, a small rural community, my classmates put me in the "brainiac" category. I routinely received the award for the best grade in each of my classes, which perhaps insulated me from the bullying that I might have received as a nerd. I suspect that it also protected me from racial hostility. And, frankly, I was fortunate that my teachers, all of whom were White, seemed to embrace my accomplishments.

Morris was a known "sundown town." When I went to school there, no Blacks had ever resided within Morris city limits, and the presumption was that none were welcome. African Americans, my family included, resided outside the paved streets of town, mostly in rural dwellings on rocky dirt roads or in a nearby historically Black settlement called Grayson, where five of my siblings attended high school. One day, a White friend and I were sitting in the bleachers of our high school football field watching the cheerleading squad practice. This was not my normal routine. I was there only because my principal, who was White and a family friend even before I knew him at school, decided that Morris should have a Black cheerleader. He chose me to be the backup for the cheerleaders who had been selected by popular vote, so I needed to learn the routines. Without any provocation, a White kid in my class, who was also standing on the sidelines, glared at me and shouted, "You're queer!" "What does that mean?" I asked my friend. She stammered, "You know. It means you like girls." I felt a creep of heat come up my body and onto my face. As I look back at my sixteen-year-old self, I have to ask myself why I was so ashamed. Was it that I so wanted to be seen as conventional and an insider? Or was it that I was embarrassed not to know what the word meant and why it had been weaponized against me? Had I stepped out of bounds by accepting the invitation to be a backup cheerleader? Cheerleading while Black? Was my male classmate's ire inspired by my GPA? I had also accepted the agriculture teacher's invitation to be on the school's soil-judging team. I was the only girl on the team. Was taking the place of a boy team member my transgression? Or was it that I had once raised my hand when a teacher polled the class to see who supported the Equal Rights Amendment, which guaranteed equal legal rights to all Americans regardless of sex? (Back then, in 1972, ERA proponents were cast as man-hating lesbians out to destroy family life.) I ignored the red-faced boy who yelled at me, and he walked away smugly content that he had shamed me. I look back and wonder why I, who had been prepared for racist name-calling, had no concept of how to respond to gender hostility.

Mine was a singular occurrence, an incidental embarrassment—what today we might call a microaggression, and not one that would pass the severe threshold of Title IX. It was not the serial behavior that continues in schools today, with no recourse short of filing complaints with the U.S. Department of Education. Schools and federal complaint systems still tolerate abuse, day-to-day slights, and insults that kids are expected to put up with.

VIOLENCE VERSUS "ROUTINE" ADOLESCENT BEHAVIOR

Ambivalence about claims of peer sexual assault is also reflected in the way it's reported in the popular press and, in one case, by the Supreme Court. The media has lambasted school districts that hold young children accountable for their sexual behavior. Cases in Boston and New York involving the disciplining of six- and seven-year-old children resulted in school administrators being called out for political correctness. The tendency to suggest that any conduct of children amounts to "child's play" is misguided and part of the problem. It might well have excused the behavior that led to a consent decree between the Allentown School District on behalf of five John Doe minors.

Children do play, but consider the facts. The allegations were that on four separate occasions a twelve-year-old fifth-grade student sexually harassed and assaulted five six-year-old first-grade students at Central Elementary School in Allentown, Pennsylvania. The fifth grader was charged with fondling the younger children. But one wonders if the age difference between the children was the driving force behind their concern. Would the matter have been the subject of ridicule if the students had all been six years old? Might the public have responded differently if two fifth graders had been involved? It's troubling that behavior that is recognized as severe in older kids and in adults is dismissed in younger children. After all, where do we think the behavior takes root?

The most startling takeaway from the stories and the research is that as early as seven years old, children's gender-based violence and aggression are avatars for adult behavior. From understanding school bullying, harassment, sexual assault, and shootings, we can see how patterns of behavior are layered into children's memories and learning. We should also recognize that some children are unable to deflect the mind-altering impact of these abuses. It's an idealistic fantasy—but only a fantasy—that somehow today's young people will spontaneously and on their own end gender violence.

And, in far too many instances, they get little or no guidance for how to change from adults. School officials' dismissiveness of peer harassment claims is as troubling as the behavior students complain about, and it's an attitude that extends to the court system. In Jaden's case, the district court was unconvinced that a school official's coaching a fourteen-year-old to participate in a scheme that resulted in her being raped was a violation of a school's duty. When a judge's dismissiveness of sexual assault becomes part of a legal opinion, it is truly dangerous, even if the opinion is a dissenting opinion. Unfortunately, that is what happened in one of the few peer-on-peer harassment cases decided by the Supreme Court.

Once, at a small gathering of women who were interested in supporting gender equality, an audience member asked if there was one particular Supreme Court decision that troubled me. I responded without hesitation: *Davis v. Monroe County Board of Education*. It wasn't the outcome of the *Davis* case that I found deeply troubling. The Court had decided in favor of a student who was suing for the protection of her right to equal education under Title IX of the Civil Rights Amendments of 1972. It was the dissent in the case that bothered me, along with the fact that the *Davis* decision was a close 5–4 decision, with Justice Sandra Day O'Connor writing the Court's opinion. The *Davis* case is the signature Supreme Court opinion defining a school's responsibility to protect a student from peer harassment. Though the Court ruled in the plaintiff's favor, Justice Anthony Kennedy's dissent demonstrates a tendency at the highest levels to accept brutal behavior engaged in by children as normal.

I began my talk by describing the facts of the case. When I said that conduct involving LaShonda Davis and her fifth-grade classmate was the basis for a sexual harassment case that went to the Supreme Court of the United States, I sensed their skepticism. Though there was no actual eye-rolling, "How bad could the behavior have been?" was written on more than one face. The boy who was the subject of the complaint repeatedly attempted to touch his classmate's "breasts and genital area, rubbed against her in a sexual manner, constantly asked her for sex, and in one instance, put a doorstop in his pants to simulate an erection and acted in a sexually suggestive manner." But the audience didn't seem fully convinced of the seriousness of the case until I told them that the local sheriff had intervened at the request of the victim's parents. Even a group of women who might be sympathetic to gender abuse started from the presumption that what happened to LaShonda was "not so bad" or that LaShonda and her mother were "making too much of" the behavior. It took a sheriff's criminal prosecution for the audience to accept that what happened might be worthy of action by the Supreme Court. I couldn't help but wonder how any one of them would have reacted if their daughter had suffered the same behavior from a classmate and was ignored by the school.

Aurelia Davis had filed the Title IX lawsuit on behalf of her daughter, LaShonda, a fifth-grade student. The complaint described the physical torture and sexually aggressive behavior LaShonda endured at the hands of a classmate. It also described the toll that the assaults had on LaShonda. Her grades dropped. She was unable to concentrate on her classwork. Then every parent's worst nightmare happened. LaShonda's father discovered that she had written a suicide note. The girl told her mother that she "didn't know how much longer she could keep [her classmate] off her." They had to act.

And yet her school failed to intervene when the Davises made their demands. Neither LaShonda's teachers nor her principal would grant her request to, at the very least, move her desk away from the boy. Noting that other girls had experienced the same behavior, one teacher asked LaShonda, "Why are you the only one complaining?" LaShonda's parents took their complaint to the county sheriff. When local law enforcement got involved, the accused, whose name was withheld, pleaded guilty to a charge of sexual battery. But the school still refused to take action to separate the two students or discipline the boy. Eventually, Aurelia Davis prevailed in the Supreme Court, and the school was held accountable for protecting LaShonda. But in a dissent, Justice Kennedy dismissed the abuse LaShonda experienced as "routine problems of adolescent behavior" and the Court's ruling in LaShonda's favor as evidence of federal overreach. He denied the harm that it caused LaShonda by calling it routine. In his way of thinking, the behavior was natural and "not so bad," and therefore the school had no responsibility to control it.

Kennedy's "boys will be boys" cavalier response to a child's ideation of suicide is shocking. One can call groping a classmate "routine behavior" or "pranks and hijinks" only if one is viewing the action from the point of view of the harasser. Kennedy's normalization of harmful behavior follows misogynist and racist tropes that have held the country back from making progress toward equality for centuries. To Kennedy, LaShonda's pain and the damage done to her education were inconsequential compared with her tormentor's freedom to misbehave and abuse. This reasoning makes sure that the cultural acceptance of sexual violations among children gets baked into law in addition to getting coded into their memories. To Justice Kennedy, politics seemed to be more important than keeping her safe. Prioritizing the abstract concept of federal overreach over LaShonda and her family's demand for protection against the physical abuse she experienced offers a disturbing disregard for girls' safety from sexual assault. It makes a right to a safe place to learn meaningless, leaving girls to fend for themselves and absolving their teachers, principal, and the federal government of any accountability to protect them. Kennedy's legal reasoning may fall short of victim blaming, but it fits squarely within a declaration that what happens to girls like LaShonda is "not so bad" as to warrant any intervention.

Kennedy's strident dissent in the *Davis* case offers a cautionary tale. In 2018, Justice Kennedy resigned from the Supreme Court. His replacement was one of his former law clerks, Brett Kavanaugh, whom Christine Blasey Ford accused of sexually assaulting her when the two were in high school. The *Davis* opinion written by Justice O'Connor is still good law. But any student of the law knows that language that starts in dissent can someday become the majority opinion.

SCHOOL SHOOTINGS AND GENDER VIOLENCE

School shootings can also be viewed as an extension of gender-based violence, especially when one considers that the shooters are more often than not cisgender, heterosexual males who express animosity or anger toward women. Marc Lépine's slaughter of women at the École Polytechnique de Montréal in 1989 should have put schools on alert that mass shootings could imperil the lives of children of all ages. Marc Lépine blamed women for the school's rejection of his application for admission in its engineering department. So one December day, he "decided to send the feminists, who have always ruined my life, to their Maker." He entered the school, separated women and men students, and killed fourteen women, reportedly saying, "You're all a bunch of feminists. I hate feminists."[19]

Perhaps the French-speaking Canadian location made the event feel distant to parents and school officials in the United States, or convinced them that Lépine's act of rampage violence was unique. But in Bethel, Alaska, in 1997, a series of school shootings began in the United States, and they have never stopped. As early as 1999, Professor Marina Angel started to notice that the school shooters were all boys or young men, they were all White, and most of the victims were girls—sometimes girlfriends or ex-girlfriends of the perpetrators, or just girls who had rejected them. In 1998, Mitchell Johnson and Andrew Golden, the thirteen- and eleven-year-old boys who killed four girls and a female teacher at their middle school, targeted an ex-girlfriend, along with vowing to kill all girls who broke up with Johnson and to shoot two other girls who had rejected Golden's advances. Professor Angel also noticed that the press was ignoring the racial factors and what she called the "gender-realities" of Golden and Johnson's and two other school rampage shootings in the 1990s.

In 2005, Jessie Klein, a professor at Lehman College in New York, did an analysis of middle and high school shootings between 1997 and 2002. Like Angel, Klein noticed the gender connection in the shooting cases, which often included the shooters expressing their anger for being rejected by or having difficulty with girls. Professor Klein also called out the media's failure to acknowledge the connection.

Professor Angel's article pointing out the gender realities of school shootings was titled "Abusive Boys Kill Girls Just Like Abusive Men Kill Women: Explaining the Obvious." But what was obvious to Angel remained uncertain to members of the public and the press. And we cannot know what lives have been lost because we failed to see clearly what provoked children to murder their female peers. Harvard professor Katherine S. Newman calls our attention to some other unfinished business related to school shootings. In her book *Rampage: The Social Roots of School Shootings*, Newman writes, "Workplace shootings and school rampages have some profound and unfortunate similarities. They represent the tips of similar icebergs, where those who feel ostracized, marginalized, and threatened with emasculation react with murderous violence." Though the settings and the way workplace and school shootings are carried out may differ, "if we want to understand why they happen it is useful to focus" on what they have in common.

And school bullying and violence are not solely the purview of the village misfit. In fact, students who seem to have it all can be powerful bullies and protectors of the conventions that make them popular. Take the case of Mitt Romney's behavior as a prep school student. Romney would be recalled by his friends as a nice guy who was a popular leader among his Cranbrook classmates. The idea that "nice boys" might engage in vicious behavior is too often met with surprise. It shouldn't be. A case that made headlines in 2015 shows that when sexual conquest becomes a school ritual, sexual assault may very well follow. On the pristine campus of St. Paul's School, an elite boarding school in New Hampshire that boasts powerhouse graduates, including the former secretary of state John Kerry and William Randolph Hearst, a secret rite known as the "senior salute" developed. Senior boys competed for the title of scoring or "slaying"—having sex with—the most girls. The language of the "senior salute" might have related to one of the video games they played where slaying was routine. Typically, they targeted freshmen and sophomores. That the boys equated sexual encounters with conquest and violence suggests that they were willing to use coercion to exploit younger girls or that they might have felt an entitlement to sex, consensual or not.

In 2014, nearing his graduation and after having been admitted to Harvard University, where he had planned to study theology, eighteen-year-old Owen Labrie persuaded Chessy Prout, then fifteen, to join him on the rooftop of a campus building. From there Labrie led Prout to a locked mechanical room. It's no coincidence that Labrie had a key to the room. The key had been passed to him as part of the senior salute rite. In fact, it was customary for the key to be passed from graduating senior class members to juniors as part of the annual ritual. Once they were in the mechanical room, Prout says Labrie raped her, despite her telling him no and that she didn't want to have sex with him. In a trial that took place a year later, Labrie was convicted of having sex with a minor and sentenced to jail.

St. Paul's alum Shamus Khan is a sociologist and professor at Princeton University. In his book *Privilege: The Making of an Adolescent Elite at St. Paul's School*, Khan summed up the culture that led to such ritualized sexual conquest as happened at his alma mater. He described a place where rituals are used mainly to impose hierarchy and where sex becomes a pathway to belonging for girls. And in their impact statement at Labrie's sentencing, Prout's parents gave their impression of the behavior and described the school as anything but welcoming. Chessy "stood up to this entitled young man," her father said. "She stood up to the entitled culture at St. Paul's School. She stood up to the rape culture that exists in our society and allows 'boys to be boys.'"[20]

INTERGENERATIONAL COMMITMENT

Yes, the data shows that younger generations have attitudes that reflect respect that crosses lines of race, gender, sexuality, and religion. But the behavior that far too many children are experiencing shows that the changes in attitudes are not enough. Each generation has laid claim to being more progressive on the equality scale than the one before. To place the added burden of evolution on a generation that has absorbed the trauma of abuse is heartless.

Past generations have passed on prioritizing violence in schools or settled for ineffective responses for too long. Yes, there are those boomers and Gen Xers who have made it their cause, but no generation has taken ownership of the problem and seen the solution as a responsibility each generation owes the next.

As a whole, my generation, though more progressive than our parents', has leaned too heavily on the notion that noxious behavior that is routine in schools constitutes antics, pranks, or boys being boys. Like the courts in the early sexual harassment cases, we've bought into the idea that harmful behavior is either natural or just not that bad. We even assure ourselves that children are resilient and will get over the abuse they experience. We rarely discuss how aggressive behaviors can cause immediate and long-term damage. We now recognize them as attempts to police gender, sexual identity, race, or any number of other identity characteristics. And though baby boomers and their Gen X children don't poll as progressive as millennials and Gen Zers, some are working to address violence that young people are experiencing.

As I read stories like Seth's and Nigel's, I think of my friend Mark Bradford. Mark, who has been described by *60 Minutes* as one of the "most important and influential artists in America today," is a gay Black man. In his late fifties, he stands six feet seven and a half inches. But in interviews and conversation, Mark recalls his eight-year-old self, when he attended a predominantly White grammar school where, as he puts it, "the boys . . . grouped up in the schoolyard" to let him know that he was different.

Mark navigated the space between the bus stop and the schoolhouse door to keep from getting his "ass whupped." After school, he escaped to the comfort of a supportive group of people who gathered in his mother's beauty shop.

Mark survived by pushing boundaries that others placed on him even as a child. "I started walking and exploring—exploring what I could—until I grew bigger or stronger or knew more." Mark's mother, Janice, not his teachers or the school, drilled into him that he had to figure out how to avoid the crap that he'd have to face as a dark-skinned, frail kid who was also queer.

Janice, a single Black mother who had grown up in foster homes in Philadelphia, eventually owning her own business in Los Angeles, was Mark's model. He and I have spoken about how his mother prepared him to address the challenges he's faced in life. "I had to navigate," he now says with confidence. "My mom navigated. I felt like if she could navigate this unusual community that she navigated in, then I certainly could. I knew that I was never going to go to formal society and ask for help. I knew that they were going to judge me as bad. I said, 'Never mind. I got this. I'll figure it out.'" And he did. And Janice enabled his navigation by offering Mark refuge from the hostility of his school in their home and the beauty shop she operated in Los Angeles. In the shop Mark listened to his mother's customers, who sometimes spent hours in the salon. From their stories of mistreatment and triumphs, he learned how each woman negotiated her own survival. And, in time, he charted his way forward.

Today, he's philosophically looking back on what he calls his "little abused path." Mark is sure that he had something "way deep down inside" that allowed him to stand up to the abuse. It shows in his art, which he describes as abstract art "with a social or political context clinging to the edges." He uses it to navigate his own painful past, too, and does so successfully, with pieces selling for millions of dollars today.

Mark is an avid reader. And among his topics of choice are feminism and mythology. In addition to helping him understand his own journey, both have influenced his art as well as his philanthropy. In 2017,

Mark represented the United States in the Venice Biennale. He titled his exhibit *Tomorrow Is Another Day*. His synchronization of Greek myths and the real-life stories of abused Black urban women, gay youth, battered and abandoned children, and women prisoners allowed viewers a glimpse into gender violence and the humanity of the people who experience it. His art made clear that the lines law and society draw between bullying and sexual assault and harassment are meaningless to the children who experience the violations. Mark's philanthropy includes programs and resources for youth who are at high risk for abuse and sexual violence.

Some have made protection of children their life's work. And that includes people like Catherine Lhamon. Her commitment comes down to something she said to me when I first met her in 2014. "I treat each case that comes into the Office for Civil Rights as if the children involved were my children," she said. "I want the same protections for them that I want for my own." There are lessons to be learned about commitment from Mark Bradford and Catherine Lhamon and many others whose work I've seen over the course of the past thirty years. No one generation started gender-based violence, and no one generation is going to solve it. In order to protect children from gender violence, each generation must own responsibility for ending it. Our duty to the next generation is to demand more of our schools and the law. Perhaps, in thinking about all of the stories in this chapter, we can disavow the myths that have distanced us from the humanity of the victims, commit to systemic change, and behave as if each child were our own and as if each child were valued within the school ecosystem. We have the chance to protect the well-being of today's generation of elementary school kids as well as the next.

Institutional Neglect

ow do I prepare my daughter for college so that she doesn't allow herself to become a victim of sexual harassment or assault?"

This question was passed up to me during a lecture I gave in 2017. I presumed that this concerned parent had read the statistics about abuse and wanted to make sure their child was protected during what was likely to be her first time living apart from her family. But sadly, rather than pressing the college to provide a safe environment for their daughter, they assumed that harassment and assault happen because students "allow" themselves to be abused.

As we saw in the previous chapter, students like LaShonda, Seth, Nigel, Mark, John, and numerous Jane Does suffered because of persistent attitudes and school cultures. Unfortunately, without interventions, the children I write about in chapter 4 won't be the last to go through the gauntlet of gender aggression and violence in those same schools. And their elementary school may not be the last place they experience harassment and bullying. Students who have been abused are more vulnerable to abuse in the future. Early experiences with abuse can put young children on a path for abuse in high school. Their schools' failures to respond to past abuses can set young people up to expect that institutions will do nothing to stop gender-based violence. As the number of students entering college increases, so does the number of students who will experience campus sexual misconduct. And from the publicized cases of widespread abuses on college campuses, we learn how the complex ecosystem of large universities might make it nearly impossible for individuals to challenge the behavior. So far, colleges and universities have failed to break the cycle of abuse that, for some students, began in elementary school.

In junior and community colleges, large and small universities, nearly every entering freshman class experiences or observes sexual harassment in some form. First-year students are the most vulnerable to sexual harassment and assault, but by the time they graduate from college, the National Institutes of Health has noted that "22% of students reported experiencing at least one incident of sexual assault." Women and nonbinary students reported the highest rates (28 percent and 38 percent, respectively), and 12.5 percent of men also reported sexual assault. It's clear that the impact of gender violence on the college student population is immense and myriad.

Of course, the college experience has enormous positive elements as well. What fuels high school students through the years of testing that culminates in a year of anxiety about whether they will get into at least one of the schools of their choice is the idea that they will be on their own, unsupervised, free to choose their classes, roommates, and new friends. The ability to explore friendships, sex, and alcohol and other drugs without parental knowledge or intervention is a freedom that students relish most. But this anxious anticipation can also contain the seeds of later problems. Freshman year is exciting, perhaps, in part, because it follows at least three years of control and fairly predictable environments; students know what to expect in high school. Unknowns can be exciting, but they can also be anxiety provoking, and without proper guidance or protections and with a load of new responsibilities and worries, students can be left vulnerable to harassment and abuse.

Today's students worry about having enough money for books, food, and extracurricular activities. They worry about their grades. First-generation college students often suffer other anxieties as they make their way through mazelike bureaucracies. And they're prone to impostor syndrome as they struggle to fit in at institutions for which others seem to have been prepped from birth, but which they sometimes find alienating and hostile. So, with all this and more on their minds, the last thing new students should have to deal with is anxiety over whether their college will do its best to protect them from harassment and assault that can take the form of intimate partner abuse, classroom harassment and hostility, rape and sexual assault in dorm rooms, and attacks that occur at social events on or off campus. They shouldn't have to doubt that schools have made their safety a priority. And yet the numbers and the stories of traumatic sexual experiences suggest that many students have reason to be concerned about whether they will have a safety net in what, for many, is their first experience away from home.

FRATERNITIES, SPORTS, CULTURE, AND COMPLICITY

Some of the most notorious cases that make the news have to do with fraternities and sports teams, so it's worth looking closely at those specific campus cultures. In large and small university conferences, whether the institution is Division I or Division III, college athletics along with fraternities have become notorious for ritualized gender-based violence. The term "hazing" does not do justice to some of the brutality that happens on campuses. One sports journalist summed it up by writing that this hazing culture has become a "rape culture." No attempts to minimize the violations with a word like "horseplay" or even "bullying" can hide the sexual and gender-based nature of the horrors chronicled in news coverage of athletic teams' customary, aggressive behaviors. Though most of the sports team assault stories involve male-on-male assault, an example of a female coach abusing a female soccer player reveals the male-oriented perspective that informed the abuse. According to an account by the student Kathleen Peay, "the coach, Bettina Fletcher, led an exercise in which a banana was forced into [three freshman players'] mouth[s] as a simulated act of oral sex. When Peay bit off and spit out the banana, another was placed in her mouth[;] then whipped cream, honey and syrup were sprayed on her hair and in her face, simulating ejaculation."[1]

Peay's story speaks to the difficulty of pursuing a claim against a university. The sports culture of the University of Oklahoma, where Peay played soccer, is pervasive, reaching into and defining the school's identity. At its core is football: the celebrated Oklahoma Sooners with iconic crimson and cream uniforms and logos, and record-holding coaches like Barry Switzer, Bud Wilkinson, and Chuck Fairbanks. Outside Oklahoma their names may not inspire adulation, but within the state they are legends. Not all sports are created equal on the University of Oklahoma campus. It's obvious even to the casual observer that at the top of the sports pyramid is football, followed by men's basketball. On some campuses, women's basketball teams have a supportive following as well. But women's soccer and the team members typically didn't come close to receiving the same attention and funding despite efforts to equalize women's sports through the civil rights protections found in Title IX. Football, with its enormous roster of athletes, coaches, and managers, gobbled up a lion's share of the athletic department's funds and drew donors and fans to the stadium every Saturday during the fall. Today, disparities, often significant, continue and are not limited to schools' treatment of women's and men's sports. In 2021, the NCAA was taken to task for providing paltry training facilities for women's basketball national tournament teams compared to state-of-the-art facilities suppled to the men's teams. Money seems to be a driving force behind large college sports programs. According to *Forbes* magazine, "The top NCAA Division I schools earn approximately $8.5 billion in annual revenue, with 58% of that revenue coming directly from men's football and men's basketball programs. But less than 7% of the revenue generated by those two sports go to its athletes in the form of scholarships and stipends for living expenses."[2] That none of the athletes, men or women, can be paid for their contribution to the system's coffers suggests that the core of the battle is about what's best for the school, not what's best for the student athletes. And schools seem to prioritize protecting their financial stream and squashing scandals, whether the topic is gender equality in sports, paying student athletes, or sexual assault scandals.

As a faculty member at the University of Oklahoma College of Law at the time that Peay attended, I served on the school's Athletics Council and witnessed firsthand the influence of Sooner Sports on the university and beyond. I'm embarrassed to say that though the episode happened while I taught at the school, I don't recall hearing anything about it. My ignorance, however, is telling and probably typical of others on campus at the time. There was no public outrage over the behavior. I realize now that the episode was probably something the administration wanted to keep quiet.

After her sophomore year, Peay left the soccer team and the school and returned to her home in Richardson, Texas. That's when a former teammate's father, after viewing pictures that were taken of the episode, encouraged Peay to complain. She sued the University of Oklahoma in federal court, claiming that her Title IX rights were denied. Peay's claim included a doctor's statement that the twenty-year-old suffered from classic symptoms of post-traumatic stress disorder, "depression, feelings of guilt, anxiety, hopelessness." There were also photos showing Bettina allegedly subjecting Kathleen and others to the hazing ritual. But ultimately, the university failed to address the harm done to Peay. Instead, it allowed Fletcher to resign her position, citing "personal and family reasons" for her departure.[3]

The ESPN sportswriter Greg Garber, who reported on the Peay case, pointed out that "one of the common justifications for hazing behavior is that group initiations foster camaraderie and chemistry." When Garber asked Peay, "How does simulating oral sex build team chemistry?" Peay gave the answer obvious to survivors of gender violence masquerading as hazing: "It doesn't." A federal judge dismissed Peay's lawsuit against the university.

It's hard to know why there was so little publicity about Peay's experience and whether it had to do with her being a woman. We can only speculate about whether a man complaining about "sexualized hazing" in college sports would have garnered more attention, though men are also discouraged from coming forward for fear of being perceived as weak. Abuse of college-age male athletes is beginning to receive public attention. A 2019 investigation of Dr. Richard Strauss, a physician at Ohio State University, revealed that he sexually abused at least 177 male student-patients over decades and that other university personnel knew of the behavior.[4] Strauss was the wrestling team physician, and some of his victims were members of the university wrestling team. The 232-page report of the independent investigator may open the door for more attention to the abuse of men in college. Most campus hazing is committed by men, and it is not the only form of gender-based violent behavior that occurs at colleges. College sports and fraternities are avenues for acting out hierarchies of power that encourage male team members and fraternity members to feel entitled to special access to better housing, to gyms and training facilities, and to the "best parties."

And some members of both kinds of groups act as though sex, consensual and sometimes allegedly nonconsensual, is a perk of their positions in the order. Incidents involving fraternities have made media headlines in the past few years. In 2010, frat brothers at Yale made a video of their annual march through campus reciting obscenities about women as their pledges, would-be frat brothers, followed, chanting, "No means yes, and yes means anal." Stories of the lewd ritual went viral, and ultimately the yearly event and claims of the school's failure to address campus sexual assault led to a student complaint filed with the U.S. Department of Education.

Fraternal organizations can serve a positive purpose for students who participate. They often provide opportunities for leadership and public service on campuses that continue to shape the students' behavior after they graduate. But fraternities replicate and sometimes amplify hierarchies, racial and gender. And their group celebration of sexual bravado, as seen in the Yale chants, and a sense of group entitlement can have a toxic effect that spreads throughout the climate on campus. It is also a zone that is often dangerously unsupervised by campus authorities, which makes it a perfect place for illegal activity that can compromise safety and implicate gender violence.

In December 2020, the University of North Carolina suspended three fraternities for operating a drug ring. Twenty-one people faced charges for distributing more than a thousand pounds of marijuana, several hundred kilograms of cocaine, and other illegal drugs valued at more than $1.5 million on the Chapel Hill campus and around the town.[5] The following month, the university's campus safety commission met to discuss the drug ring and "how it relates to campus health and safety—particularly with regard to sexual assault prevention." Safety commission members "expressed disappointment that this discovery was long overdue," but others noted the limitations the UNC police faced in monitoring the fraternities, because fraternities operate on private property. Although the school is working with the town to expand jurisdiction to the fraternity houses, the current lack of oversight means that other crimes in fraternity houses, like sexual assault or abuse, also fly under the radar or go unaddressed. In January 2021, Nick Papandreou brought attention to the issue in an op-ed in Northwestern University's campus newspaper. Papandreou, the head of the school's interfraternity group, called out the "racial discrimination, sexual assault and harassment, hazing, classism, homophobia/transphobia, abuse" within fraternity life at Northwestern. He pledged to address fraternal groups' lack of accountability and awareness.[6]

Athletic teams don't operate as private entities. The hierarchies that exist in athletics involve coaches, athletic directors, and student athletes. Like fraternity membership, athletic participation has been a gateway to success in life, including public service during college and after. And while research finds that more sexual harassment and assaults are traced to fraternities than other college organizations, athletics paint a better picture of how the pecking order on campuses contributes to colleges and universities excusing violations of campus sexual assault rules. The case of Larry Nassar, a team doctor who took advantage of his connection with sports to sexually assault hundreds of students, demonstrates institutional complicity in the abuse. The former USA Gymnastics team doctor's abuse of more than 350 survivors and victims, over two decades, is well documented. But it could have been short-lived had Michigan State University officials acted when they were first informed about his so-called treatment sessions, the guise under which he masqueraded his sexual assault. Beginning in 1997, young women told at least four coaches and trainers about Nassar's predatory behavior. One coach reported the accounts to MSU officials, and one victim reported to a university general counsel and university police.[7] In 2004, another victim of Nassar's, Brianne Randall-Gay, reported that when she saw him for back pain, Nassar tried to "penetrate" her vagina with his bare hand, "massaged her breasts and manipulated her genital area."[8]

Yet no one took the complaints seriously enough to take action to protect the women, some of whom were as young as sixteen. The Meridian Township Police Department chief, whose office failed to refer Randall-Gay's complaint to prosecutors, admitted that the office was so taken with Nassar's standing that it did not question his explanation for seventeen-year-old Randall-Gay's claims.[9]

Hundreds of women were assaulted by Nassar not because they were silent but because the system failed them.[10] As part of their independent investigation of Nassar's abuses, Joan McPhee and James P. Dowden looked into any "systemic deficiencies, failures of oversight, cultural conditions or other factors contributing to Nassar's serial sexual abuse of gymnasts over an extended period of time." They ultimately concluded that Nassar had "acted within an ecosystem that facilitated his criminal acts," adding that "numerous institutions and individuals enabled his abuse and failed to stop him, including coaches at the club and elite level, trainers and medical professionals, administrators and coaches at Michigan State University."[11]

An important element in the systemic complicity was the license Nassar was granted to operate within the university and sports systems of both USA Gymnastics and the U.S. Olympic Committee. Like the Meridian Township Police Department, these organizations all deferred to Nassar. Eventually, the then president of Michigan State University, Lou Anna Simon, was charged with lying about her knowledge of the criminal behavior to Michigan State Police investigators. A court dropped those charges, and Simon resigned her position as MSU president, apologizing that "a trusted, renowned physician was really such an evil, evil person," but she took scant personal or professional responsibility for the system that enabled his behavior.[12]

CAMPUS ASSAULTS: FACT AND FICTION

Cases involving sports teams have gotten an enormous amount of media attention. In 1989, I was teaching at the University of Oklahoma and observed a frenzy of news coverage over a rape that occurred in the athletic dorm. Of course, that was more than thirty years ago, but looking back, knowing the statistics on campus sexual harassment and assault, I have no doubt that there were many more cases of assault that didn't involve athletes and were not reported on, similar to the Peay case.

I had managed to either ignore or avoid the experiences during my own undergraduate years. The only warning I had about student-sponsored parties came from my oldest brother, Albert. "If you go to a party off campus, don't drink the punch," was all he said. I had just turned seventeen and had never drunk alcohol. I figured out that punch could be spiked, but it took me a while to catch on that what he meant was that drinking spiked punch might lead to sexual assault. No one ever confided in me that they had been sexually assaulted by one of our classmates, and no one mentioned being harassed or "bothered" by a college or law school professor. But in fact, harassment and assault were just some of those things women didn't talk about. In 1977, Catharine MacKinnon, a Yale Law School student, set out to change the way we see sexual harassment in universities by demonstrating that colleges had a legal responsibility to protect students and faculty members. At the time, the term "sexual harassment" had not caught on in popular discourse. Like many Ivy League schools, Yale's undergraduate student body was men only. But in 1969, the school admitted 278 women to its freshman class from the 2,800 applications it received. By the late 1970s, women students at Yale College increased to 37 percent of the student body. Sexual harassment also grew.

MacKinnon joined forces with lawyers and the Yale Law graduate Anne Simon to address the problem. They interviewed and brought together five students and one faculty member to sue Yale University, arguing that sexual harassment prevented them from receiving the educational experience they had come to Yale to get. The claim—that these victims were deprived of equal educational opportunities as provided by Title IX and the educational amendment to the Civil Rights Act of 1964—was a somewhat novel one at the time. What's more, the students' various experiences and the addition of the male faculty member stretched the breadth of Title IX's protection. But the similarities between the five students' experiences gave us a glimpse into how perversely the problem had become entrenched in campus culture in the few years after Yale went coed.

I started law school at Yale in 1977, nearly sixty years after the law school first admitted women to its program. I had no idea that three years later that lawsuit, *Alexander v. Yale*, would completely change the way students viewed the gender-based aggressions they experienced in schools. *Alexander v. Yale* was named after one of Simon's clients, Ronni Alexander. A senior at the time of the lawsuit, Alexander came to Yale with a dream of becoming a professional musician. According to her court filing, Alexander's flute teacher forced her into sexual intercourse when she was a freshman. Alexander also complained to the court that she had no one to talk to and nowhere to report it, and that she had abandoned both majoring in music performance and playing the flute as a result.

A second student, Pamela Price, a survivor of the Ohio juvenile justice and foster care systems, reported that a professor of political science, her major field, offered her an A in exchange for sex. When she refused, she got a C in the course.

Lisa Stone, Price's classmate, said she had spent a good deal of time with a friend who had been sexually harassed and had not been able to do anything about it. Stone concluded that if she were sexually harassed, she, too, would be left on her own by Yale; as a result, she began to fear and shun interactions with male faculty members.

Margery Reifler, the manager of the women's field hockey team, asserted that her life had been made miserable by sexual harassment from the team's male coach.

And some faculty and coaches who were not alleged harassers said sexual harassment had an indirect impact on their ability to teach effectively. Jack Winkler was a classics professor who argued that he could not do his job as a teacher if his women students were in a constant state of anxiety about male faculty members, well aware that the university provided no way for them to make complaints, let alone have them resolved.

Ann Olivarius, the student who had been most active in investigating the persistent reports of sexual harassment at Yale, claimed that when she tried to file a complaint on her own behalf as well as others', the university rebuffed her. A senior Yale administrator told her that if she did not stop complaining about faculty who verbally or physically came on to students, she would get sued for defamation and Yale would not help her.[13]

The court dismissed all the claims except for Price's, and even she personally did not recover any damages. Yet the judge, in deciding Price's claim in the 1980 case of *Alexander v. Yale*, required schools to establish reporting systems to enable students to file sexual harassment claims. In this way, the case set a precedent for protecting the rights of future students, if not those who brought the suit. For the first time, a court declared that Title IX prohibited sexual harassment, but it denied its victims the full educational benefits they were entitled to receive. And though the complaints of the six *Alexander* plaintiffs involved faculty harassment, peer harassment existed as well.

It took nearly fifty years for some of the accounts of abuse and harassment to come out. Writing to the *Yale Alumni Magazine* in 2019, Sarah

Birdsall, who graduated in the first class of women from Yale in 1972, described the seniors during her time there as "pretty horrible [her] first year. We girls had, after all, ruined their perfect fraternal experience. . . . To them, girls existed for weekend fun." Birdsall remembered the sophomore and freshman boys as "funny, sweet," and welcoming. Yet another member of the class of 1972, Debra Herman, wrote that on the final day of classes her second year, she was sexually assaulted by a junior whom she'd been in the same class with for the prior nine months. The assault came shortly after the two students learned about their final grades for the math course they shared. Herman received a grade of Honors, and he got a grade of High Pass. Nearly fifty years later Herman writes, "He let me know his grade and expressed anger that I had bested him." Later, when the two were alone briefly, he assaulted her. "When it was all over, I told no one. #MeToo." Though the actions by faculty as described by the students in the *Alexander* suit were largely behavioral, Yale administrators' reactions to them show what would become standard practice on the part of universities: protecting faculty and institutional reputation at the expense of students. Even if they believed the students, they chose to ignore them or defend their attackers.

Even when the behavior wasn't physical in nature, there were other ways in which women were harassed and undermined, including in the classroom. In her 2006 oral history published by the American Bar Association, the civil rights lawyer Judith Lichtman told a story about her experience as a University of Wisconsin law student in 1961, when she was one of two women in her class of 150. Lichtman describes a tradition of her criminal law professor, Ed Kimball. Kimball called upon women students only once per semester, and that was to discuss "the rape case." Accordingly, Lichtman "only had to respond to the question: What constitutes rape?" And if she managed to say, "Penetration, no matter how deep," she "could rest assured, [she] would never have to speak again the entire semester."

Yet, despite knowing that Kimball's practice "was wrong" and provoked the "feeling of humiliation," neither Lichtman nor the one other woman in her class complained to their dean. It was 1961, and "that was part of what we signed up for in this system, so we took it." Kimball's routine was the subject of law school legend. It's hard to know how many women were similarly humiliated in public. The administration should have acted years before to check his behavior. And neither of the students should have had to complain to the dean about a known problem that both robbed the students of the same experience that their male colleagues had and positioned them to be perceived as competent enough only to talk about rape. Kimball's behavior continued unchecked as long as he taught the course.

In one medical school, a decade after Lichtman and her classmate endured Kimball's demeaning practice, things were little better. One female medical student, one of 12 in a class of 120, had to put up with "naked *Playboy* pictures [displayed by] professors in lectures. The professor was not disciplined despite our complaints."[14]

THE STRUCTURAL BALANCE OF POWER

These experiences are just the tip of the iceberg of the harm that can arise from institutionalized sexual harassment. In 1991, Dr. Philip Hart, at the time a college chaplain, wrote to me about his experience counseling students, staff, and faculty who had experienced campus sexual assault. When I contacted him in 2014, he offered further insight into how sexual aggression on campuses was supported by institutional hierarchies that protected faculty in general:

> Over the 38 years at Plymouth State, I acted as an "advocate" for a number of women that had been assaulted. This was an awkward position, especially when it came to the accused being members of the Faculty. (That is one element about which little has been mentioned, to my knowledge.) Most of my counseling, of course, dealt with students who had been assaulted by other students. Assaults by faculty members or students were kept fairly quiet . . . handled "in house" by the University.[15]

Protecting high-profile professors or those who brought in large grants was and remains common. And in some cases, the will to cover for valued faculty had widespread and long-lasting consequences. Recently, I came across an article by Professor Molly Hite of Cornell that told the tragic experience of a graduate student who was the victim of gross sexual exploitation at the hands of her program director. The story, which was written in 1991, has stayed with me. And studies like the one conducted in 2019 by the National Academies of Sciences, Engineering, and Medicine's Committee on the Impacts of Sexual Harassment in Academia indicate that something very similar could happen today. Professor Hite wrote about a student, whose name or college she did not name "for legal reasons," whose experience shows how institutional interests are often prioritized over survivors' well-being in schools, and adds context to what Hart describes as "in house" handling of complaints against faculty.[16]

The story starts when the university was looking for a director of a program that was part of a large university department. After a national search, a high-profile candidate rose to the top of the stack of applications. He was hired after being lured by the committee with perks and promises. The noted specialist in his field came with great fanfare, lauded by colleagues and superiors as a great find and good match for the institution. Shortly after the director arrived in his new post, he began having affairs with certain female graduate students whom he had attracted to the program. He succeeded in getting these students the most prestigious grants, fellowships, and, ultimately, jobs.

Troubled by the director's behavior, the only three women faculty in the program left it for positions at other universities because they could no longer tolerate what they saw as institutionalized rewards for sexual favors. One student did complain to the department chair, who was the director's boss. The department chair dismissed her complaint about the affairs, concluding that the student was merely jealous because the director showed her no sexual attention. He based his conclusion on conversations he had with the program's male faculty, who also pointed out that the director's behavior was normal for a man in his position. In addition to being famous in his field, the director was single.

So far in this story at least three women's careers have been altered. And given that one student had not received the funding and prestige benefits afforded her peers, she has had to come to terms with the idea that to get ahead in her career, one must sleep with a powerful man. Her burgeoning career, too, was likely impacted because of the financial support she missed out on. The amount of support graduate students get as students often determines what they get in their first job. Foundations are part of the power structure of higher education. And they are not always great equalizers. In some cases, they replicate the behavior of banks, giving more money to people who already have money and less money to people who don't. Later, the three faculty members who resigned to escape what they felt was their director's harmful and reckless actions thought they had been blocked from getting grants.

What Hite describes as a crisis involving the entire university soon occurred. A young woman who was undergoing psychological counseling for parental sexual abuse went to the program director to disclose her situation. Fearing that her mental health condition might cause her to act inappropriately in some situations, she sought his counsel about how her condition might affect her academic prospects. The director elicited her family story over dinner. From there he invited her to his home and had sex with her.

The next day, the student complained to two faculty members. She then committed herself to a mental institution. The following turn of events shows the ways in which institutions avoid investigations into how their systems allow sexual harassment to continue. The faculty members went to the university ombudsman, who investigated complaints of maladministration. The growth of the office on college campuses started in the late 1960s as universities were becoming more diverse and restless. The term "ombudsman" is Swedish in origin, translating loosely to "representative of the people." One major university in the South describes the office as "a safe place where all [university] staff, faculty, students, and administrators are welcome to come and talk in confidence about any campus issue, problem, or dispute" informally. The role has evolved to one of neutrality as opposed to championing. This particular ombudsman was moved enough by the story to trigger events that eventually resulted in the university's giving the director the choice of resigning or being discharged. He chose to quit and soon got another position at another institution. It's not clear if the professor's new university was aware of why he left his former position. It's often the case that institutions don't disclose the reasons behind a faculty member's departure, which allows for the possibility that an abuser will go on to hurt more people. And there is no evidence that the college at which the story unfolded did anything to proactively guard against the same kind of abuse happening again.

The nuances of this kind of campus power imbalance are presented in the playwright David Mamet's 1992 play, *Oleanna*, which is written as a conversation over three acts between a male college professor, John, and a female student from one of his classes, Carol, who visits him in his office. Over the course of the play, their interactions become increasingly tense as Carol accuses John of sexual assault. When, in the third act, the accusation escalates to rape, John viciously attacks Carol.

Responses to the play reveal just how deeply rooted is our societal acceptance of violence against women and our misunderstanding of what lies at the root of gender-based violence. Audiences reportedly cheered John's reaction, as if beating women who step out of line, so to speak, was just what men do—or, more disturbingly, what we want them to do.

Roger Ebert wrote glowingly about the drama. "Experiencing David Mamet's play 'Oleanna' on the stage was one of the most stimulating experiences I've had in a theater," he wrote in a review. "In two acts, he succeeded in enraging all of the audience—the women with the first act, the men with the second. I recall loud arguments breaking out during the intermission and after the play, as the audience spilled out of an off-Broadway theater all worked up over its portrait of . . . sexual harassment? Or was it self-righteous Political Correctness?"[17]

One university professor opined that the play "is not about sexual harassment. It is about power"[18]—as if one could ever divorce the two.

Another academic, an English professor, without acknowledging the fact that sexual harassment exists or that it's wrong, wrote in 1998 that the play was about the "political correctness of American colleges' treatment of sexual harassment."[19] His conclusion suggests that as late as 1998, nearly twenty years after the *Alexander v. Yale* case, some faculty members were still clinging to the idea that sexual harassment on campus was "not that bad" or, even worse, something weaponized in a liberal takeover of higher education. One criticism rejected the notion that the power play in *Oleanna* had anything to do with gender and only to do with the university hierarchy, as if one could separate gender from academic hierarchies. A number of the reviewers seemed fixated on what Carol, the student in Mamet's play, was wearing. Professors' resistance to the play as a vehicle about sexual harassment is troubling and sheds light on how entrenched the problem is and why it's been so hard to combat, especially for students who are trying to get their degrees and at the same time calling the university to account for harassment or assault.

While Mamet contends that he wrote the characters to muddle audience allegiance, he missed one point. His audiences, as a reflection of society, had been conditioned to believe that women could not be trusted to be truthful about the severity of their unwanted sexual experiences. In 1992, most of us, including theatergoers, were predisposed to view the issue of sexual assault from the abuser's point of view and to blame women for violations. Without addressing the sway that myths hold over us, Mamet's muddling was pointless unless his goal was to uphold conventional thinking about women's credibility.

The *Alexander* case reminds us that twenty years prior to *Oleanna*'s debut, women were excluded from enrolling in some colleges, and that once they were allowed to enroll, women experienced harassment. And certain programs continued to deny women admission even after they were accepted into the schools. Against this backdrop, setting *Oleanna* on a college campus provided a great opportunity for a discussion of the role of power in sexual harassment. But Mamet missed this opportunity by failing to contextualize the central conflict in the play. Instead of exploring the rich terrain of power on college campuses, which resulted in student protests beginning in the 1960s and any number of reforms in campus structure in the following decades, Mamet relies on a worn-out canard. He imagines that Carol's claim of sexual harassment comes from her having joined a feminist group. *Oleanna*'s most obvious flaw is that the interactions between the professor and the student are limited to one setting, the professor's office.

By erasing the classroom experience, the deans and department heads, the grading system, the tenure system, and other students, Mamet deprives his viewers of the chance to witness the fuller spectrum of interplay between hierarchies of power within a university. We are left to interpret what happens between Carol and John as a "she said, he said" incident, in which some perceived Carol as weaponizing sexual harassment through her diabolical manipulation of the facts to some purpose other than merely confronting an assailant. We are meant to believe that a student armed with words alone can shift the balance of power to her side, which we are also led to believe is dangerous.

Despite this flawed and problematic setup, *Oleanna*, which *Time* magazine named one of the ten best plays in 1992, continues to be staged even after 2017, when #MeToo presumably changed the conversation about sexual harassment. And the interpretations of the play have not come very far. Responding to a 2017 production, one critic was so convinced that Carol held all the power, for instance, that she left the performance "feeling sorry for the professor who was gradually annihilated as Carol sets on him like a rabid dog, eyes bulging, spitting with rage."[20]

In 1992, the same critic described "the professor as presumptuously concerned with protecting the fruits of the patriarchy" and "deserving of his punishment at [Carol's] hands as comeuppance for his patronizing complacency." She also referred to Carol as an "acute verbal warrior, wielding 'the facts' as weapons to skewer the man in charge."[21] Her reaction to the 2017 production and choice of dehumanizing words to describe Carol leaves one to wonder if race and gender both figured into the seasoned journalist's review. While the latter version starred Johnny Lee Davenport and Obehi Janice, two Black actors, the play's world premiere in 1992 starred William H. Macy and Rebecca Pidgeon, two White actors.

What *Oleanna* misses by presenting this conversation in a silo is how college structures work together to silence victims, often sweeping incidents and complaints under the rug. Interpretations of the play relied on personal biases rather than a grounded understanding of how institutions are set up to fail victims and, in many cases, facilitate abuse.

Countless letters from students who shared their stories of campus sexual violence with me in the 1990s showed me that the issue had always been lurking. What most stood out were the lacking institutional responses they outlined, because colleges ineffectively "dealt with" harassment, assault, and extortion. My first helpful insight into why efforts were failing came in the letter that Dr. Hart, the college chaplain, wrote to me in 1991. He explained that the chaplain's office, where he and his wife both worked, had become the de facto location for addressing harassment and assault complaints from students, staff, and faculty. The clergy staff had no special training, no set procedures for investigating, and no power to punish offenders if they concluded that a violation occurred.

In 2020, I tracked Dr. Hart down, hoping to draw on his decades of representing victims and survivors to help me understand how the behavior lived on in colleges. He had retired by then, after twenty-five years as a university chaplain, but continued to teach and represent students in sexual harassment and assault hearings. He provided chilling insights about sexual violations from the past as well as those that continued to occur:

> I have seen the statistics of "one in five" being publicized in recent months. In all honesty, it seems on the low side. My encounters with young women who, in their Junior or Senior year, realize that they were, in fact, raped (some as First Year students) led me to understand that the forced sexual encounter was dismissed by many of them as "college life."[22]

What the students' assessment misses is the role institutional hierarchies play in normalizing the aggressive and violent sexual behaviors that they view as just "college life." Until I started digging deeper into the issue of gender-based violence, I didn't understand that sexual harassment and assault were prevalent even when I was in college and, as Nick Papandreou noted in his op-ed on the fraternity culture at Northwestern, continue today.

STUDENTS: THE FORCE AWAKENS

In 2011, the U.S. Department of Education's Office for Civil Rights issued a guide to colleges struggling to address problems students had complained about for decades. Schools took notice and began to institute policies for addressing rape, assault, and harassment claims. It was a good first step, but more changes were in order. Those began to materialize in 2014, when millennial student activists started calling for reforms to the way colleges handled Title IX claims, and the Department of Education submitted additional directives to the schools. Schools began requiring antiharassment training for students, faculty, and staff. Around the same time, students started complaining that schools were withholding information about campus sexual assault as required by the Clery Act. Stepped-up enforcement of the mandate that schools report violent crimes on campus followed. A requirement that all on-campus sex be consensual began at Antioch College in the 1990s. It was ridiculed around the country as creating absurdly unrealistic expectations of young people. Yet despite being mocked, by 2014 the notion took hold, and the University of California system put in place an affirmative consent policy. Consent was defined as an "affirmative, unambiguous, and conscious decision by each participant to engage in mutually agreed upon sex." Critics have called it overburdening and unfair to students accused of sexual violence. But what was once an outlier approach to campus sexual assault has been touted as best practice with the potential for changing campus culture.

One might think that in a post–Chanel Miller world, given the attention her sexual assault case garnered, things might have changed significantly. Miller was sexually assaulted at Stanford University in 2015, and her assailant was tried and found guilty. But believing that one case on one campus can change what has been described as campus rape culture throughout the country is not realistic. In fact, that thinking is dangerous, allowing us to close our eyes to what is happening every day and everywhere at colleges around the country. A simple Google search for news on "campus sexual assault" nets scores of 2020 stories in college newspapers as well as larger outlets.

GATHERING THE FACTS AND ALLIES

In 2020, *The Chronicle of Higher Education* surveyed colleges and universities nationwide to gauge change on how institutions handle complaints. With the government effort to offer guidance and the push internally on campuses to fix systems, one might think that things have improved greatly. But while the survey noted a good deal of change, it painted a dismal picture of progress.

Among the most common steps institutions have taken to deal with sexual misconduct are revising policies, hiring or appointing a Title IX coordinator, reforming the investigation process, holding mandatory training (for students, staff, and faculty members), and supporting bystander intervention, a type of prevention that encourages students to step in if they see a potentially risky situation. On the whole, campus officials were more likely to say they had taken certain steps than to report that those steps were effective. In other words, the changes being made offered institutional cover but did not appear to have made a difference in students' experiences.

In 2019, Paula Johnson, co-chair of the National Academies of Sciences, Engineering, and Medicine committee, testified to Congress about her committee's findings. Including interviews of graduate students and undergraduates, the research revealed that in higher education "over 50 percent of women faculty and staff" and, "depending on their field, 20–50 percent of [women students] will experience sexual harassment from faculty and staff while at their institution."

But perhaps the most distressing revelations were the frequent "perceived tolerance for sexual harassment in academia, which is the most potent predictor of sexual harassment occurring in an organization," and the "increased focus on symbolic compliance with Title IX and Title VII [that] has resulted in policies and procedures that protect the liability of the institution but are not necessarily effective in preventing sexual harassment."

I have been a university professor for nearly forty years and presented at an early gathering of the National Academies' Committee on the Impacts of Sexual Harassment in Academia. And still the National Academies' findings are hard for me to stomach. It's no wonder that the term "rape culture" has become synonymous with "campus culture." The problems Johnson's committee documented could have been resolved more than forty years ago if colleges and/or the federal government had acted and followed the law announced in one of the first sexual harassment in education decisions. Is it reasonable to believe that what happened to the student in Professor Hite's story could happen today? Paula Johnson pointed out one factor that contributes to the likelihood of sexual harassment and suggests similar abuse of graduate students is happening today. Johnson notes that "strong dependencies on those at higher levels (as is the case in many competitive graduate programs) . . . are more likely to foster and sustain sexual harassment." And competition for funding along with the weight of favorable faculty references contributes to graduate students' being dependent. Johnson warns that "when power is highly concentrated in a single person, perhaps because of that person's success in attracting funding for research students," subordinates are less likely to complain about abusive behavior.

Over the past five decades evidence of universities' failing to live up to their institutional responsibility to curb student and staff harassment and assault is growing. And, whether through neglect, dismissiveness, or blatant abuse of power, the National Academies' research indicates that the same failures continue today at universities. Importantly, in a post #MeToo moment of reckoning around the issue of sexual assault and harassment, students, alumni groups, and media outlets are stepping up to hold academic institutions responsible for protecting victims and survivors.

At Princeton University a battle erupted in 2017 over its treatment of a sexual harassment claim made by a graduate student, Yeohee Im. Im had traveled from South Korea to study with a renowned engineering professor, Sergio Verdú. Following an investigation, the university validated Im's claim that Verdú's behavior toward her was harassment. The university required Verdú to attend an "eight-hour training" session on sexual harassment. He continued to teach yet was denied the opportunity to plan for a sabbatical for nine months. But the deeply entrenched power dynamics were made clear by what followed, starting with Verdú's cutting off funding that had been promised to Im.

In a petition signed by about nine hundred Princeton community members and published in *The Daily Princetonian*, many students, faculty, and alumni advocated on behalf of the student. "We the undersigned write to express our deep concerns regarding the University's handling of the recent sexual harassment case against electrical engineering professor Sergio Verdú," the petition said. It requests that the university "elevate its disciplinary actions" and "firmly establish that sexual harassment will not be tolerated in our community." This forceful response is the culmination of years of student complaints and protests against institutional neglect of sexual harassment and assault on college campuses that surged in 2014 but began in the 1970s.

Verdú's engineering colleagues from around the country also got involved, writing a letter supporting him. It chastises the university for overreacting to Im's charges and calls Verdú "an innocent victim of the

fallout from the national hysteria on the subject." This was a reference to claims of "political correctness" and hysteria arising from the
#MeToo movement.

The MIT graduate and former engineering professor at Cal State
Bob Gray, on the other hand, wrote an open letter urging his professional colleagues to discuss the issue of sexual harassment and open up
more general discussions at professional workshops, at symposia, and
in articles. Gray warned the 500,000 members of the IEEE, the world's
largest technical professional organization, that "failure to take substantive action will put us on the wrong side of history."[23]

A year after the turmoil involving Yeohee Im, Princeton revoked
Verdú's tenure and dismissed him from his teaching position after
finding that he had broken university policies by having consensual
relationships with other students of his. In turn, he sued Princeton
under Title IX, claiming that the university had fired him because of
his gender.[24] The court rejected Verdú's claim.

The question at the top of the chapter is worth revisiting. Behind
the question "How do I prepare my daughter for college so that she
doesn't allow herself to become a victim of sexual harassment or assault?" is the notion that the sole responsibility for preventing sexual
violence falls on potential victims and their families. Of course, parents need to talk to their children about all the challenges of college.
Students should be aware of the sexual assault rates and procedures for
their college before they decide to attend it. But the responsibility for
students' safety on campuses must ultimately fall squarely on the shoul-
ders of college administrators. As a professor, I know that most college
staff and leaders take this role seriously. But there are lingering questions. Do we believe that ending sexual harassment and assault on college campuses is in everybody's best interest? If so, we will stop putting

the burden of change on victims and survivors to tip the balance of power in their favor. As hard as they are to read, studies like the National Academies' and the *Chronicle of Higher Education* surveys, reports in college newspapers, and overdue cases of individual accountability are encouraging because facts that matter are finally coming to light. So, too, are the growing involvement of parents and alums committed to safer campuses and the increasing attention of media to campus violence. Rather than seeing this parental and alumni involvement as coddling or contributing to students' fragility, we should welcome these efforts for their ability to produce what's in everyone's best interests— better information, transparency, and committed engagement that might lead to broader institutionalized changes that can lead to much-needed cultural change. In the university ecosystem, money matters. And the scores of people and foundations that donate funds in the forms of gifts or grants to support institutional programs, research, and infrastructure often have a tremendous influence over schools. Many donors are alums. Some are not. But by joining with alums and parents, they can use their influence to make sure leaders do everything in their power to keep campus members safe. This community approach to ending university harassment and assault might help plant the seeds of change among a population poised to enter our workplaces.

The Millennial Workplace

The number of millennials currently working or looking for work outnumbers any other generation. At 38 percent of the labor force, they eclipsed Gen X in 2016 and will continue to grow. And though a miraculous overnight transformation of society's attitudes about gender is not happening, one might think that millennials' attitudes about equality and active engagement in social movements might make a difference. Is it possible for a new generation's experiences and ideas to move workplaces to, over time, become less tolerant of sexual violence and more likely to embrace equality in a range of forms? Or is radical change the only way to de-systematize our tolerance of workplace abuses?

INTRAGENERATIONAL DISSONANCE

For all the criticisms of the generation born between 1981 and 1996 as being pampered, selfish, and disengaged, conventional wisdom positions them as liberal when it comes to race and discrimination. And why wouldn't they be? In terms of demographics, U.S. Census numbers show that Gen Y, also known as millennials, is the most visibly racially and ethnically diverse population in American history. And the General Social Survey, which, since 1972, "has provided politicians, policymakers, and scholars with a clear and unbiased perspective on what Americans think and feel" about issues such as gender equality, found that millennials have the most progressive attitudes about gender equality of all population groups. Millennials' leap in egalitarian attitudes is stark. Egalitarianism among Gen Yers is considerably broader than among their predecessor generation. Three-quarters of millennials believe that women should be equal both at home and at work.[1] Unfortunately, even though the workplaces they are now in are changing in many ways, millennial liberal leanings are no match for entrenched anti-diversity cultural biases and workplace structures that demand compliance with tradition.

The #MeToo revelations show that diversity alone, or support for equality, does not necessarily mean that men will abandon their demands to control women using sex or violence. And that liberal persuasion is by no means uniform. Hostility persists. A recent article by the sociologist Barbara Risman about the generation's advancement toward gender equality had Gen Y detractors. One comment posted by a reader dubbed Lucifer A cited "toxic" feminist ideology and its "cancerous effect" on families as the reason for "increasing violent crimes, domestic violence, [and] increasing sexual assault numbers," among other social problems. So that there was no doubt, Lucifer A stated, "I myself an 'older' millennial, early 30s now, don't for a second think men and women are equal, they never have and never will be equal."[2]

Lucifer A's antagonism toward feminism echoes that of a prominent journalist from the silent generation. The syndicated columnist George Will said that numbers supporting what he called a "supposed campus epidemic of rape" were based on bad math. He criticized administrators' response to the well-documented problem as an invention of progressive feminists bent on promoting "victimhood [as] a coveted status." But attitudes like Will's and Lucifer A's are just one contributor to the acceptance of sexual harassment and assault among millennials. Despite their progressive attitudes about equality, the fact is that Gen Y students and workers inherited university and workplace cultures where gender aggression is practiced to the point of normalization. And like Dr. Hart's students, they assume that it is just "college life." These young women's take on their college experiences with sexual assault are similar to how generations before them viewed college and work life. The feminist icon Gloria Steinem famously said that when she was young, sexual harassment didn't yet have a name. She and her peers, victims and abusers, were conditioned to see the behavior as "just life" rather than as a violation of a basic civil right.

Concerns about gender equity should have taken a positive turn following the revelations of the #MeToo movement. But not all millennials are on board with the #MeToo agenda of prioritizing anti-harassment efforts. According to a Gallup poll, only 55 percent of men aged eighteen to forty-nine currently consider sexual harassment a major problem, and that's a sixteen-point drop since 2017. Generation X, millennials, and Generation Z are considered the most socially liberal groups in modern history. The majority of them have grown up in households with working mothers. Yet in her book *Brotopia: Breaking Up the Boys' Club of Silicon Valley*, Emily Chang makes clear that the generation that claims to be disrupters of everything traditional has left the old boys' club intact. In fact, the tech industry is known for a "bro culture" that lacks diversity and exhibits both race and gender bias, as well as for documented cases of bullying LGBTQ+ colleagues. Bro culture is not limited to tech, and no one generation is going to miraculously overcome the misogyny that has plagued the world from time immemorial. It provides as much of a challenge as changing the way we promote gender hierarchy for children and younger adults in college. We must also create the tools and strategies to disincentivize long-standing and toxic behavior in our workplaces.

What kind of workplace will millennials inhabit throughout their life span? Will the workplace be the continuation of a stream of abuse that children witness and face beginning in elementary school? Will gender aggression and violence continue to be baked into pay and promotion incentives or assumed to be acceptable depending on whether the violators are in positions of power—top moneymakers or simply managers? These are significant questions given that millennials came of age during, as well as spearheaded, campus protests against sexual assault, Occupy Wall Street, and Black Lives Matter. These movements might easily have bent that generations' politics toward greater gender, race, and class equality. But all too many older observers write them off as the wasted generation that the journalist Morley Safer of *60 Minutes* described as "narcissistic praise hounds now taking over the office."[3]

Safer's comments drew lots of attention at the time but strike me as absurdly elitist and a bit paranoid. Most millennials are not headed greedily for corporate offices, and they're not out to take our jobs or deprive us of anything. Many of their goals are expansionary and inclusive. Their advocacy in support of economic, racial, and gender equality moved the issues forward on campuses and off, as did concerns they raised about global warming. Safer's brand of intergenerational sniping is not new. And baby boomers, like generations before, want to protect their legacies even when those include classism, racism, sexism, and damage to the planet. Gen Y women and people of color are challenging the obstacles they face in workplace settings, from food and janitorial services to high-tech jobs to news and entertainment. But the story is bigger than a few high-profile news accounts. Harassment continues to be "just life" for many workers. Rather than write them off, we need to meet them in the places where they are working and see for ourselves what conditions they really face.

THE FOOD INDUSTRY: LOW WAGE AND HIGH RISK

Three of the top five occupations expected to see the most growth in the next decade are women dominated and low wage. Personal care aides, food industry workers, and home health aides are the three minimum-wage jobs with the most predicted job growth between 2016 and 2026. And according to the National Women's Law Center report on jobs of the future, "If policymakers do not take action to ensure that all of the jobs our economy creates allow working people and their families to be economically secure, the future of work for women threatens to be increasingly characterized by precarious jobs with poverty-level wages."[4] But low wages are not the only challenge facing the millions working in the food industry. These jobs are also rife with sexual harassment.

In the restaurant and food prep business, the average age of fast-food workers is twenty-nine. Forty percent are twenty-five or older, 31 percent have at least attempted college, and nearly 60 percent are women. The Bureau of Labor Statistics projects that 40 percent of female fast-food workers have been sexually harassed on the job, with Black and Latinx women being most affected.[5] And while many servers, cashiers, and bus people work in low-paying jobs at fast-food chains, sexual harassment of restaurant workers is an industry-wide problem up and down the ladder, not just at McDonald's.

High menu prices are no guarantee of a safer work environment. In 2017, twenty-five women working in celebrity chef John Besh's corporate entity Besh Restaurant Group and his restaurants complained of a "bro culture" throughout the enterprise of several high-end restaurants in New Orleans. The offenses allegedly included "vulgar and offensive comments, aggressive un-welcomed touching and sexual advances [that] were condoned and sometimes even encouraged by managers and supervisors," according to *The New Orleans Times-Picayune*. Those who complained were shunned or ignored. Some managers used their authority to attempt to extort sex from restaurant workers. One alleged regular event was the poolside workday scheduled by a company supervisor, which included alcohol and female workers in swimsuits. Male chefs and "businessmen in suits" were invited to visit the pool and introduced to the female staff. Not surprisingly, the pool days resulted in lewd or sexually suggestive comments toward the women, according to the *Times-Picayune* exposé. One woman, whose name was withheld, accused Besh himself of coercing her into a sexual relationship and others of retaliating against her when she tried to end it.[6] The suits are still being decided, but Besh was asked to leave his post as head of the company named after him.

The ubiquitous McDonald's brand with its family-friendly marketing and product names, like Happy Meal, was also the subject of a nationwide worker protest over alleged rampant sexual assault and harassment. In 2019, "systemic sexual harassment" was alleged in as many as fifty claims filed by the National Women's Law Center on behalf of workers against the chain.[7] On record were allegations from "a 15-year-old cashier in St. Louis who said an older male employee said to her: 'you have a nice body; have you ever had white chocolate inside you?'" A Chicago worker said she was asked by her manager if she wanted to see his penis and "how many penises she could take." She held that when she reported it, she was fired. When a New Orleans worker complained about a co-worker groping her, she stated that the manager told her she should take it to the "next level" with him. When a second employee tried to sexually assault her in the restaurant's bathroom, she explained that she did not report it because her first complaint had been ignored.[8] In 2021, those lawsuits and a class-action lawsuit were pending.

The vulnerability of workers in the food industry, putting them at high risk for workplace abuses, are myriad. Disparities in power, race, and ethnicity of the workforce, low and sporadic wages, lack of advancement opportunities, and uncertain hours are just a few of the elements that promote a troubling environment. But one factor that is often overlooked is the sexualization of the restaurant experience. Some chains or individual outlets hire women servers based on how they look in skimpy required uniforms. Other women servers complain of managers who encourage them to flirt with customers as a way to increase their tips. Both are setups for harassment.[9] Speaking about her time as a Hooters waitress, Brittany Anderson, currently a chef and restaurant owner, told *GQ* magazine, "It is an entire job based on sexual harassment. You are paid to be sexually harassed and objectified. Everyone at Hooters is aware."[10] The name of the restaurant itself encourages ogling, at the very least.

And the all-American chain McDonald's is hardly a model. In a stunning turn of events in the middle of the claims brought against the company, its CEO was charged with breaking company policy by having an affair with an employee. Like Besh and Mario Batali, another celebrity chef accused of sexual misconduct, the British-born executive Steve Easterbrook was forced to resign his position with McDonald's, initially receiving a whopping $42 million in severance pay. A year later, NBC News reported that McDonald's was suing Easterbrook after evidence emerged that the CEO had affairs with three other employees and had lied to the company about them.

While reporting on the #MeToo movement focused largely on women actors and models, the activist and migrant worker organizer Monica Ramirez stepped in to make sure low-income workers were not ignored. Rather than "call out" the movement for overlooking women of color and "blue-collar" and "no-collar" workers, Ramirez's "Dear Sisters" letter stood in solidarity with #MeToo on behalf of 700,000 "farmworker women across our country suffer[ing] in silence because of the widespread sexual harassment and assault that they face at work."[11] The TIME'S UP Legal Defense Fund, money raised by Hollywood actors and producers, supports the attorneys representing the women suing McDonald's. The idea for the fund was sparked, in part, by Ramirez's call to action on behalf of women overlooked in the movement. And a PBS *FRONTLINE* documentary, *Rape on the Night Shift*, spotlighted the night-shift office-cleaning staff's vulnerability to sexual harassment and assault.[12] The film, along with organizing and a four-day hunger strike on the lawn of the California state capitol, led to state legislation requiring training for all janitorial workers, not just managers.[13] Yet we cannot underestimate the gaps in attention to the multiple hurdles that home health-care, restaurant, factory, and janitorial workers face merely to be heard and to lobby for change or fund lawsuits. It's disgraceful that underpaid women must camp on the ground to raise awareness for a problem that has been documented and shown on national television. But it is also telling of how low-wage women's claims may be the last to be heard, let alone addressed. This is a reality not only in the public sphere but in their workplaces as well.

Women in Hollywood did a great public service by coming forward and sharing stories of the rank abuse they experienced. Their vulnerability was made obvious by revelations of an industry culture of silence. Ultimately, though, public enchantment with a depiction of a harassment victim as a glamorous starlet, in part based on the rape myth of the perfect victim, did a disservice to those who were featured in the initial #MeToo stories as well as many others, such as service workers. The term "Me Too" was coined in 2006 by Tarana Burke, an African American activist, to help Black and Brown girls who had been sexually assaulted, as Burke was. It's a shame that the narrow representation of sexual assault and harassment coming out of the #MeToo movement left out Burke's intended survivors as well as lesbian, gay, trans, queer, and bisexual people's broad range of experiences. Statistics show that LGBTQ+ individuals are at higher risk of violations than straight and cisgender women. LGBTQ+ and gender-nonconforming narratives were presented more clearly in publications after 2018. *Grabbed*, a book of ninety-one essays edited by Richard Blanco, Caridad Moro, Nikki Moustaki, and Elisa Albo, fills in some of the gaps we need to close. It shows how people of different sexual identities, ages, races, and ethnicities react when their body or brain is taken over for the "amusement or pleasure of a predator."[14] More work is needed as well to challenge the shaping and presentation of #MeToo stories solely within a White, heterosexual, upper-class, male framework.[15] The spectrum of gender violence covers a range of behaviors that impact its victims in a variety of ways. The acts themselves vary, as do their consequences. Attending to the many stories and acknowledging the factors that make people vulnerable to abuse increase our chances of making the world safer for everyone.

HIGH TECH, HIGH FINANCE, AND GENDER HOSTILITY

Key to the harassment in the food industry is the culture and history of worker exploitation. In tech and finance, a history of gender and racial exclusion lies behind the current obvious and pronounced hostility toward women.

Every generation has its so-called dream job, and those typically involve working in offices of a big corporation. For the youngest baby boomers, IBM was an aspiration and a symbol of the American dream, according to *Mother Jones* magazine.[16] As they aged, what baby boomers discovered was a workplace where policies promoted as worker friendly actually favored the corporation, not the workers. In the case of career-long IBMers, the betrayal came in the form of age discrimination, or as one confidential planning document put it, a strategy to "correct [its] seniority mix."[17]

Not all millennials aspire to work in the new tech industry called

Silicon Valley, but it's been a powerful lure and symbol. Yet tech, where leadership roles are increasingly held by the generation born between 1981 and 1996, shows both the best and the worst of the "modern" workplace. There are fast fortunes to be made, but at great sacrifice, especially for women, who remain a distinct minority in Silicon Valley environments. What many millennials are learning is that corporate protections, structures, and policies against sexual harassment, where they exist at all, are often toothless or geared toward protecting those in power. Though tech leaders are quick to say that their generation of companies are all about innovation and disruption, when it comes to addressing workplace abuses, it's their grandfathers' values that emerge.

Ellen Pao's lawsuit against the venture capital firm Kleiner Perkins in Silicon Valley gives us a glimpse into what journalist Emily Chang describes as a brotopia culture, where men make their own rules and where the systems of rewards in place limit women's chances of succeeding in high-paying jobs. Some view the jury decision against Pao in her gender discrimination case as evidence that challenging bias in tech is fruitless. But putting aside the glitz and lure of Silicon Valley, I see that case as just the beginning of a new way of understanding the intricacies of gender discrimination, including sexual harassment in the industry, as well as how millennials can navigate those complexities. The high-profile suit that Pao brought against her powerhouse venture capital employer and the issues raised by Susan Fowler at Uber, which prompted a massive worker walkout, pull the curtain open to reveal how unacknowledged bias can dominate hiring, promotions, and sexual harassment investigations in an industry that is presumed to be a liberal bastion.

The core of Pao's lawsuit against Kleiner Perkins Caufield & Byers was her claim that because of her gender her employer refused to make her a senior partner. The stakes for Pao were high. Partnership would have put her in a position to earn as much as $3 million a year, according to a Recode article titled "Follow the Money: Did Men Earn Quintuple What Women Made at Kleiner Perkins?," with a summary that read "Pro tip for an aspiring VC: Be a managing member. That's where the money is."

But lost in the coverage of the discrimination claim was the significance of the everyday atmosphere of the office, the routine discussions of strip clubs and pornography, and the retaliation against her because, according to Pao, she broke off a romantic relationship with a colleague. She was excluded from a firm-sponsored dinner that turned out to be a "bros"-only affair where influential clients were entertained. Pao only found out about the dinner because it was coincidentally being held in a restaurant on a lower floor of her condo building. Though not the basis of the suit, the hostility Pao experienced seems more than enough to interfere with her ability to do her job. By 2012, when Pao sued Kleiner Perkins, the term "hostile environment sexual harassment" was familiar but didn't play a role in her legal claim, though the facts suggest that it could have.

Kleiner Perkins, which had early on funded the tech behemoths Amazon and Google, was seemingly inattentive to discrimination. Pao considered a formal complaint about her colleague's retaliation against her after she'd broken off what Pao described in her book, *Reset*, as "a short-lived, sporadic fling" with him. But she was told that Kleiner Perkins had no internal process for sexual harassment claims. Pao learned that another woman at the firm, Trae Vassallo, had an experience similar to hers. The same colleague with whom Pao had been involved had attempted to coerce Vassallo into a sexual relationship.

Again, there appeared to be no formal complaint process and no anti-harassment training. When Kleiner Perkins did hire an investigator to look into Vassallo's complaint, they brought in a man who was open about his interest in getting a job at the firm. Despite the obvious conflict of interest, Kleiner Perkins later hired the same person to do antiharassment training.

Not to be lost in Pao's experience is the connection between the performance evaluations and the culture that paints women as persona non grata. In her annual review, the Kleiner Perkins partner John Doerr encouraged Pao "to soften your style, to be more collaborative, supportive, particularly of those with whom you don't easily work" in order to improve her ratings. This is a familiar phrase to women who've been told forever just to try to "get along, to fit in, not to rock the boat," or to not "come off as so bossy," or to not act like "a cynical bitch," as a CEO called one female subordinate during a meeting. The same workplaces often applaud boorish and even angry behavior in men. One wonders how far Pao was expected to go to support "those with whom [she didn't] easily work" if those were the very colleagues who she believed were attempting to exclude her or wanted to engage her in lewd conversations. In *Reset*, Pao acknowledged that before Doerr hired her as his chief of staff, he had requested an Asian woman for the position. Ellen is the daughter of Chinese immigrant parents, both of whom are scientists. Pao would testify in her trial that Doerr "liked the idea of a 'Tiger Mom–raised' woman." Ellen might have fallen into the model-minority trap as described by the Pulitzer Prize–winning author Viet Thanh Nguyen: "to be invisible in most circumstances because we are doing what we are supposed to be doing, like my parents, until we become hypervisible because we are doing what we do too well."[18]

Pao's gender discrimination claim ended up in court. And after two weeks of an intensely public trial, Kleiner Perkins prevailed. But Pao's revelations were just the tip of an iceberg of sexual harassment complaints against venture capitalists throughout Silicon Valley. In 2017, a range of disturbing sexual harassment charges started to emerge. Women entrepreneurs told stories of behaviors ranging from inappropriate comments to sexual extortion. As start-up funders, venture capitalists have an immense amount of power and influence over would-be entrepreneurs. This power differential, along with the "bro culture" in the sector, allows for harassment to flourish. The absence of company policies to handle harassment cases and lax external regulations on venture capital operations also contribute to the high level of abuses.

The ambient impact of tolerance for harassment extends to the climates of the companies that the VCs fund. Ginny Fahs, a technology policy fellow at the Aspen Institute, wrote for *The Atlantic* about having to travel from San Francisco to Menlo Park, California, to read one company's sexual harassment policy because the firm's HR chief would only allow Fahs to view the policy in person in their Silicon Valley offices. Fahs was not allowed to take photos or notes about the contents.[19]

In her work, Fahs concluded that funder harassment and tolerance for discrimination trickled down to the tech companies they invest in. "When toxic workplace cultures pervade any of their portfolio companies, VCs are in a strong position to force these companies to confront the problem." But that doesn't happen, according to Fahs, and the only remedy is outside pressure. For Fahs, that means new laws need to be passed to rein in the toxicity that she and others have witnessed or experienced.[20] Some investors have taken the step of posting their anti-harassment policies to distance themselves from the toxicity.[21] And the problem of sexual harassment among VCs became so well-known that institutional investors took notice. Universities, pension funds, and limited partners, which is where the VCs go to get funds, are taking matters into their own hands to guard against losses related to harassment and other bad behavior. One way institutional investors protect their risks is by identifying and avoiding investing with VCs who are known bad actors.[22] The threat of not having access to money works to some extent, but only if practiced throughout the industry. So far harassment is so entrenched and so loosely regulated that the culture has not evolved. Ultimately, absent a major lawsuit or extensive regulations, it's up to the leaders in the VC industry to change the toxic culture and practices.

Fowler's now famous blog post about the noxious environment at Uber led to changes in that organization's culture and practices. Freada Kapor Klein, the pioneer in antiharassment work that dates to the 1970s, along with her husband, Mitch Kapor, both tech investors, wrote an open letter that pushed Uber to reform its practices.[23] And Ellen Pao established Project Include, a nonprofit that works with tech companies to accelerate diversity and inclusion within the industry.

Pao's and Fowler's experiences are reminiscent of episodes chronicled almost twenty years earlier by the journalist Susan Antilla in her revelatory book *Tales from the Boom-Boom Room: Women vs. Wall Street*, about a landmark sexual discrimination and harassment suit filed against the brokerage firm Smith Barney. On 1980s Wall Street, in workplaces owned and operated by members of the silent generation and baby boomers, sexual harassment and assault went hand in hand with exclusionary, male-centric practices that discouraged women from applying for jobs as brokers or from succeeding if they did manage to get hired. In the 1990s, women did get hired, but little changed in the offices they entered. The variety of rampant sexual harassment, assaults, and other sorts of discrimination in the financial industry was stunning.

Smith Barney ultimately paid $150 trillion in arbitration awards and settlements to the twenty-three women who brought the class-action suit in 1996. Throughout Wall Street, companies began drafting sexual harassment policies and hiring antiharassment trainers. But any gains were short-lived, and the commitment to change all too shallow. More than two decades after the case settled, Antilla offered a grim reminder of the fragility of the gains toward ending sexual harassment. She followed up with the parties involved in the Smith Barney suit that she chronicled in *Tales from the Boom-Boom Room* and in 2019 wrote an exposé revealing what happened to the women who had filed sexual harassment and equal pay violations in the 1990s and early 2000s. Antilla's editor sums up the largely discouraging findings:

[A]s women filed discrimination complaints, Wall Street forced those claims into arbitration, where hearings are behind closed doors, documents are filed secretly, and awards are less. Most women lost those battles, and even those who won faced career disruptions. We found those who stayed in the industry took years to get their careers back on track; others dropped out and settled for lower-paying jobs. One is a baker. Another is an Uber driver.

The men they accused, meanwhile, did quite well. Serial harassers carried on despite their histories; financial regulators never required them to publicly report the harassment cases they lost. One man settled a sexual assault lawsuit confidentially; ten years later, a second woman sued him and won $2.5 million. He's still in the insurance and securities businesses—and neither case appears in his securities industry records.

Some men did suffer: the ones who testified on behalf of women they say they witnessed being harassed. Two such men lost high-paying jobs in the industry after testifying on behalf of women. One is now a handyman; the other is an emergency responder.

39 years after the EEOC set a goal that 25% of Merrill's new brokers should be women, the data is grim. Only 17% of brokers today are women. And 60% of female financial advisers said in a recent survey that they had personally experienced sexual harassment at work.[24]

Whether in finance or tech industries, harassment in Silicon Valley companies in the first decade of the twenty-first century follows the same patterns as harassment on 1970s Wall Street. It took Fowler's blog on Uber and multiple lawsuits to bring attention to how institutional protections allowed powerful men to flout antiharassment laws. And a common ingredient in multiple cases was a climate, pervasive in tech, that accepted and even embraced reckless and often unlawful behavior by men.

The twenty-thousand-worker worldwide walkout in 2018 to protest Google's multimillion-dollar payouts to executives with long histories of harassment might have made the biggest impression on industry leaders and the public. The walkout might also have become the model for worker demonstrations at e-commerce companies, such as those at Amazon and Wayfair, as well as essential-worker protests at Target and Instacart. But the story of the Google walkout did not end happily for everyone. Its organizers, Claire Stapleton and Meredith Whittaker, have left the company, claiming they faced retribution for their efforts. Google denied having retaliated against the two women. Yet less than a year after the global demonstration of resistance to a culture that Whittaker and Stapleton thought would make them and their colleagues safer, Stapleton was demoted, and Whittaker's responsibilities were revised. They both left the company within a year of the walkout.[25]

Millennial women in low-paying jobs, whether in tony communities like those in Silicon Valley, in urban areas, or in rural communities, will likely not have the flexibility or freedom or money to sue, nor are they likely to have the platform to write a viral blog. No matter the location, women working low-paying jobs experience employment violations with some of the same markings as those with eye-popping revenues and salaries.

Companies throughout the country have taken the steps of establishing policies and procedures to address sexual harassment in the workplace. And a majority of them, more than 70 percent, have instituted anti-sexual-harassment training, with 20 percent of American companies requiring employees to take the training. But even years after the #MeToo movement, training remains a "check the box" exercise for many companies. Research found that trainings focus on legal definitions rather than getting rid of sexual harassment. And though some revamping of these trainings is taking place, questions remain about whether the changes will result in safer workplaces.[26] In fact, the Harvard University sociologist and veteran researcher Frank Dobbin says that sexual harassment programs actually result in women losing ground—a 5 percent drop in the number of women in management.[27]

Institutions have to take responsibility for their own structural failures. Management can help solve harassment by first recognizing it, then taking action as soon as it appears. Supervisors can act to stem abusive behavior before it rises to the severe and pervasive standard of a federal antidiscrimination claim. Also, bystander training has been shown to be effective at empowering colleagues to take action, reducing the burden on victims to step forward. Multiple reasons back a more proactive approach to resolving conflict and supporting gender and racially inclusive working groups. In many tech enterprises, teamwork and trust are critical. Harassment costs employers. There is no business interest in tolerating the harassment of any one individual or group of individuals. There is a growing body of social science research that verifies the increased productivity of diverse work groups. Studies show that gender and racially diverse and inclusive workforces make good business sense. Researchers in the United States and Europe have discovered that groups with equal numbers of women and men performed better at negotiations, moral decisions, and brainstorming and are more profitable than groups where men outnumber women. But even this may not be enough to get business to break the pattern of gender aggression and violence in our workplaces. What really makes a difference is the tone set at the top of an organization, where eliminating harassment is presented as a value proposition that is part of the organization's culture. That kind of leadership coupled with problem solving (as opposed to compliance to regulation) is an effective approach to ending the problem in the workplace.

When it comes down to it, the possibility of a new generation changing structures that have become business as usual also depends on external factors like finances and regulators. Without systemic changes and industry-wide demands, it's hard to imagine that individual workplaces will evolve. Precise prescriptions for change in finance may vary from those in the food industry, but each requires shifts in the cultures, structures, and systems that have locked gender and sexual harassment and hostility in place.

GENERATION NEXT

I've taught for more than three decades. But I count the experience in terms of the numbers of generations I've encountered in the classroom and on campuses around the country. By that calculation, I'm on my third life. I started teaching in 1983 to a class of boomers. By the end of the decade, my classes were largely made up of Gen Xers, who had been labeled cynical, know-it-all slackers. I found that not to be the case among that generation's law students. But there was a difference between Gen X, also known as the hip-hop generation, and my own baby boomer generation. And even though I was only a few years older than some of my students when I began my career at Oral Roberts University, just a few years later, I realized that they had different role models. Born in the years between 1965 and 1980, they had not experienced the civil rights movement as a drama of resistance broadcast in real time. It was as if I were talking about the Civil War. It was history to them, not current events.

My students in those days were mostly White men. Only a handful of them, mostly Black men and a few women, ever gave me any indication that Dr. Martin Luther King Jr.'s rhetoric or goals held any resonance for them. The women's rights movement was equally abstract. First-wave feminism, at best, was something that might have inspired their great-great-grandmothers to march for the right to vote. And second-wave feminism was just as likely to have been portrayed as a threat to family life as an urgent call for gender equity. Even the students who valued the achievements of the rights era weren't devoted to their parents' and grandparents' integrationist strategies.

The social critic and University of Southern California professor

Todd Boyd even went so far as to say that there is "no unifying force when it comes to bridging the generation gap between those of the civil rights era and those of the hip-hop generation."

In 1995, when I was asked to give a talk about the role Generation X could play in promoting gender equality and preventing sexual harassment, I became even more sensitive to the gap. Even the label *X* seemed to signal our alienation from our progeny and our insecurities about them as our successors. Nevertheless, I presented them with four challenges. The first was to understand the interrelationship of various forms of oppression. I mentioned racism, sexism, homophobia, and classism by name while acknowledging that other forms of bias were just as pernicious. The second challenge was to comprehend the global scope of gender oppression. The United Nations Fourth World Conference on Women had just taken place in Beijing, promising a new global women's rights movement. First Lady Hillary Clinton's "women's rights are human rights" was the takeaway message. And while the movement has not jelled, pockets of it exist and have sparked changes in women's and girls' ability to oppose violence in their lives.

Third, I warned them that individual oppressive behavior was only possible because institutions sanctioned it. I cited the case of the graduate student whose sexual exploitation went unacknowledged because the university was concerned more about maintaining the "prestige" one abusive director brought to the school than in mitigating the harm his behavior did to the entire community. But my final admonition was that Gen X take care not to pass a culture of oppression to the next generation. Now I know that I was asking more than might have ever been possible. Every generation is connected through our biases, conscious and unconscious. When these biases go unacknowledged and unaddressed, the next generation and the next will suffer them.

And what about connecting through pop culture? Through its storytelling and technical creativity, Hollywood has the power to influence society to model the systemic change that the BLM and #MeToo movements insist upon.

But in 1994, rather than promote a film that encouraged a deep conversation about sexual harassment in the workplace, Hollywood chose *Oleanna* and *Disclosure*. *Disclosure*, like *Oleanna*, chose to tell the story of harassment from the point of view of accused men as victims. Just as in *Oleanna*, in which a male professor is accused by a student of rape, the male lead in *Disclosure* evolves into the sympathetic character. Billed as an erotic thriller and set in the corporate office of a tech company, *Disclosure* starred Demi Moore as Meredith Johnson, the recently promoted manager of her ex-lover, Tom Sanders, a character played by Michael Douglas. When Sanders refuses some (but not all) of Johnson's sexual overtures, Johnson retaliates by weaponizing sexual harassment—filing a claim against Sanders. Sanders counterclaims with his own suit—a sexual harassment claim. Johnson's scheme is revealed, and the movie concludes with Johnson losing her job for having filed the false claim against Sanders, who, of course, takes her position in the business. The 2005 film *North Country* was the first with a realistic portrayal of the dynamics of power and abuse abundant in the workplace. In one scene, workers use a backhoe to topple a portable toilet that one of the women has just entered. Community members and, in some cases, the women's family members side with the company and ostracize the women workers. Set in the early 1990s, the movie was based on the horrifying real-life story of some of the first women to work as miners in an iron field located in Minnesota. And the experiences of women in 1980s and 1990s Wall Street boom-boom rooms were just as despicable as those brought to the screen in *North Country* from the mine in Minnesota.

Fast-forward to 2019. Hollywood might have finally started asking the correct questions about sexual harassment and power in its own living room. Fittingly, the animated Netflix series *Big Mouth* started a new conversation about sexual harassment in an episode called "Disclosure the Movie: The Musical!" *Big Mouth* is the brainchild of the millennial Nick Kroll, who turned the 1990s movie into a cartoon that takes on sexism, racism, and homophobia. The episode is filled with lines that reflect society's understanding (or misunderstanding) of sexual harassment claims more precisely than *Oleanna* or *Disclosure* was able to do. Is *Disclosure* a story of women's empowerment or a "misogynist fantasy"? the *Big Mouth* kids ponder. Or is it "an exploration of the dangerous times that we men are now forced to navigate? This play dares to harass the very notion of sexual harassment and say, 'Uh, yeah, Me Too,'" as one *Big Mouth* teacher opines. After watching the movie and the cartoon, I have faith that maybe somewhere in the future there is a generation that will get the answers to sexual harassment right.

Meanwhile, we—advocates, legislators, consumers—have to keep pushing industry to change. By the time people reach the workforce, they have experienced, witnessed, or participated in systems where some level of abuse is tolerated. Most have watched countless movies or television shows, and an increasing number have played video games that reward violence. Effective training should be called untraining, because workers unlearn the bad lessons about how violence and aggression signify success. Bystander and implicit bias training are improvements over compliance training, but not all bystanders are equally equipped to challenge violators. To quote Dr. Mary Rowe, an expert on antibias training, policies, and the role of ombudsmen, "In my experience incredibly important constraints on very powerful people are other powerful people who act, and act frequently, as effective peers and bystanders."[28]

Yes, powerful people can change the bad behavior of other powerful people. But the questions that opened this chapter remain. Is incremental change that comes from altering individual behavior enough? Rowe also proposes that powerful people use their clout to intentionally change the systems—even those that give them their power. Millennials can begin that work by recalling the demands to change structures that they made in the anti-racism, anti–campus rape culture, Occupy, and climate change movements. And what about the rules outside work? Radical ideas must also apply. Where is the antiviolence and antibias training for intimate relationships, encounters on the streets or in restaurants and bars, and civic engagement? Though progress in our schools and workplaces can have profound influences on other locations, gender-based violence extends well beyond schools and workplaces. We are only beginning to cover the range of violence and aggression that derives from gender bias, antiwoman dogma, and misogyny. Despite a sustained campaign for gender equality in the United States, gender aggression and violence remain a drag on the social fabric of our country, including our democracy.

SEVEN

A Woman's Worth: Representation, Violence, and Equality

Kamala Harris knocked off a host of firsts when she won the vice presidency in 2020. She is not only the first woman to be vice president but also the first Black person, child of immigrants, and person of Asian descent. Many were dancing in the streets when the election—one of the most consequential in recent history—was called, after days of nail-biting as several key states counted and recounted a historic number of votes.

In 2016, when Hillary Clinton became the first woman to win a presidential primary, we were given a high-profile lesson in how political races bring out intense and open resistance to women seeking office, even to the point of absurdity. Rather than offering an opportunity to showcase our achievements, recurring questions about credentials are lobbed at women candidates to knock them out of the running for public offices.

"WHAT QUALIFIES YOU?"

Consider the journalist Matt Lauer's opening questions to Hillary Clinton in 2016, during what was billed as MSNBC's Commander-in-Chief Forum. Rather than probe her professional capacity, Lauer cut directly to one of Clinton's personal practices: her use of a personal email account and server to communicate while she was secretary of state.

"You've said it's a mistake," he said. "Why wasn't it more than a mistake? Why wasn't it disqualifying, if you want to be commander in chief?"

In contrast, Lauer launched his interview with Clinton's opponent, Donald Trump, with a softball, open-ended question: "What have you experienced in your personal life or your professional life that you believe prepares you to make the decisions that a commander in chief has to make?" Rather than point out that Trump had no foreign policy or diplomacy experience and that his personal flaws were notorious, Lauer gave Trump the privilege of making his case. In this instance, the idea was apparent that men are presumed credible and women have to prove it. That sentiment tainted the 2020 election, for example, when a female swing-state resident explained that she had voted for Trump in 2016 because she "couldn't see two women [Clinton and Nancy Pelosi] running the country."

By 2020 this sort of misogynist questioning and name-calling had become such a predictable staple of political discourse that TIME'S UP, the organization formed in response to the #MeToo movement, created a new initiative. Recognizing the damage that misogyny and name-calling do to women candidates' chances of winning, "We Have Her Back" pledged to call out "sexist and racist tropes about the ambition, likeability, looks, or attitude of women candidates across parties, especially women of color."[1] When women who win offices propose gender-based policies, antiwomen statements make it easier to defeat the proposals. And alt-right groups have mobilized election-cycle misogyny to recruit followers and undermine gender equality protections. In 2018, the Southern Poverty Law Center added two male-supremacist organizations, A Voice for Men and Return of Kings, to its list of U.S. hate groups. Paul Elam, the face and voice of AVFM, in 2010 began a blog declaring October "Bash a Violent B—— Month." He later called the piece satire but justifies his hateful, violent rants as necessary to galvanize the men's rights movement. ROK, founded by Daryush Valizadeh (known as Roosh V.), has called for repealing women's suffrage as the path to saving Western civilization and the legalization of rape on private property.[2] After the 2016 election, Roosh V. reacted with exuberance over the country's selection of "a President who rates women on a 1–10 scale" based on "their appearance and feminine attitude." Roosh V. wrote on his website to his followers, "We may have to institute a new feature called 'Would Trump bang?' to signify the importance of feminine beauty ideals."[3]

Two months into her run for the presidency, in a televised interview on PBS, Senator Kirsten Gillibrand posed the question "Do we value women?" She responded, "The answer is no." Gillibrand based her candidacy on being a champion for women, and she was outspoken about her belief that a woman leader could heal the divisions in the country.

The senator from New York had also been a prominent voice in Washington in support of victims of domestic violence and sexual assault. Gillibrand cited the failure to prosecute rapists along with the increasing rate of sexual violence in the military, despite "every promise by every general and every secretary of defense" to address the issue.[4] But Gillibrand's campaign failed to gain traction, and after she dropped out, discussions of how candidates might address the country's well-documented gender-based violence were virtually nonexistent on the campaign trail and during the primary debates. And midway through 2020, the Defense Department was once again accused of failing survivors of sexual assault in just about every branch of the military.[5] Gillibrand's attention to gender violence was not enough to qualify her candidacy. And gender violence didn't qualify as a topic worthy of primary prominence.

Senator Harris's candidacy and win were tainted by the same sexist scrutiny all women candidates face, compounded in Harris's case by her race. Eric Trump, the president's son, for instance, "liked" a tweet calling Harris "a whorendous pick." His father, speaking of Harris's debate performance against Vice President Mike Pence, twice called her a "monster" whom Pence "destroyed." Though not as direct as Trump's prior references to women as pigs and dogs or his campaign adviser's reference to Harris as an "insufferable lying bitch," "monster" is a trope often enlisted to dehumanize people of color.[6]

But the demonization and denigration of women voters, candidates, and leaders are only two of the headwinds women face in the pursuit of full political participation. Whether demanding equal pay or ending gender violence, issues that promote gender equality languish in political processes. Early in 2021, months after its expiration, the Violence Against Women Act was yet to be reauthorized by the Senate. One of the major impediments was disagreement over the "boyfriend loophole," which allows abusive dating partners access to guns even if they have a criminal record of domestic violence. As of March 2021, the Paycheck Fairness Act, which addresses gender pay inequity, had sat in the Senate without action for nearly two years. When it comes to women's well-being, economic equality and basic safety against violence are two inextricably linked factors. And since the first-wave women's movement in the United States, both have been recognized as indicators of women's full political participation.

WOMEN'S ECONOMIC WORTH

At the root of the collective disbelief in women is the idea that we are inherently underqualified and of limited value, socially and economically, despite all evidence to the contrary. And the question "What qualifies you?" isn't just aimed at women seeking political office but lobbed against working women all over the place to undercut their accomplishments in all fields. Women servers and CEOs alike tell stories of having their credentials challenged for no other reason than their gender. A friend, I'll call her Angela, a tenured faculty member in one of the top engineering programs in the country and a tech entrepreneur, said she still faces bias when she approaches male funders about backing her projects. She once entered a conference room to discuss financing for one of the many innovations she has developed during her career. The bankers had already received a professionally developed portfolio of information that included her business card and résumé. After introductions, my friend presented her idea as she'd done many times before. The first question she got from the group was whether she had a degree in engineering. Who knows whether the men seriously thought that a woman in 2010 couldn't have an engineering degree or whether they were joking. But Angela wasn't amused. "Can't you take a joke?" is often the response when anyone is called out for a sexist comment. Regardless of intent, language can be demeaning and discriminatory. And unfounded challenges to women's competence couched in gender terms can serve as precursors to denying women workplace assignments and opportunities for the advancement they deserve. Presumed incompetence or lack of qualification has a disastrous impact on women's wages and economic growth. Despite movements for gender equity in this country and around the globe, women remain undervalued economically. The Institute for Women's Policy Research offers grim news for pay equity. The pay gap is stubborn:

> The ratio of women's and men's median annual earnings was 82.3 percent for full-time, year-round workers in 2019, a statistically insignificant change from 2018 when it was 81.6 percent. This ratio means that the gender wage gap for full-time, year-round workers is 17.7 percent. Women's median full-time, year-round earnings in 2019 were $47,299, compared with $57,456 for men.

Even grimmer are the chances that millennial workers, who make up a large contingent of today's workforce, will see the gap close during their work lives:

> The rate of progress toward closing the gender pay gap did not increase in 2019. If the pace of change in the annual earnings ratio continues at the same rate as it has since 1960, it will take another 39 years, until 2059, for men and women to reach

parity. This projection for equal pay has remained unchanged for the past four years.[7]

A 2012 Yale University experiment demonstrated that all things being equal, both women and men will presume women's incompetence. In a blind study, identical résumés, some with female-sounding names and some with male-sounding names, were sent to science faculty from research-intensive universities who rated students' application materials. Faculty were more likely to offer the applicants they thought were men bigger salaries and rate men as significantly more competent and "hirable" than presumed women applicants. And despite efforts at universities toward increasing diversity, women applicants were less likely to be offered mentoring. Other research shows that female life science graduates get less money to cover their start-up costs than their male colleagues. It's no wonder, then, that women are still lagging behind: talent isn't the villain; bias is the culprit.

This research reveals something more than men's immediate economic advantage. When scientists, like those in the Yale study, downgrade a candidate's abilities based on a female-sounding name alone, their decisions can last a lifetime. Some make gender-biased presumptions that women may not be as serious about their careers as men or that they will take blocks of time raising children and become less productive team members. Of course, this kind of preemptive elimination of women from jobs is illegal discrimination. Paying women less up front or not hiring them at all for something they may or may not do in the future is just as sexist (and I would argue just as illegal) as hiring or asking only male employees to a business lunch because men have families to support. In science, entry-level job opportunities, salaries, and funding for building labs can determine the breadth of scientists' work and how they advance their ideas and, of course, their careers. Ultimately at stake are grants, publications in leading journals, and professional recognitions, which can, in turn, lead to more government and private funding and potentially greater discoveries. Many women and people of color are drawn to science and tech to address problems that impact their communities and are overlooked by White men in their fields. I met a young Black woman studying engineering at MIT who was raised by an elderly grandmother. She told me that her inspiration for staying in the field came from watching her grandmother face mobility challenges. Her goal is to develop products to help the elderly live day to day with comfort and independence. Assuming that students like her are a bad risk based on their gender or race hurts science and innovation. And that hurts everyone who might have to do without or wait for science that will change their lives. Underrepresented candidates' contributions to ending disparities in access to science and tech is a compelling reason to consider the value of their candidacies. However, their credentials for positions in the industry stand on their own regardless of how they choose to use their training.

In the United States, we are slowly, painfully waking up to the gender wage gap, and the result has been numerous legislative as well as political actions over the past decade. Pay equity, childcare, family leave, and better economic opportunities are issues that appear routinely on Democratic Party political platforms. March 24, 2021, Equal Pay Day, marked the day the average woman's past fifteen months of earnings had finally matched what her male peer had earned on December 31 for twelve months of work. The Biden administration's national recognition of the day was notable, particularly for its acknowledgment of the disparate economic hardships women have faced during the coronavirus pandemic.[8] Any equal pay advances made in the past few years are tiny and unequally distributed. As with most aspects of gender bias, the brunt of the wage gap falls most heavily on women of color. Latinx women, for example, make only fifty-five cents for every dollar a White man makes. The economic disparities persist throughout the labor market, and the ripple effects can be devastating and deadly. Low wages and high debt that women often face make it harder for them to leave abusive homes and family and work environments, and leave them little safe space to recover from sexual assault. In one bizarre and repellent twist of policy, before the passage of the Affordable Care Act, some insurers considered medical treatment related to domestic violence and rape a preexisting condition that would preclude survivors from getting insurance.[9]

THE EGG OR THE HEN

The struggle to overcome the invalidation of women and so-called women's issues is, of course, not new. But it became particularly pronounced when women sought political participation in the form of the right to vote. In 1848, Elizabeth Cady Stanton and Lucretia Mott gathered at the Wesleyan Chapel in Seneca Falls, New York, for what is known as the first women's convention in the United States. The meeting produced the Declaration of Sentiments, an appeal for recognition of the social, economic, and political rights of women. The women at the convention perceived little light between women's social, economic, and political freedoms, rightly viewing them as inseparable parts of the whole of equality. Stanton based their claim for equality on their citizenship but focused largely on the rights of White women only, leaving the rights of disenfranchised Black citizens, as well as enslaved, Native, and Asian immigrant women, waiting to be addressed. The Seneca Falls thinking was that the recognition of women's value would follow from White women's enfranchisement.

On that afternoon in the Wesleyan Chapel, a hundred men and women, including the former slave Frederick Douglass, signed the declaration on behalf of free White women who were seeking equality through citizenship. Mott, a Quaker minister who on religious grounds believed that slavery was against the laws of nature, also signed. They started by going after the right to vote, a bold opening salvo given that in public law and public opinion women were presumed to be unqualified to make political decisions. And Stanton and her followers wanted more than just a say in who got elected; they wanted a part in passing laws, too. They wanted representation. But it appears that no one raised concern about how the Declaration of Sentiments served the political interests of enslaved, immigrant, and Native American women.

Personal safety has been an uncertainty as long as women have been economically disadvantaged. As energy for women's suffrage mounted, the early advocates started to fully embrace the idea that voting was essential to their personal safety as well as political autonomy. They also knew very well that their rights to vote and exercise other freedoms were only as secure as their personal safety from physical abuse by men, in particular fathers and husbands, who could prevent them from voting, attending school, and gaining employment. But the approach that Stanton and Mott took was tepid compared with what others had suggested before them. Sarah Grimké, a nineteenth-century abolitionist and feminist, had been more direct in confronting the problem of patriarchy and violence. Grimké refused to marry to resist being subordinated to her husband. She spoke directly to men, instructing clergy and legislatures on the rights of women and Black people. And in

1837, a decade before the Seneca Falls meeting, on behalf of women, she brazenly implored men to "take their feet from off our necks." Grimké was a radical predecessor of the twentieth-century suffragists.

And on the political front, Grimké's successors in the cause knew that if women's contributions could be reduced in the eyes of the public, the public was unlikely to be concerned about the physical, economic, and sexual abuse women routinely suffered. Not deterred, and still aiming for women's political representation, in 1866, Stanton ran for a seat in the U.S. House of Representatives. She received twenty-four votes of twelve thousand that were cast.

More than seventy years would pass between the signing of the Declaration of Sentiments and the ratification of the Nineteenth Amendment, invalidating laws that denied women suffrage. Black people's citizenship rights were codified in the U.S. Constitution, but states continued to limit their rights to vote. Similarly, even though Congress enacted the Indian Citizenship Act in 1924, states refused American Indians the right to vote. Given the disenfranchisement of Native and Black women, the Seneca Falls group's concept of universal rights and suffrage was an illusion well into the twentieth century. Even then, the question of who would represent the interests of women of color remained, and their experiences with gender-based violence went largely unexplored.

Some early suffragists blamed the unfettered physical and sexual abuse men wielded against women on male lawmakers, jurors, and judges. Winning the right to vote for women was their antidote to sexual assault in the home, on the streets, and in workplaces. But women's newly gained right to vote did not yield policy and verdicts that brought an end to gender violence. In 1931, Mary Hamilton, the first policewoman appointed in New York City, observed that "there hasn't been a conviction of a man for rape in twenty years." Hyperbole aside, Hamilton's point was well taken. Even after the Nineteenth Amendment's passage, women's political participation in ways essential to ensuring their right to protection against sexual assault was never fulfilled.[10]

Though today we enjoy far greater freedoms than the women of the Seneca Falls Convention, what Stanton called "the greatest movement of human liberty recorded on the pages of history" remains unfinished. Limits to women's political, economic, and social agency continue to dog us, making freedom from violence or the threat of violence impossible. And the question of whose freedom from gender violence mattered continued to plague women's movements into the twenty-first century.

In short, the vote did not guarantee full recognition of women's worth, and we're left to wonder if recognition of women's value must come before we can secure full political participation. Which brings us back to the question Gillibrand raised: "Do we value women?" Do we value women enough to accord them full participation in our democracy or enough to dedicate our democracy to putting an end to gender-based violence? A look at three types of gender-based violence and where we stand in addressing them shows how far we have to go before we can say that we truly value women.

INTIMATE PARTNER VIOLENCE
AND POLITICS

Politics govern how much of our public resources we are willing to invest in challenging gender-based violence. And the politics of gender-based violence is fraught with victim blaming. When public officials categorize intimate partner violence as a private matter, the victim blaming becomes built into our structures. It also shows in our calculation of the cost of the behavior to individuals and the greater society. Classifying gendered violence as a private rather than a public issue has many effects. It reduces the significance of the problem and serves as an excuse for lack of public funding for solutions. We tell ourselves that it's not so bad. And then we ignore the costs in lives and human resources it causes. Personalizing the impact of gender-based violence is a kind of denial that allows us to tell ourselves "it's not our problem." Why should government funding be spent on individual personal problems? Labeling intimate partner violence a private matter has a social effect—stigmatizing victims and marginalizing them in our communities. All of the above reductive approaches to gender-based violence devalue women who experience abuse, silencing the witnesses preemptively.

Victim blaming plays a role in suborning gender-based violence. But it is never more problematic than when it happens to intimate partner violence survivors, who often encounter sexual assault, emotional abuse, beatings, and financial extortion at the hands of partners. Shaming, for "allowing themselves to become victims," by friends, family, or people to whom they reach out for help can further trap them in abusive situations they are trying to escape. I had read about this part of the cycle of abuse as well as the role that abusers themselves play in entrapping victims of gender-based violence. But I had not witnessed it firsthand until 1992, in a shelter for what we then called "battered women" and their families in Detroit.

The Women in Detroit

Long before I ever visited Detroit, it loomed large in my imagination. As a place of near-legend status, for the economic opportunities and the music it created, Detroit is important especially among Black

Americans. Its spectacular prosperity in the first half of the twentieth century, shared by Black people who landed there during the Great Migration, and spiraling economic decline in the second, which hit Black neighborhoods hard, make it a true example of the urban American story. I've now visited the Motor City twice, and both my experiences exceeded my imagining. I'd grown up in Oklahoma, a Black child in a rural community with a population that was as White in the 1950s, when I was a child, as Detroit's was Black in the 1990s.

Even with the downturn in its economy, the city had an allure. My ancestors were not a part of the Great Migration that brought families north to escape racism and restrictions on our basic rights. To those who joined the throngs who left, mobility gave them a newfound freedom. Many were just one generation from severe beatings for being caught off the land of their slaveholders. When I studied the scant section on the Great Migration in my small-town rural high school American history course, I wondered how my life might have been different had my mother been lured to Chicago or Detroit as many girls and women were. The migration north was not something my family experienced firsthand, but it was part of my history as a Black American and a part of American history. Many of their families had arrived in Detroit decades earlier, looking for the freedoms they could only dream of in the South. They wanted more for themselves and their children. The toll that racism, dating back to slavery, had taken on the migrants to the North was palpable and enduring. But stories about the cost of gender violence on Black women's bodies, families, and entire communities were largely unspoken, often consigned to the experience of slavery. On this visit to Detroit, what had been a continuing tax on Black America, the unacknowledged price of intimate partner violence, was evident on the faces of women in a domestic violence shelter. Like their mothers before them who abandoned their homes to escape Jim Crow laws that threatened lives and stifled freedom and opportunity, children led the women in Detroit shelters to abandon their homes to escape an abusive partner who threatened their lives, their freedom, and their opportunities. The former danger was state imposed. Too often, the latter danger has been neglected by the state.

Had my family moved north, would my chances of being a victim of domestic abuse and ending up in a shelter have increased? Intellectually, I knew that domestic violence victims came from all backgrounds. From my experiences with the women's center in Norman, Oklahoma, I knew that small-town and rural women were abused. But for that brief moment, I thought that somehow the circumstances of living in an economically depressed city were the cause of the violence instead of one more thing that made it hard for some victims to escape. And though it plays a role in intimate partner violence, including options for escaping it, financial hardship is not a determinant of who gets abused.

Sandra Kent, a Detroit native and nurse who worked to reform the state's health-care system and who devoted her spare time to women's empowerment and community services, organized my trip to what was once a Black mecca. More than the lure of my romanticized images of the Great Migration, Sandra's passion for the Motor City was what persuaded me, with just one phone call, to travel there. Buckets of ink had been spent describing Detroit's various woes—job losses, failing schools, abandoned houses, and ravaged neighborhoods. But rarely did any of the media I read focus on the injury the city's woes caused women whose livelihoods and bodies were imperiled by the economic downturn. After I landed at the airport, our first stop was a trip to a local intimate partner violence women's shelter, where I encountered a group of women who had suffered violence that drove them and their children from their homes and landed them in a shelter with other women in the same situation.

Perhaps it was anxiety, but for a moment I wondered what I would say once I got to the shelter. For a year I had been speaking about gender equality and women's empowerment. A speech wasn't appropriate. But I was out of my comfort zone. I had never spoken to a group of survivors. Though I was on the board of a local service provider for domestic violence survivors in Norman, where I lived in 1992, I'd never visited their shelter. For privacy and security reasons, not all board members visited the house where women who had no place else to go were sent.

Sandra explained to me that the women had watched the Thomas hearing. As with women around the world, the senators' dismissive and hostile reactions to my experience with harassment had resonated with them. How many times had they been asked why they didn't just leave at the first sign of abuse? The connection between me and them was clear. And upon reflection, I realized that to believe in their own ability to weather this dark time in their lives, they needed to see me as a survivor. I also realized that I needed to see them where they were in their journey—as victims, survivors, or somewhere in between. To understand the complexity of gender-based violence, I needed to know what it was like for them to suffer physical and emotional trauma and have to decide whether to stay or to leave. To really understand, I had to hear how, in the face of trauma, they decided whether to call police, where they would live if they had to leave their homes, what might happen with their jobs and to their relationships, and most of all if their children would suffer more harm. All emotional decisions, but all decisions with concrete consequences that had to be worked through even as their bodies ached from the blows and their brains were on alert for the next battering.

On a cool, sunless day, I and about two dozen Black women who had mustered the courage to escape home violence sat on gray folding chairs. The setting was austere, but the safety the women found was enough for them to remain there for the time being. Facing one another in a circle provided a sense of intimacy that made me uncomfortable at first. But there I heard and felt face-to-face how that threshold question to victims (Why didn't she just leave?) lingers well after they find help. Even the people who love them question survivors' credibility to make sense of their own stories. The economic turmoil the city faced made their personal struggles for survival even more difficult to overcome. Many shared, through tears, the guilt and responsibility they felt for being beaten. They spoke about what they wanted most. Most of their desires were pretty basic—to be able to wake up in the morning, get themselves and their children ready for the day, and return from work all in the safety of their homes. They also wanted to know that they were valued members of the community.

HARD "CHOICES"

While often a strong motivator, children can also make leaving more difficult. Survivors on social media describe the dilemma in painfully immediate terms. In a 2014 article compiling accounts of women's stories, Catherine Woodiwiss wrote that they "paint a heartbreaking picture of just how ubiquitous and varied abuse can be," as well as how complicated the decision to leave is. Woodiwiss pointed to tweets from partner violence survivors and victims that illustrated her point. Ellen

G., the daughter of one victim, tweeted, "My mom had 3 young kids, a mortgage, and a PT job. My dad had a FT paycheck, our church behind him, and bigger fists. #WhyIStayed." Fear of losing her children and the support of her church complicated Ellen G.'s mother's decision. Madge Madigan's post showed that mutually inconsistent feelings about the best course for their families can keep victims in abusive relationships: "#WhyIStayed—I thought it was best for the kids. #WhyILeft—I realized that was what was really best for the kids." Jewels tweeted, "#whyileft Holding our 4 wk old baby & told to put him down or both of us get hurt. Me & my black eye got a restraining order the next day." Jewels reached the precipice of imminent injury or death to her child before taking the bold step of leaving her abuser.[11]

The dueling hashtags of these posts show the conflicted feelings survivors have about whether to leave or to stay. Often either of those questions is nothing more than a slightly veiled accusation. "You should have stayed. Why didn't you?" or "You should have left, or left sooner. Why didn't you?" Victims and survivors often stay and try to negotiate their or their children's safety with their abusers. This rarely works. And as Jewels makes clear, the final straw may be that after beating a spouse for a period, the abuser begins to strike out at their children. Madge Madigan stayed before she came to the realization that staying was worse than leaving, and that can sometimes take longer than those of us who have not been in an abusive setting can imagine. While leaving may be best for children, it can come at a huge cost. Imagine walking out of your home with three young children in the middle of the night and nothing but the clothes on your back and bus fare to the shelter. Amid such heartbreak, it was hard to rally these women to hope without seeming callous. They had been told that they had no worth, so I listened to those who would talk.

When a situation is dire, like what the women in Detroit experienced, we often think calling the police is our best recourse. But calling the police to protect you from someone whom you love or whom your children love is in itself traumatizing. Some women don't feel safe in the presence of police officers when they and their children live in communities in which police abuse is notorious. But not engaging the police was hardly an option for some of the women I saw in 1992 who were in danger of losing their lives without intervention. And the dilemma of resorting to law enforcement continues. At a recent national conference for survivors of sexual and partner violence, victims and survivors stated that they often feel criminalized by police officers' approach to addressing their complaints. In pleading for an alternative to the criminal legal system for community safety, the conference attendees spelled out their concerns.

There are currently limited strategies that survivors have available to them when navigating harm, because too many of our current strategies that purport to protect the safety of survivors are rooted in the criminal legal system. This means that police serve as responders in situations they are often not trained to handle and, in turn, exacerbate the trauma of the survivor; methods of resolving violence lead to incarceration over survivor-centered, community-driven accountability or healing processes. Moreover, one in four women (24 percent) reported they had been arrested or threatened with arrest during a partner abuse incident or while reporting a sexual assault incident to the police. Additionally, sexual misconduct claims accounted for the second-highest category of complaints against law enforcement officers, after use of excessive force, meaning the very systems tasked with providing safety often perpetuate harm and fail survivors.[12]

And myriad circumstances factor into why a person stays or leaves an abusive relationship. Economics and children are obvious ones, but sexual identity can be another. One should also not underestimate the importance of community and family support. In 1992, social support for same-sex partners was limited; same-sex marriage was far from being legal, let alone accepted. Community support for a victim of same-sex intimate partner violence followed suit. And attitudes in some regions have not changed. LGBTQ+ individuals may remain in a relationship because they have no other place to live. Stigma associated with sexual identity works against them. Victims also stay because an abusive partner threatens to out gay or lesbian partners to employers, family members, or workplace colleagues. Again, police may be unsympathetic. They may blame victims' abuse on their "lifestyle choices," challenge their credibility, and leave people to fend for themselves based on sexual and gender identity.

The basic question of where to go when a victim leaves an abusive relationship is extremely difficult to navigate. Often the victim has relied on an abusive partner's income to afford housing. Without that income housing options are limited; available affordable housing in many locations does not cover the demand for it. And for victims the need to find a sanctuary away from their abusers dictates their options. In her book *No Visible Bruises: What We Don't Know About Domestic Violence Can Kill Us*, Rachel Louise Snyder says that the three thousand shelters nationwide that have been opened in the past four decades have undoubtedly saved lives. But shelters alone will not provide even the basic safety needed. In fact, according to Snyder, "Shelter is necessary and saves lives, but it is also an abysmal fix." Despite best intentions of providers, shelters lack consistent funding and are a short-term solution, even if there were enough places to house everyone in need of a haven from abuse. Some women are housed with their children in single budget-hotel rooms that have no cooking facilities. If they're in a shelter, they are at a greater risk of work absenteeism or job loss, leaving them to cover financial costs without a reliable source of income. Abuse triggers a chain of consequences that are often insurmountable. And victims' lives can be forever changed, because the choices are not real choices, just temporary responses to a long-term complex problem.

I have never had a partner who beat me. But neither my education, my job, my marital status, nor any of the other things that we claim will protect women from intimate partner violence would have shielded me. I think about what happened to my friend Beverly Guy-Sheftall, a women's studies professor at Spelman College and one of the country's leading Black feminist scholars. I met Beverly in 1992 at Spelman, where she has taught since 1971 and went to school as an undergraduate majoring in English before getting her PhD in American Studies at Emory. Beverly's experience with intimate partner violence is terrifying. And while she didn't have to decide what might happen to children or other family members or her job or home, the abuse she experienced and her decision to extract herself from the relationship were nevertheless traumatic.

Shortly after her fortieth birthday, Beverly broke off a relationship with a colleague at Spelman. His possessive nature and extreme distrust of women convinced her that they would never be a good match. She thought it would be an amicable split, given that they had dated for a short period. Beverly did not imagine the terror that the fellow faculty member, now ex-boyfriend, would subject her to for "one seemingly endless year . . . from hell." He forced his way into her home and threatened her with a fireplace poker, stole and torched her car, and stalked her at her home late at night and sometimes all night. And in what Beverly describes as the "most aggressive and dangerous" behavior, he wrote her name, telephone number, and address in numerous public telephone booths and men's bathrooms throughout Atlanta with the invitation "I have good p—y." Strangers started to call her at all times of day and night proposing to "accommodate the bogus invitation." Beverly's former husband discovered her name on the wall of the men's bathroom at a restaurant near her school that was popular with faculty members. She was determined to stop her former partner's nightmarish behavior as well as stem the flow of phone calls and drive-bys from strangers who had read the messages he'd posted about Beverly. Outraged and frightened, she reported the problem to the police. A sympathetic detective pursued her case for months, the Atlanta police ultimately charged the ex-partner, and local prosecutors decided he should be tried. What followed were additional months in and out of court attempting to have the ex-boyfriend prosecuted for simple battery, car theft, and arson.[13]

In the end, the court found Beverly's ex guilty only of the arson charge. He was put on probation for five years with no prison time. With the conviction, he lost his job, and Beverly and a friend were free to go about town with Windex and paper towels to remove the evidence of her abuse.

Certainly the conviction and loss of a job amounted to accountability. However, the court's acquittal on all charges except for the damage to Beverly's car leaves an especially bitter taste in my mouth. Did the jury reach its decision because damage to property is more easily proven under the law? One can easily wonder whether the acquittal on the abuse charges might have been the result of something more noxious, a propensity to value market products over women's lives. And perhaps, as is often the situation in rape cases, because Beverly was not bearing scars or black-and-blue bruises, her injury was not apparent under the law. The outcome raises questions about how much harm intimate partner violence victims must show to meet the legal standard of proof.

Beverly was savvy, superintelligent, and financially independent, and she reported her ex's violence to the police. And among all of the other lessons from Beverly's year of terror, it's clear that leaving an abusive situation or one that smacks of the potential for abuse will not always save you. When women exercise their right of mobility, whether within the same community or across state lines, their decision to leave nearly always involves the legal system, police, criminal courts, or family courts—a system that many survivors of domestic violence find unwelcoming and are fearful of accessing. And even though Beverly went to the police and found some relief from her torment, the process itself was brutal and the outcome, to some extent, unsatisfying.

I had no solutions to offer the women in Detroit other than those available in the shelter. Funding for shelters was limited. In the end, I found words to let them know that they deserved better than the life they had. They deserved to have dreams for themselves as well as for their children. At the very least, they deserved services not available at most shelters throughout the country: education, safe and affordable housing, and wages that allowed them to escape abuse or even avoid it altogether. And they should have had all of those things without having to endure abuse. While many cash-strapped cities, towns, and rural areas are doing the best they can, more federal assistance should be available to address a problem that impacts the entire nation. What's more, these women deserve laws and law enforcement aimed at protecting them, as well as educational and work opportunities throughout their lives. The critical lessons from the pandemic are that the resources victims and their children need to survive are sorely lacking. And when economic and health crises happen, domestic violence victims will suffer.

Thirty years after my trip to Detroit, what we offer to victims of intimate partner violence still falls short of what they need to recover from the health, social, and financial setbacks that can result from such violence.

So the next time you hear someone ask, "Why don't women just leave abusive relationships?" remind them that people who think that's an easy solution are mistaken. People who ask the question don't take into account the enormous financial, social, and emotional costs associated with leaving and for which our government offers paltry support. Those people should know that for some women the fear of leaving outweighs the penalties associated with staying.[14] A high level of empathy is needed in order to fully understand the dilemma victims face. Like all of us, they want to maintain their lives, their identities, and their family's security, but despite the development of some supportive and secure shelters and associated social services, there is no consistency in quality or resources throughout the country. Let people know that victims' social support—friends and relatives—may abandon them out of safety concerns, or because of the social stigma that goes with being a victim, or because some people just don't want to associate with someone who has been abused. Tell the questioner about the social cost of intimate partner violence, how very often, as when any couple splits, relatives and acquaintances may feel compelled to pick sides, and how victim blaming, financial resources, or simple power dynamics can favor the male partner. Some former associates distance themselves from the abuse victim's experience by denying that a close relationship with the victim even exists or by telling themselves that an acquaintance's abuse is "not my problem."

SHARED RESPONSIBILITY

The cost to individuals is real and sometimes devastating. But intimate partner violence is a community problem. It comes with a monetary price that the community must pay. Estimates of costs vary, and recent calculations are hard to find. According to the World Health Organization, for example, in 2004 intimate partner violence in the United States cost $12.6 billion, including health-care, lost productivity, and judicial costs.[15] That amounts to $16.5 billion in today's dollars but does not account for population growth. Other researchers found that in the United States the losses would be between $16 billion and $107 billion in today's dollars due to costs to the criminal justice and health-care systems along with business losses. To adequately address the violence, the study concludes that an effective response requires "the involvement of both government and private organizations if it is to be addressed over the long term."[16]

Every community has a stake in ending intimate partner violence. The costs that communities and states incur due to partner violence and the costs to victims are inseparable. And the cost is not limited by geography. The entire nation bears the cost of intimate partner violence. In 2020, when the pandemic struck and a huge swath of the U.S. population was laid off from work or transitioned to working from home, intimate partner violence escalated. The new public health and safety crisis of COVID-19 combined with the existing health and safety crisis of intimate partner violence increasingly imperiled the lives of mostly women and children, and especially nonbinary youth. The tanked economy, lack of COVID-19 relief, and the politics of domestic violence all combined to spark an economic conflagration that disproportionately set women back. And when women lose jobs and become economically dependent, they are more vulnerable to abuse and at greater risk of becoming financially dependent on state resources.

On November 9, 2020, the Monday after Biden was declared the winner of the 2020 presidential election, the majority of the ten million unemployed were women. Prior to the job losses caused by the COVID-19 spread, women made up 39 percent of the national workforce. In this pandemic economy, women have suffered 54 percent of the job losses. A *Harvard Business Review* article called this backslide "not just a blow to women and societal progress but also to the economy and business."[17]

In a stable economy, victims might avoid going into shelters, and there had generally been a movement away from shelters as the way to keep women safe. However, during the pandemic, in cities from New Haven to Houston, shelters are operating above capacity.[18] One report from Denver was that abusers were using the virus to convince victims that they "have no place to go—and if they try to escape, they'll die of a terrible disease."[19] In that respect, the coronavirus simply put a spotlight on intimate partner violence as a problem that will be exaggerated by any health and economic crises and victims' long-term unemployment. This points to the need for a more thoughtful intervention that recognizes just how tenuous safety is for many individuals.[20] And when basic safety is lacking, political freedoms are easily lost.

For intimate partner violence sufferers and their communities, recovery from the pandemic will require more than herd immunity from massive vaccinations. The Great Recession offers a cautionary lesson for what will likely be the fallout from the pandemic for intimate partner violence victims. Less than a year into his presidency, Barack Obama's plans to restore communities throughout the country suffering from the Great Recession were just taking shape. Neighborhoods were still devastated by the collapse of the U.S. housing market, and some families were barely able to cover the cost of food. But help was coming too slowly for those already in crisis. And economic downturns are precursors to increases in other social issues that can crop up seemingly out of nowhere in communities. Hard economic times nationally are bellwethers for surges in gender-based violence that occurs on the local level.

In a small town in New England,* intimate partner violence became "a serial killer." The "spree" started at the height of the recession. Forty-six-year-old Amy Williams, who was working three jobs to support herself and her two children, was the first victim. She had a dream of owning her own cleaning business in the small New England town where she lived. But on March 22, 2009, a paramedic was dispatched to an apartment and found Williams's body sprawled across the living room floor. She had been strangled. Strangulation is a prevalent and underreported form of intimate partner violence, though not always fatal. But the attack on Williams resulted in her death. Her long-term boyfriend and the father of one of her children was found guilty of murdering her. Williams's sister testified at the murder trial that she had witnessed the accused act out in anger in Williams's home. Within six years, four more women would be murdered in the same town, all by their partners.

By November 2010, the economic hardships of the Great Recession were abating, but domestic violence persisted. That month, Jane and Michael Smith, both forty-eight, were found dead by local police in the couple's kitchen. The cause of death was gunshot wounds. An in-

---

* I have changed the names of individuals involved in this section out of respect for the victims' families.

vestigation by the district attorney's office ruled the deaths a murder-suicide. Michael Smith shot his wife, then turned the gun on himself, the local district attorney said. Neighbors and the couple's children all said that the Smiths appeared to have a happy marriage.

Unlike the two earlier victims, Jane Jones, who was killed in 2013, left a trail of information about the events leading up to her death. The twenty-nine-year-old mother had taken out a temporary restraining order against her boyfriend, the father of her four-year-old daughter. Family members described him as volatile, possessive, and violent. The day before she was found dead in her apartment, when Jones failed to show up at a hearing to extend the order, her boyfriend was released from jail. Later, he went to Jones's apartment and stabbed her to death. Their daughter was at home during the attack. The boyfriend and father pleaded guilty to Jones's murder.

Nancy Adams, forty-two, worked two jobs to help support her family, which included her, her husband, Ben, and two sons. On Christmas Eve in 2014, Adams asked Ben to move out, explaining that she was ending the marriage. On New Year's Eve, Ben returned to the couple's condo and stabbed her twenty-one times. There had been no history of abuse, according to friends.

Following up on a family member's request for a well-being check, police went to the home of Ann and David Taylor. Ann, a server at a local restaurant, had not shown up for work the previous evening. It was unlike Ann, whom co-workers described as the nicest person they knew. David was a retired police officer. Checking inside the home after getting no response when they rang the doorbell, the officers found two bodies. In another apparent murder-suicide, David shot Ann and then himself. Ann was fifty-two.

The scars left from these victims' traumatic deaths are perhaps incalculable. Their families were left to reckon with the tragedies—in some cases being forced to bury both parents, one a killer, the other a victim of intimate partner violence. Family, friends, co-workers, and neighbors lived with the pain of loss likely mixed with guilt that they did not save their loved ones.

The death of these five women touched the clients of a beautician, patrons at a restaurant, regular shoppers at a supermarket, special needs children who were driven to school each day by one of the victims, and scores of children participating in local youth sports. As one youth hockey parent said, "He [Smith's husband] didn't just take her from her family, he took her from all of us."

These women have a few things in common. They were all employed. In some cases they had a supportive network of family and friends. There is no evidence that they knew one another. But they all lived in the same small town, and they all were killed by their husbands or partners. And there is little known about them or their community that suggests that any of them were more prone to being in a violent relationship than any woman who has escaped their fate. The issue of intimate partner violence is complex. We know that poverty, substance abuse, guns, and isolation can be factors in fatal family abuse. But what makes the mix of these and other factors toxic is unknown.

The number of deaths due to intimate partner violence is larger than what is typically considered. Overall, such violence contributes to more than one in ten violent deaths. This includes victims who are killed by their partners, family members and friends of victims, and suicides in homicide-suicide events such as those that happened in New England.[21] One study of intimate partner homicides found that 20 percent of homicide victims were family members, friends, neighbors, people who intervened, law enforcement responders, or bystanders.[22]

Whether the victims sought police protection prior to their murders, or whether their deaths involved homicide or both homicide and suicide, government systems are ultimately involved. And it is becoming clearer and clearer that our focus on police intervention as the primary approach for preventing homicide-suicides or other outcomes of abuse is not serving the needs of victims or communities.

As researchers look ahead at the impact of COVID-19 on individuals, localities, and the nation, they express concern about a surge in intimate partner violence, including domestic homicides, murder-suicides, and sexual and other physical abuse of children. But the pandemic, like the Great Recession and the economic downturn in Detroit, merely exacerbated abuse; it is not the source of the violence. We've made some progress in empowering survivors and victims politically. Today, women are emboldened to call out the problem with policing around sexual and other kinds of gender-based violence. That's not a solution, but it is progress. We've also made progress with how we describe intimate partner violence. We've changed our language and no longer talk about laws against "wife beating" or refer to victims as "battered women," language that does a disservice to survivors and victims who don't survive. But any progress we've made is not nearly enough. Because these crises shine new light on festering problems that are gender based, they provide an opportunity for gaining new knowledge and offering new solutions to issues that flourish in good times and in bad. Our elected representatives at every level have a responsibility to "all of us," surviving family and friends as well as the communities in which these horrific acts of violence occur. And we can begin to own that responsibility by acknowledging that what happens in households is, far too often, a matter of public concern. Our leaders' failure to recognize the public interest in intimate partner violence will result in more deaths and more communities left wondering whether their representatives believe that their loved ones' lives are worth saving. Neither our anatomy nor, as some argue, our career choices justify the income gap. Consider how our choices are limited by cultural assumptions about what work is valuable and misguided ideas about our credibility that keep us from getting justice in criminal courts. Think also about how women struggle and often fail to recover financial setbacks caused by sexual harassment and assault and discrimination in the workplace. And our political and legal systems, including our courts, have throughout our history locked those gender-based disadvantages and losses into place.

SEXUAL HARASSMENT AND SECOND-CLASS CITIZENSHIP

In 1991, many people were so unfamiliar with the legal concept that they didn't even know how to pronounce the term "sexual harassment." Following the Thomas confirmation hearing, that changed. The phrase went into common use, even though in some cases judges were uncertain of what constitutes illegal sexual harassment until 1986, when the Supreme Court ruled on the issue, despite the fact that Spottswood Robinson mapped out the legal theory in 1977. Eventually, the law changed. And with the legal changes, clearer understandings of harassment as a civil rights violation emerged. Corporations and schools put in place policies and procedures for addressing the sexual extortion and aggressive and demeaning sexual behavior that women had been complaining about for decades. But the idea that ending sexual harassment was in the best public and business interest was starting to wane.

As the employee protections developed, so did employer resistance. Nondisclosure agreements that prevented workers from discussing settlements in harassment claims and forced arbitration, typically favoring employers, became popular. And, after cases in the 1990s produced decisions that followed the spirit of Spottswood Robinson's broad interpretation of the guards against workplace abuses, courts took an increasingly miserly view of the protections offered to workers and increasingly shielded employers from liability.

The blinkered perception that gender-based violence is a personal matter rather than one of public concern can have consequences that shape the protections against it. For intimate partner violence it has meant government attention to survivors' and victims' health, housing, and financial needs are underfunded. Even when legislators pass laws that demonstrate the public's interest in women's safety and well-being, courts may view the protections as outside congressional authority to safeguard women's rights. One pivotal Supreme Court case decided in 2000 that involved a claim of sexual harassment dealt a significant blow to workplace and school anti-sexual-harassment efforts. The ruling in *United States v. Morrison* chipped away at a woman's right to file a federal claim for abusive behavior—a right that had been secured with the passage of the Violence Against Women Act of 1994. The act had been in effect less than a decade when the Supreme Court's *Morrison* decision invalidated critical portions of the landmark law. Though the particulars of the case involved the Court's review of a student's right to have her sexual assault case heard in a federal court, the Supreme Court's language in denying that right was sweeping, gutting gender violence protections put into place just a few years earlier. The Court found that Congress had no authority to provide a federal civil remedy for gender-motivated violence. Chief Justice William Rehnquist justified the Court's decision as an effort to maintain "a distinction between what is truly national and what is truly local." But the decision left victims to fend for themselves through state and local systems where protections were uneven at best and antiquated at worst.

The U.S. Constitution gives Congress the authority to pass laws regulating commerce among states in the Union and to pass laws to prohibit the interference with commerce. In 1964, rather than serve Black patrons, the owner of Ollie's Barbecue, Ollie McClung, argued that Congress had no power to enact the Civil Rights Act of 1964, the law prohibiting discrimination on the basis of race. McClung's suit made its way to the U.S. Supreme Court. There, the acting U.S. attorney general, Nicholas deBelleville Katzenbach, argued that the burdens placed on interstate commerce by racial discrimination gave the federal government the authority to intervene against private acts of discrimination. The Supreme Court agreed and upheld badly needed civil rights protections against racial discrimination. But for the commerce clause, the federal government may well not be authorized to address racially motivated violence that happened in local communities. Congress passed the Violence Against Women's Act to confirm a "national commitment to condemn crimes motivated by gender in just the same way that we have made a national commitment to condemn crimes motivated by race or religion."[23]

Since the *McClung* decision, congressional authority to protect civil rights, whether based on race or gender, has been assumed as long as the legislators show a burden placed on commerce by related discrimination. In *Morrison*, despite the mounds of evidence documenting the effect that violence against women had on interstate commerce, the Court concluded that the law exceeded congressional authority. According to the *Morrison* decision, the various forms of violence against women covered by the VAWA were not activities that substantially affected interstate commerce. Rehnquist's reasoning was based on his assessment that women's contributions to commerce and the interference to commerce caused by gender violence were inconsequential—not worthy of the federal courts' or congressional attention. By denying women the right to sue in federal court, the ruling severely diminished the federal government's role in protecting women and others from violence visited upon them because of their gender. The message in *Morrison* was that half the population of the United States was not worthy of federal protection against a well-documented threat.

Rehnquist's limited view of the significance of women's contribution to commerce hearkened back to a case that was decided more than a century earlier in which the Supreme Court appeared to be swayed by the notion that women were fit only for work in the home. In 1869, Myra Bradwell had succeeded where few women had ventured. She studied law, took and passed the bar, and met the ethics qualifications for licensing in Illinois. Yet that state's supreme court upheld a state board's decision to deny Bradwell her occupation because she was a woman. As if to prove that she was qualified to practice law, Bradwell took her case to the U.S. Supreme Court in an effort to protect what she argued was her constitutional right as a citizen not to be discriminated against on the basis of her gender. In essence, she argued that as long as we deny a woman's personal economic freedom, we deny her citizenship. The U.S. Supreme Court denied that the Constitution gave Bradwell a right to work in any profession of her choosing, despite having qualifications that equaled male lawyers. In a separate opinion, one Supreme Court justice went even further in justifying Bradwell's disqualification. Joseph Bradley cited "the law of the Creator" to justify blocking Bradwell and upholding the idea that a "women's sphere" was the home. Bradley dismissed the validity of women's efforts to break out of traditional roles. Bradwell's freedom to practice law was eventually granted by Illinois. But her case was singular and does not address the myriad ways that individual women's economic viability are undermined.

And the *Morrison* case went further. The Rehnquist opinion denied that women's labor contributed to the nation's economy in ways that transcend state lines. In doing so, Rehnquist also established that gender-based violence that affected that labor or women's mobility failed to affect interstate commerce. But the assumption that the import of violence against women extends only to the home or to local communities, like the belief that women should be limited to these spaces, is a fallacy that denies their full protection under the law. Rehnquist's misperceptions amount to a blatant denial of women's worth. Despite being easily refuted by the facts, the Supreme Court's conclusion continues to serve as a structural barrier to women's ability to challenge abuse. In the *Morrison* decision the promise of equality under the law got completely lost, just as it did in *Bradwell v. State of Illinois.*

Women's inability to work in safe environments—whether it's at a university, in a restaurant, or in a local bank—affects not only their own economic standing but also the nation's political health. A McKinsey Global Institute report makes clear the link between gender parity in the workplace and the exercise of women's political voice. McKinsey's *Power of Parity* analyzed fifteen gender-equality indicators across four categories. These helped illustrate the "strong link between gender equality in society and gender equality in work—and has shown that the latter is not achievable without the former," according to a *Harvard Busines Review* article on women's economic setbacks in the pandemic.[24] It's worth noting that "political underrepresentation, and violence against women" were two of the four factors that combine to diminish global growth.[25] Despite gains made to women's freedom and rights in the United States, political underrepresentation and gender-based violence continue to muddy and stifle these advancements. The shrinkage of institutional accountability also presented itself socially. Rather than see sexual harassment as diminishing workplaces, public opinion turned against civil rights causes. Victims were labeled whiners, and legal protections were viewed as problematic, unnecessary, or overreaching.

In 2018, the reckoning brought about by the #MeToo movement rocked the entertainment industry and continues to reverberate in others. Sexual harassment is present in workplaces throughout the global economy, and no industry in the U.S. economy is exempt. The McKinsey report, the tidal wave of social media posts, and key sexual harassment cases refute the assumptions about women's limited economic influence on commerce. Jewelry store chains like Jared, Kay, and Zales promote their products in ways that romanticize women. But in 2019, shareholders garnered a $240 million settlement in their suit against their parent company, Signet Jewelers, accusing the Akron, Ohio–based company of concealing an operation that was "rife with sexual harassment" of female employees for behavior that allegedly occurred at Sterling Jewelers, a Signet subsidiary. Charges included forcing female employees to trade sex in exchange for jobs, promotions, and benefits. Led by the Public Employees' Retirement System of Mississippi, Signet's investors were eager to have the company account for the losses caused to the State of Mississippi employees and others around the country.

Alphabet, the parent company of Google and the fourth-largest technology company in the world, settled with stockholders for $310 million to fund the DEI Advisory Council. Among other activities that affected the value of their stock, shareholders claimed that Alphabet had covered up payments made to company execs who had sexually harassed employees. In 2020, a settlement in the Alphabet case required the company to spend $310 million over the next ten years on diversity, equity, and inclusion initiatives. Alphabet also agreed to allow its employees who settle claims to discuss publicly the facts of their harassment and discrimination complaints.

Shareholders have filed suits against Wynn Resorts, Fox News, and CBS, all showing that sexual harassment in the workplace has an impact on interstate commerce.

Even our beloved national parks offer no safe haven. According to Ken Burns's documentary *The National Parks*, it was the writer and historian Wallace Stegner who dubbed the U.S. park system "America's best idea." But for scores of women park rangers, scientists, superintendents, and administrators, the park system is a dangerous workplace. According to an article in *The Atlantic*, by 2016 as many as sixty women throughout the country had complained about various forms of sexual misconduct, from verbal harassment to sexual assault.[26] A survey of National Park Service employees found that the 22,000 permanent, temporary, and seasonal staffers and 340,000 volunteers had to endure what a *BuzzFeed* article described as a "toxic workplace culture for the stewards of some of America's most beloved public lands."[27]

For decades, human rights activists claimed that the food that lands on America's dinner tables was harvested by women who suffer abuses that range from groping to sexual extortion to routine rape. After years of ignoring complaints by farmworkers and their advocates about sexual harassment of migrant workers on large American farms, the Equal

Employment Opportunity Commission finally responded. Between 1999 and 2014, the federal agency brought roughly fifty complaints against farm operations throughout the country, from Maine to Arizona. In 2017, the EEOC brought the last case that I could find against a large farming operation in Florida. Favorite Farms was charged with sexual harassment, rape, and retaliation.

These reckonings occurred only after horrendous treatment of women that went unchecked in many cases.

RAPE AND THE JUSTICE SYSTEM

I ask, that you can contemplate that rape is not just one moment of penetration, it is forever. Whether that rape exposes a victim to a lifelong disease, a pregnancy, injury, mental disorders—the impact will last a lifetime.

—FROM THE VICTIM IMPACT STATEMENT OF JESSICA MANN, WHOSE TESTIMONY HELPED CONVICT HARVEY WEINSTEIN

Rape is a peculiarly heinous crime. And the exercise of full civic participation demands that individuals be able to fully engage the criminal justice system—including demanding justice when they have been raped.

Jessica Mann's statement describes how it impacted her life. Harvey Weinstein was sentenced to twenty-three years in prison for third-degree rape and first-degree criminal sexual act because the court allowed multiple women to testify to Weinstein's predatory behavior—showing that he was a threat to women, not just a single victim. But legal analysts noted that in many jurisdictions the case might never have gone to a jury because prosecutors might have dismissed it as a "he said, she said" situation.

Rape victims' responses are not identical. The personal harm of rape and sexual assault on its victims is singular and indeterminable in terms of both scope and duration and should never be underestimated. A sexual assault or rape can have long-term health outcomes that affect individuals for their entire lives, and by extension their families and communities. Reports of a single rape send shivers through any community, but the alarm doesn't stop at the city limits. Reports of a series of rapes are nothing short of gender terrorism, which is the systematic use of violence and intimidation, especially as a means of coercion. While most sexual assault cases fall under the jurisdiction of local law enforcement, the boundaries of the terror these cases can evoke are limitless.

When I was a teenager, I saw the film *The Boston Strangler*. It scared me. For the first time in my life, I felt that women, especially those living alone, were not safe simply because they were women. The claims that the movie was largely fiction didn't matter. I was only mildly comforted by the fact that the Strangler lived in a city some sixteen hundred miles away from Okmulgee County, Oklahoma, where I lived, or that the women were mostly White and elderly and I was a Black teenager. If a killer and rapist could roam free for two years in Massachusetts, it could happen in Oklahoma. Like a bucket of red paint spilled on a map of the United States, the horror oozed onto places far outside the reach of the individual who sexually assaulted and raped thirteen women in Boston between 1962 and 1964. Decades later the mark is still there. The Strangler's story emerges each time there is a serial rapist in the Boston area.

Researchers suggest that even absent a serial spree like the one described above, in the "shadow" of women's fears of crime is the fear of sexual assault. But the sociologist Mark Warr put it more bluntly, writing that "fear of crime *is* fear of rape" with real and measurable consequence on the "individual and social level." The constant fear of rape is a terror both unique to and widespread among women and other groups targeted for their gender or sexual identity, which together make up more than half of the population. Yet these abuses are often downplayed or ignored in media coverage compared with other kinds of crimes. Meanwhile, our police and other city officials fail us as thousands of rape kits are shelved and ignored, leaving serial rapists to continue their assaults. Police and prosecutors still look for the perfect victim in order to pursue a conviction for rape. The rapist counterpart to the perfect victim is the beast or deviant that can be distinguished from the people women might encounter every day.[28] This rape myth makes it difficult for victims of all rapists to press criminal charges. The rapist stereotype makes rape by a family member, partner, or acquaintance even harder to reconcile in a victim's mind. It might also contribute to the failure to confront sexual assault in the military, where members of units are trained to trust and think of each other as comrades.[29] And the public might demand that the accused be a perfectly horrible monster in order to believe the victim, even the "perfect victim." If the threshold for proving rape is nearly impossible to meet because we look for the perfect victim or the monster rapist, should we still call rape a crime? When we think about violence against women, our mind often goes to sexual crimes. We need a cultural shift in the way we think about rape and all forms of gender violence and the common link between them—subjugation of women. When taking into account the full spectrum of the terror of sexual assault and rape, we don't have a proper scale to measure the damage they cause, physically, emotionally, financially, and politically.

We need a sea change in our thinking about the harm of gender violence. Examining just a few cases shows the consuming grip that the collective violence against women and others based on gender or sexuality has on the entire country. And I'm not referring to our fear of rape and sexual assault. Gender-based violence, whether rape and sexual assault, harassment, stalking, trafficking, or intimate partner violence, is terror. Viewing any form of the issue as anything less keeps us from ending these behaviors.

One hundred years ago in the United States, our grandmothers and great-grandmothers were asked what qualified them to vote. Early suffragists saw the vote as key to all women's personal as well as political autonomy. But a hundred years of women's suffrage has shown that gaining the right to vote or run for office will not be enough as long as we're threatened with emotional, physical, economic, or sexual abuse at work, at school, or in our own homes.

When the abolitionist and feminist crusader Sarah Grimké prescribed the country's cure for gender inequity, she demanded "our brethren . . . take their feet from off our necks." Grimké was speaking both literally and figuratively of how women were being held back. Like early suffragists, she linked physical safety to political empowerment. The lesson is lost on us because we still don't value women as social, economic, or political contributors. We continue to demand that women political candidates have superior credentials, experience, demeanor, and temperament to White men. And many don't flinch at the fact that a man who has been called out for alleged sexual abuse by multiple women and who has bragged about his entitlement to sexually assault women resided in the White House.

POLITICAL WILL

Some legislators, like Senators Gillibrand and Patty Murray and Representative Ayanna Pressley, have placed survivor justice at the center of their legislative agendas. Pressley shared her own story about surviving childhood sexual assault in print and on the floor of the House of Representatives as she rose to support an anti-sex-trafficking bill. But the Democratic Party's full support for ending gender violence must be conspicuous and forceful. For starters, language in the Democratic Party platform describing the party's commitment to anti-gender-based violence measures must be stronger, matching the severity of gender-based violence evident in our country. Democrats in office must lead by stepping up their support of tactics and measures to protect women from the well-documented abuses they face. That can begin with a clear statement in the party platform that violence against women is an existential threat to our democracy. While President Biden's COVID $1.9 trillion recovery plan dedicates millions to curtail domestic violence, this is just a start. Women and the behaviors that impede their progress must be considered in every aspect of an economic recovery package. Our employment, education, and health and welfare systems, to name just a few, as well as public safety, must invest in the prevention of violence.

In 2020, a hundred years after the passage of the Nineteenth Amendment, gender-based violence persists, and neither political party has a plan in place to end it. Four years prior, Donald Trump had been elected to the country's highest office despite a massive global protest led by women following his own admission that he felt entitled to "grab" women by their genitals and charges by scores of women who claim he had sexually assaulted them. Many thought this would spark a new energy on the issue, buoyed by the waves of pink "pussy hats" in the 2017 Women's March. Throughout the 2019 presidential election primary season, gender advocates waited to hear the issue of violence against women raised by the slate of candidates vying for the title of Democratic Party presidential nominee. Yet again, the cause deflated, and after Gillibrand's departure from the race, gender-based violence was largely ignored as a political matter in the 2020 election. The issue gained only nominal media attention when Tara Reade accused the presumptive nominee, Joe Biden, of sexual assault, where it was rightly raised to question Biden's personal character.

With the nominee's vulnerability on the issue and without any demand for addressing gender violence during the primary, the question of whether the Democratic Party would acknowledge the myriad problems that had sparked a woman-led global movement in 2017 hung in the air. Under the heading of "Healing the Soul of America," the DNC announced its plan for addressing civil and gender rights, gun violence, LGBTQ+ rights, racial justice, free press, and ending violence against women in its platform.

Ending Violence Against Women

Democrats are committed to ending sexual assault, domestic abuse, and other violence against women. We will act swiftly to overcome Republican obstructionism and reauthorize and expand the Violence Against Women Act to better protect Native American women, women with disabilities, children and young women, transgender women and other LGBTQ+ people, and other groups who are disproportionately affected by sexual assault and domestic abuse. Democrats will expand services for survivors of violence against women, including by expanding access to housing, legal assistance, and victim advocate services. We will support danger assessment and lethality training for law enforcement officers and community partners to help curb domestic violence homicides. We recognize that sex workers, who are disproportionately women of color and transgender women, face especially high rates of sexual assault and violence, and we will work with states and localities to protect the lives of sex workers. We will enforce and provide tools and resources for schools to implement Title IX, which requires schools and institutions of higher education to properly investigate sexual misconduct, including peer-on-peer sexual harassment and violence; take appropriate action; and prevent future sexual misconduct. Democrats will increase resources to eliminate the national backlog of untested rape kits so that more survivors can see justice be served. And we will support federal and state legislative efforts to make "revenge porn" and other unauthorized disclosures of intimate images a civil and criminal offense.

Meanwhile, the Republican Party simply punted #MeToo and its aftermath by readopting its 2016 party platform.

While all the issues that the Democrats listed are critical to women's well-being, nowhere in the laundry list of persistent social disorders is any sense of the political impact gender-based violence has on our country, nor of its deep roots that need addressing in the broadest terms. Instead, the Democrats fall back on the tired strategy of anodyne descriptions and piecemeal solutions that fall painfully short of sparking any actual change. The equally urgent issue of gun violence, on the other hand, is introduced with this: "Gun violence is a public health crisis in the United States." Climate change is called "a global emergency." Religious freedom is described as a "core value of the Democratic Party"; the free press as "essential to our free democracy"; and the arts as "essential to our free and democratic society." It's true that climate change, gun violence, threats to religious freedom, and access to the arts demand concerted national attention. These are complex problems that cannot be ignored. But none are more essential to democracy than the elimination of the physical, psychological, sexual, and economic abuse of individuals based on their gender, because this foundational inequity hinders our efforts in all other areas.

Women's rights to vote and to run for office or participate in party platform building do not by themselves secure our full rights as citizens or ensure that efforts to address gender violence will prevail. As Gillibrand has said, having representative bodies of only 20 percent women makes it difficult to pass legislation to address abuse. And while ending gender-based violence is every legislators' responsibility, having a critical mass of policy makers who understand the problem from the point of view of survivors is essential. Research still shows a gap between men's and women's understanding of the severity of the problem and their ideas about how it can best be solved. But beyond the numbers, a key to recognizing the political significance of this abuse is understanding how our thinking about women's lack of credibility is built into the processes our government employs to address it. When it comes to gender-based violence, women's presumed untrustworthiness, another name for incompetence, becomes the basis for denying us our rights as citizens.

Both political parties have failed to see how gender-based violence does more than imperil our bodies: it limits our ability to exercise our rights as citizens. The Democrats' platform reflects the same cultural response that existed when the country was founded. Rather than a problem with political repercussions that deserves collective attention, we continue to see violence against women, no matter the location, as a personal problem to be resolved primarily by victims.

In 2018, when confronted with Christine Blasey Ford's claim, the Senate Judiciary Committee seemed more concerned about how the committee member Dianne Feinstein had handled Ford's complaint than about understanding the significance of getting to the truth of Ford's statement. The committee and the president decided in concert that only Kavanaugh and Ford would be called to testify and gave the FBI only three days to wrap up an investigation that might surface other witnesses. The question of Kavanaugh's fitness for the lifetime appointment was deferred to political convenience. It was simply easier to dismiss Ford's experience than acknowledge the importance of a sexual assault claim. But both Thomas's and Kavanaugh's behavior is of the utmost political significance.

For now, *United States v. Morrison*, with its faulty reasoning and false assumptions about the value of women, should be overturned, or Congress should commit to correcting the decision through legislation. One can't help but wonder how the federal government might have played a larger role in ending violence against women had the reasoning of Justices Stephen Breyer, Ruth Bader Ginsburg, and David Souter prevailed. Consider that the Justice Department brought the suit in *Morrison* because Virginia Polytechnic Institute allegedly failed to adequately address a student's claim that she had been raped in a campus dormitory by two fellow students. Had the dissents prevailed, Congress might have been able to put more pressure on schools and states, in cases involving public universities, to end college sexual violence. As pointed out by Souter in his dissent, the Court's majority ignored "the mountain of data assembled by Congress, here showing the effects of violence against women on interstate commerce."[30] But our policy makers should not. Since 1999, evidence of the harms of violence against women that Souter acknowledged has continued to mount, and so have the rates of abuse, including the numbers of deaths. And there are states that do not include violence motivated by gender or sex as a category of hate crimes. While Massachusetts, for example, lists gender identity as a factor in determining whether a crime is motivated by bias or hate, as late as 2021, it did not list gender. Attorney General Maura Healey proposed reform to have gender added to the hate crimes provisions.[31]

Denigration, dismissiveness, and denial of women's worth are exhibited throughout society and reflected in the actions of policy makers and the courts. What's most disturbing is that these ideas show up in our government's deficient attention to the problem of gender violence. It's time for us to acknowledge how gender-based violence impacts national commerce, imperils our local communities, and undermines our individual basic safety, rights, and freedoms. And as a nation, if we are sincere about stopping gender-based violence, we will commit our political collateral as well as our financial resources to ending it.

EIGHT

Victim Shaming

Two weeks after Donald Trump lost his bid for a second term as president in 2020, a portrait of a determined Black girl appeared on the cover of *The New Yorker* holding a small American flag. The girl looks hopeful. She wears a blue iris in her hair that the artist, Kadir Nelson, said in an interview with *The New Yorker* reflects "hope and promise." Her rolled-up sleeves represent "the work it took to achieve the results of this election, and the work we'll have to do in the months and years to come." Kamala Harris was set to become the first woman vice president of the United States, and Nelson hoped to show girls around the world "that there are no barriers they can't overcome."[1]

In the week following the election, as the results became clear, I felt grateful to be witnessing the first Black and Indian American woman VP. But while I love Nelson's portrait and its portrayal of the future of democracy in this country, I couldn't shake my own apprehension. For four years, Trump openly made racist and misogynist statements, some especially targeted at Black women journalists. His failure to denounce his *Access Hollywood* statement about assault eroded the nation's hope that the administration's policies would not reflect the beliefs he shared. As his presidency drew to a close, the chasm between the work that was done to advance women's issues and my vision of equality seemed wider than ever.

Trump's own statements weren't the only troubling signals of his administration's lack of interest in tackling these issues. Within hours of Trump's inauguration, the White House staff had removed the LGBTQ+ rights page from the White House website. When I tried to visit the site that night, I got a message thanking me for my interest in this subject and ultimately directing me to the Obama White House Archives. But I was also instructed, "Stay tuned as [they] continue to update whitehouse.gov." Within six months, the Trump administration had also removed all data on sexual assault from the White House website. This followed an announcement that the Office of the President was considering closing the White House Council on Women and Girls, under whose auspices the data was gathered. Made up of representatives from every government agency, the council had hosted several summits under the Obama administration and published *Rape and Sexual Assault: A Renewed Call to Action*,[2] which offered a range of policy approaches to violence directed at women.

When it came to LGBTQ+ equality, or sexual assault, Trump seemed to be delaying or deliberately neglecting to provide the information necessary for us to find solutions. I was beginning to see a pattern. Was this how a post-fact world began, with facts and figures vanishing in the middle of the night? The disappearance of the proof of inequality is worse than any symbolic whitewashing of the problems the data revealed. Government-collected data has historically been a reliable source of information from which to develop policy. And it's proof not only of the situation but of what an administration cares enough about to study and make public. As early as January 2017, the signs were clear that the Trump administration was going to resist and stall progress that had been made by law and leadership toward ending sexual harassment and assault.

BELIEVING THAT CHANGE IS POSSIBLE

In October 2017, Kathleen Kennedy and Nina Shaw, two entertainment industry powerhouses, had asked me to join them in building and chairing the Hollywood Commission. A group of entertainment industry leaders from the unions, guilds, studios, talent agencies, and academies of television, motion pictures, and music, among other fields, backed the project. Our goal was to find ways for entertainment to police itself and end the array of workplace abuses that had ignited a social media movement that reverberated around the globe. Joining forces with industry leaders was a shift for me. I had always felt that my role as an advocate against abuses was to use legislative protections and court decisions to pressure employers to make needed changes. But in October 2017, I knew that the multiple credible charges of assault and rape against Trump compromised his ability to use his power as president to end sexual assault in the country. My lack of faith in the Trump administration's intention to be proactive in ending gender-based violence led me to seek other avenues for change. Shifting from depending on government and legal recourse as the route to ending harassment, assault, and bias to working with businesses and workforce representatives to correct cultures and systems that condoned abuse required a leap of faith. I also understood the effort's potential reach beyond Hollywood. As a reflection of social mores and values, the entertainment industry was primed to serve as a microcosm for the problem in other industries; all eyes were already on Hollywood.

Criminal charges continued to mount against Harvey Weinstein and Bill Cosby that included behavior that spanned decades and multiple accusers. Les Moonves and Andrew Kreisberg would eventually lose their jobs at CBS and Warner Bros., respectively. Moonves was terminated following accusations of sexual harassment and assault that went back several years. The sexual harassment charges behind Kreisberg's dismissal also went back years. That it took so long for these powerful entertainment industry fixtures to be held accountable made it clear that some decision makers in the industry were reluctant to engage even if not disinterested in self-correction. Putting my hope in Hollywood to correct its own course was a challenge not unlike the challenge of getting the Trump administration to act to address its own sexual misconduct. Networks and famed studios had huge financial investments in offenders. The entertainment industry's content and workforce policies had largely been unregulated. And the fact that contract workers rather than employees often created the movies that made Hollywood famous meant that countless workers were not automatically covered by civil rights protections. As one industry veteran explained to me, "Entertainers are the original gig workers." Much of the work was doled out through connections and word-of-mouth recommendations. Who you knew and their willingness to put in a good word could make or break a career. Outside what had been negotiated by industry-based unions, I found that there was something essential missing in previous efforts that prevented the collaboration necessary to solve complex problems. There was no history of information sharing among rival organizations that would help future employers to identify abusers. Instead, the rumor mill served to brand women who might complain about abuse as "difficult to work with." The entertainment industry taught me volumes about how informal systems, or lack of formal systems, intersect to silence victims.

But even in the presence of strong headwinds, as I sat in the room with the group of industry leaders, all men, along with Kathy, Nina, and Freada Kapor Klein, the tech financier and early antiharassment trainer, I was hopeful. We urged the heads of talent agencies and movie, music, television, and labor organizations, many with conflicting business interests, to see the recent revelations as a call to alter the Hollywood modus operandi around sexual harassment. With glaring clarity, #MeToo revealed the cultural acceptance of the problem. Ironically in doing so, #MeToo and TIME'S UP showed just how influential individuals in the industry could be in reshaping public perception of the acceptability of the behavior. Audiences were awaiting their response and in some cases so were company shareholders. Fortunately, I found some allies in the entertainment industry who were ready for cultural change and who were demanding accountability for bad behavior that had been unchecked and often glamourized. I honestly believe that if Hollywood can change, it can be a model for the business world and perhaps even impress upon Washington the need to move toward elimination of the problem. But I knew that the commission was competing with a narrative, both inside and outside the entertainment industry, which held that Hollywood would never change. Convincing industry workers that transforming the Hollywood culture is possible is no easy task.

By the time Biden and Harris were elected, after three years of determined effort by the Hollywood Commission, I was certain that both public and private efforts were needed to end gender violence. Our work began with getting leadership from all sectors in the room for buy-in on the need for change. Next we got their representatives to talk about and build on what they were doing to protect the people for whom they were responsible from harassment and other forms of discrimination. But the biggest challenge was finding a way to hear from workers throughout the industry about a range of abuses, including bullying, gender and sexual harassment, racial and ethnic discrimination, sexual assault, and extortion and their consequences. Two years into the commission's existence, we had begun to build proven-practice systems to serve the unprotected, address the need for greater diversity in hiring to improve decision making related to problem behavior, and provide platforms and resources to fill gaps in coverage that exist because of the transient nature of the workforces.

As we approached our third anniversary, we launched the largest-ever industry-wide survey and gathered data and stories about the culture and conditions in industry workplaces and what 9,600 workers thought the commission should do to make them better. We realized that we were able to see just the tip of the iceberg, but we had opened a portal for seeing the whole of issues that were holding the less powerful people back from achieving their full potential. Our findings forced us all to hear workers in a way that had never been done before. And what stood out as most important to workers in all identity categories was the desire for accountability—consequences for abusers who violate laws, company rules, and policies or who bully and abuse fellow workers, and consequences for leaders who fail to hold violators responsible. Our work at the Hollywood Commission is ongoing. Even after women in the industry spoke out against harassment and assault and

spurred millions of disclosures worldwide, many entertainment industry workers still fear coming forward. That fear will only be lessened
by leadership action that demonstrates a commitment to accountability.

Fundamentally, women's ability and willingness to speak up about
harassment, assault, and abuse wherever it happens is hampered by their
inherent value in the eyes of society and in the eyes of our government.
Our tolerance of anemic policies and years of neglecting gender violence demonstrate our unwillingness to acknowledge the harm this does
to us all. Myriad credible accusations against a sitting president and his
combative and dismissive reactions to the claims further undermined
the valuation of women's voices. Trump's exit from the White House
renewed my hope that girls could again take on the challenges to their
safety and citizenship. But as I looked at Nelson's portrait of democracy on the cover of *The New Yorker,* I knew that a mere change in administration was never going to be enough. We all needed to raise our
voices—and I needed to continue to raise mine—to break walls of
silence that still surround individuals who want to complain about
abuse. That means the end of denials—"it's not so bad" or "it's not our
problem"—and the unfounded notion that through natural evolution
the problem will fade away, as Trump once said about the coronavirus:
"One day—it's like a miracle—it will disappear."

In part, effectively raising our voices means returning to a basic
question that clearly had not yet been adequately answered: What is
our vision for gender justice? There is no one-size-fits-all solution or
single administration that will put in place instant reform. But a concept of universal equality that considers how a victim's race, sexual identity, politics, and wealth (or lack thereof), among other things, combine
to complicate their experience with gender-based violence should shape
our vision. Previous efforts have tried blanket solutions for problems

that spanned the gamut and called for specific, targeted approaches. An individual's identity often determines whether we recognize the urgency of protecting them when they experience violence because of gender. Socially imposed nondisclosure agreements about abuse are often reinforced by racism, homophobia, transphobia, and politics. Bias and fear of losing political standing keep people of certain identities from coming forward. Confronting various forms of oppression directly in the face, one by one, and calling them out for the destructive roles they play in the battle for gender equality is not easy, but it is key to eliminating gender-based violence.

In chapter 7, I examined the question "Do we value women?" In this chapter, I ask more specifically, "Do we value all women?" Different women of color face sexual stereotypes that are peculiar to their race and/or ethnicity, putting them at a higher risk for abuse. Black and Native women's heightened risk of experiencing abuse is well documented.[3] Vestiges of Black and Native women's unrepresented status continue to prevent them from enjoying protections against gender-based violence. Cultural presumptions that no woman, other than the mythical perfect victim, is a credible witnesses to her own abuse serve as an invisible gag that prevents victims from coming forward. Where sexual and partner violence are concerned, women of color are at risk of being gagged on multiple fronts. The journalist and political science professor Melissa Harris-Perry places shame at the root of this self-silencing, saying that shame "sometimes keeps Black women from asking for the political help they deserve as citizens." For example, Black and Native women, often the targets of humiliating racial stereotypes, may stay silent about their experiences with violence to avoid public scrutiny tinged by racist beliefs. Harris-Perry explains that they retreat "rather than be exposed to the shaming experience of presenting their needs" to a system that attributes their problems to their race or Native ancestry.[4] Self-silencing can also derive from a collective allegiance to one's racial or ethnic community. Revealing their abuse, especially when it was at the hands of a Black or Native man, carries with it the fear of tearing down their own people. LGBTQ+ members of communities of color suffer from similar forms of silencing, and the apprehensions of women and LGBTQ+ people of color about hostility from their communities are real. Speaking out requires overcoming significant cultural and structural barriers and weathering public humiliation. R. Kelly, the R&B singer who was federally indicted on charges including child sexual exploitation, child pornography production, and kidnapping and is currently in federal prison, still has supporters who discredit his critics and claim that they are contributing to the destruction of a Black man, a representative of the Black community.

For many who have studied violence against women, the March 2021 slayings in Atlanta of six women spa workers of Asian descent was clearly a hate crime. But public officials' and public confusion about whether to categorize it as such is another example of societal erasure of bias against women of color and the failure to recognize racism's role in their experience with sexual violence. The alleged assailant's claim that his actions were motivated by his sexual addiction point to a gender motive behind the shootings. That the White shooter allegedly targeted massage parlors where Asian women were employed at a period in time when anti-Asian violence is on the rise is another clue to the hate behind the killings. That misogyny is not a hate that counts in some states is reflected by the fact that some do not list gender in their hate crime laws, and this hurts all women. But the inability to see the Atlanta slayings as a hate crime was also likely due to the lack of education about the history of anti-Asian violence in this country and the racist and sexualized tropes about women of Asian descent. What may have further confounded some observers about the Atlanta shootings was the intersection of racism and misogyny that might have fueled the violence. The fetishization of Asian women has been documented as myth by researchers but accepted as truth by some. Thus the dominant culture's perception of sexualized violence against Asian women is cloaked in a narrative that reads sexual violence against them as acceptable. It is one more form of denial that inhibits protests against the sexualized abuse of women of color—even when the victims are killed.

Over the years, I've heard from many women who would not speak up about abuse they experienced because they didn't want to shower more collective shame on a community that has suffered systemic bias from the larger society. Religious women want to protect their churches or clergymen. Students want to protect their colleges. Musicians want to protect the reputations of their orchestras or chorales or directors. The force of racial and ethnic silencing, like other forms of bigotry, extends beyond a single organization or industry. It is a compounding factor that implicates victims individually and acts as a barrier to ending gender-based violence. And as with other forms of bigotry, oppressed communities have a stake in ending the silencing of gender-bias sufferers.

I've witnessed dominant-culture and community muzzling as well as self-silencing in different kinds of communities. Efforts to silence those who identify as boys and men begin at an early age as a form of indoctrination into manhood. Cultural tropes from literature, films, animation, and video games offer the strong and silent male as the masculine ideal. Boys learn to internalize their emotions about most everything that might suggest that they don't fit the stereotype. They also learn to enforce the silencing of those who act outside of the prescribed character. Statistics tell us that one in every six men have experienced sexual assault in their lifetime, whether as boys or adults. Those figures might underrepresent the actual rates of unwanted sexual contact, because men are hesitant to report. Before the first abuse, they are programmed to keep quiet about it out of shame, fear, or both. Even when they do speak, those in power to respond ignore them. Recall the report on Richard Strauss's behavior discussed in chapter 5. Years before the university called for an investigation, students had told university employees about the behavior. Yet Strauss abused young men there for two decades.

Racism and misguided notions of masculinity combine with misogyny to silence victims. Simply having a procedure in place is not enough to empower all victims to come forward. This combination of biases shapes the attitudes of those responding to gender-based violence, the processes used to assess claims of violence, and the resources survivors need to recover or seek justice. Yet some individuals hobbled by this toxic mix have broken through. We can learn from them that ending gender violence is possible if, and only if, we commit to fight against all forms of hate that contribute to violent victimization.

NATIVE AMERICAN WOMEN

As antiviolence advocates often remind us, gender-based violence reflects men's power over women and their fear of losing it. That power is also wielded to promote class and race differences and gender conformity. It's a tool to enforce entitlement to citizenship, rights, and political power. Sexual abuse has figured into conquest in wars throughout the world, but one need not look further than American history: think

about the rape of Native women in the United States during colonization, or how White men have justified lynching and political disenfranchisement of Native and Black people in the name of protecting
White women, in turn claiming ownership over their bodies. If Native
women and their tribes are to survive, legally sanctioned structural
barriers to justice for Native women will have to be upended.

"Stunning and shocking" only begins to describe Native women's
experiences with violence. In a legal brief filed in federal court by the
National Indigenous Women's Resource Center, a section title offers a pre-
scient warning: "The Current Rates of Violence Against Native Women
Constitute a Crisis."[5] Whether on tribal lands or in urban areas, Native
women are at a high risk of sexual and/or domestic partner violence. André
Rosay of the National Institute of Justice found that more than half of
Native women report being victims of sexual violence and that an over-
whelming majority of the violence is perpetrated by non-Native men.[6]

The Urban Indian Health Institute found that in Seattle, 94 percent
of indigenous women had been raped or coerced into sex in their lifetime.[7] According to the Obama administration's report on rape and
sexual assault, Native women are particularly vulnerable to sex trafficking, though they are largely overlooked as victims.[8] And the number of missing and murdered indigenous women is only starting to
gain attention. One study found that in four locations where Native
Americans were 10 percent of the population, "an average of 40 percent of the women involved in sex trafficking identified as American
Indian/Alaska Native or First Nations."[9] Among these striking statistics, one fact stands out: sexual assault and missing persons are underreported offenses, which means that the problem is even larger than
what existing data indicates. Many women stay silent because of the
discrimination and stereotyping Native communities face from local

law enforcement. During a community meeting sponsored by the Urban Indian Health Institute, participants shed light on the kind of shaming that Native women are likely to experience when they report to local police. One person spoke to the stereotypes that discouraged families from reporting missing women: local police believe that "Native Americans have a 'reputation' of having alcohol/drug abuse and prostitution." Another person said that officers sometimes will not take the report because of perceived "reputation of drug/alcohol issues, criminal history, or mental health."[10]

The histories of Native people vary from tribe to tribe. Native Americans are not one homogenized group. But for Native Americans for whom rape was a tool of colonization, sexual assault of Native women is an assault on the tribe.[11] The myths of Native women like Sacagawea and Pocahontas, who were removed from their homes and enlisted in the building of America while the rights of indigenous people en masse were denied, are now replaced with the stereotype of Native women as undeserving. Protecting tribal and family reputations from humiliation, especially by White people, is a survival tactic adopted by Native peoples since colonization:

> There is often a belief that whatever you do in life affects the clan/family system, which often numbers in the hundreds. If the victim is already feeling guilty about the incident, she may not want to subject her "family" to further humiliation due to the gossip and negative backlash from misconceptions about rape.[12]

According to Sarah Deer, Native women's inclination to minimize their experiences with violence is in response to centuries of systemic and strategic dehumanization. Deer is a Native American legal expert who formerly provided survivor services that included accompanying Native women to hospitals, police stations, or courthouses. Deer says that Native women's victimization dates back to what she calls the colonial project, when, as far back as Christopher Columbus, Native women were viewed as expendable or even as people who "needed to be done away with," such that rape against them was not recognized as an offense. This has led to consistently high rates of rape of indigenous women in the United States for more than five hundred years. Deer warns that Native women are often the targets of predatory behavior by people who exploit their vulnerability and lack of credibility with law enforcement, viewing them as "somebody who is not going to be believed or supported." She's also learned from "survivors who have been brave enough to speak" that perpetrators often look for victims in urban neighborhoods more likely to be inhabited by Native people.[13] Deer found that rape has become such an everyday occurrence in Native women's lives that it had come to be expected, as was the lack of response by local police.

State and local government response systems were not the only ones that betrayed Native people. In 2011, an attorney named Blaine Tamaki announced that he was suing the Ursuline sisters of the Western Province and the Roman Catholic Diocese of Helena for abusing Native children under their care at the Ursuline Academy in St. Ignatius, Montana. Tamaki is a Japanese American whose family lost everything after their internment during World War II. "When [my dad] told me that because of our race he lost his freedom, I realized as a young child that race does matter in America," Tamaki said. "It matters so much that it could wind up depriving you of your freedom, and it made me committed to seeking justice for all people regardless of their race or ethnicity, or sex or sexual preference, or any other trait that has been discriminated against throughout history."[14] Still, charging Catholic clergy with abusing Native children in their care at the Ursuline Academy in a small community in Montana was a bold act. The Ursuline sisters' school had been embedded in the lives of the Bitterroot Salish, Kootenai, and Pend d'Oreille tribes since it was introduced in the 1940s and continued to be part of the Flathead Indian Reservation community in Montana into the 1970s. The suit against the Ursuline sisters listed thirty-seven men and women as the victims of sexual molestation. Eventually, additional victims represented by other attorneys would become part of a massive suit.[15]

The victims, most of them Native Americans in a five-state area from remote Alaskan villages to reservations in the Pacific Northwest, were sexually or psychologically abused as children by Jesuit missionaries in those states. "I came from a very strict Catholic family and this would have stressed out my parents," said Jackie Trotchie, a Native American woman who attended a Catholic school in Helena, Montana, according to court documents. "When things happen like this to Native American women people say, 'It's your fault, you got what you deserved,'" Trotchie said, adding that "people told her when she was young that she would burn in hell if she told."[16]

Tamaki's suit against the Ursuline nuns settled for $4.45 million in 2015, which the nuns paid through selling assets because the order did not have insurance to cover the claims.[17] In 2011, the Pacific Northwest chapter of the Roman Catholic Church's Jesuit order agreed to a record $166.1 million settlement, which was paid into a trust to "resolve approximately 524 abuse claims."[18] In addition to a formal apology to each of the victims, the Northwest Jesuits agreed to stop referring to them as "alleged victims," thereby validating their claims.[19]

In part, the abuse among American Indian tribes took place because the government abdicated its educational responsibility to Native populations, transferring it to the Roman Catholic Church, which resulted in generations of abuse. In essence, the Ursuline Academy acted in place of the state or the federal government in providing education for the tribes. But the federal government failed the tribes in three ways: first, by not providing tribal members with a quality education; second, by not monitoring the Ursulines' behavior as they took on the educational responsibility to the tribes; and finally, by not prosecuting the clergy who were abusing tribal children.[20] This negligence was a glaring display of racism and colonialism that predated the Ursuline Academy's presence in Montana, but there is no apparent governmental accountability for its role in putting the tribes in harm's way.

The connection between citizenship, racial equality, and gender-based violence against Native women is inextricable. Bonnie Clairmont, a Ho-Chunk woman and an anti-rape activist, is adamant that the future of American Indian nations depends on gender justice. In a 2007 essay, Clairmont writes about the connection between individual autonomy and tribal independence: "Women's sovereignty is central to Indian sovereignty because nations cannot be free if their Indian women are not free."[21] It's become clear that state and local police are committed to securing neither tribal sovereignty nor Native women's freedom. Some steps have been taken at the federal level. In July 2010, President Obama signed the Tribal Law and Order Act to support the infrastructure of tribal court systems and give tribes the authority to prosecute and punish criminals for sexual assault and intimate partner violence.[22] And thanks to the Violence Against Women Reauthorization Act of

2013, anyone accused of domestic violence, dating violence, and violations of protective orders in American Indian country can be tried in tribal or federal courts.

These protections were fortified by a case decided by the U.S. Supreme Court in the summer of 2020. The case, one of the last of the Court's 2020 spring term, surprised legal experts and some tribal leaders with its expansive view of tribal sovereignty. Justice Neil Gorsuch, writing for the five-justice majority in *McGirt v. Oklahoma*, ruled that the federal original land grant given to the Mvskoke tribe in 1899 remained American Indian country today. The tract covers three million acres of land in eastern Oklahoma, land that my family farmed and that I grew up on. In a joint statement, Sarah Deer, a citizen of the Mvskoke Nation, and the Cherokee tribe member Mary Kathryn Nagle declared this Supreme Court decision a victory for Native women in the "fight for the sovereignty of our Nations—and our bodies," adding that for these women, "it is more than a legal question. It is a matter of life and death."[23] In light of the seminal decision, advocates' work to ensure that tribal and federal courts do not replicate the state systems that have treated Native women abysmally seems more important—and promising—than ever.

BLACK WOMEN

Judge A. Leon Higginbotham Jr. was a giant of a human being, intellectually and physically. His 1978 treatise on enslavement and the role of the law in debasing Blacks was essential to a generation of lawyers' and legal scholars' understanding of equality. His articulation of these concepts of justice was made all the more effective by his booming voice.

He was fearless. As a mentor, he counseled me to think boldly about my work. Higginbotham was what we might have called "a race man." Judge Higginbotham passed away in 1998, but one thing he told me in the early 1990s continues to guide my work: "I never talk about race without talking about gender equality." I realized early that it takes boldness to shout into the darkness that hides the truth of how being Black in America stymies one's chances for bringing claims of all forms of gender violence, but especially sexual violence, given the social and racist stigma attached to it.

In October 1992, I gave a talk in Minneapolis titled "Racism, Sexism, and Power," in which comments from the audience revealed the extent to which people struggle to understand how race and gender work together against both men and women. In response to my presentation on burdening stereotypes, relationships between Black and White women as advocates, and the challenges Black women face within their own community, some wondered whether ending racism in the African American community should take precedence over ending gender-based violence. It's uncanny that these questions came from an audience in a city that would in 1993 become known for electing Sharon Sayles Belton as their first Black and female mayor and, in 2020, for being the location of George Floyd's killing by police. Nearly three decades later, questions and comments that aim to understand the complexity of intersectional gender and race issues are still being raised. Some are spot-on; others miss the point. Here are some I've heard over the years:

> Do you have any thoughts on sexual racism—the objectification of the Black female as the embodiment of dirtiness, badness, and desire?

How do you think Black and White women can work together toward gender equality?

It seems as though one were forced to choose between supporting a battered woman versus a victim of racism.

Some in the Black community feel that sexism erased the problems of racism in this country—that you sold out the community.

Some commentators have recently indicated that the fact that you are both Black and a woman has been ignored.

Do you feel the relationship between Black men and Black women has improved or worsened?

Do you think that the Senate would've confirmed Clarence Thomas had the charges of sexual harassment been brought by a White woman?

Would you speak to the racist undertones in sexual harassment and how your testimony against a Black man dislodged the unspoken rule of not speaking against a brother and opened the possibility of addressing abuse across all racial barriers?

Thank you for breaking an African American cultural taboo by speaking out in the public arena against a Black male.

With the continued criticism you've received from men and women in the Black community, if you could do it all over again, would you?

Young African American men are facing a crisis in our society today. How can we meet these needs within a feminist agenda?

What's striking is that every one of these questions is still being posed today, thirty years later. The country still wants the answers. Young Black women still struggle with how they can bring complaints of any kind given the stereotypes about Black women that render them untrustworthy or not worthy of protection from gender-based violence. The conflict is even more complicated when Black women complain about the behavior of Black men. Still, increasingly, Black men want to know how they can be allies to Black women while they are themselves at risk of being stereotyped in ways that imperil their safety.

From Rosa Parks and her predecessors to the plaintiffs in the early sexual harassment cases discussed in chapter 1, Black women have taken up the cause to end violence they experience in and outside our homes and communities. One such woman is Beverly Guy-Sheftall, the women's studies professor at Spelman College. In the previous chapter, I told the story of her year of hellish harassment inflicted by an ex-boyfriend. I met Beverly in 1992 at Spelman. I didn't know at the time that she had written about the Thomas hearing.

I had been shamed by Black people for testifying about Thomas's harassing behavior toward me. One woman approached me angrily in an airport and yelled, "What you did was horrible!" before walking away. While many Black people had written their support, some painted me as an ingrate who had ruined the life of an important African American man who had helped my career. But four other Black women came forward at the time of the hearing to say that they had experienced or witnessed the same behavior from the Supreme Court nominee. They agreed to testify before the Senate Judiciary Committee, but their testimony appears only in written form because the chairman, Senator Biden, declined to call them. In an article in *The Black Scholar*, Guy-Sheftall had this to say about why some Black people had reacted so strongly to my testimony:

> Perhaps the best explanation of this tendency on the part of large numbers of African Americans, men and women, to vehemently oppose Anita Hill's public exposure of Thomas's sexual harassment of her (I wonder if the response would have been different if the hearings hadn't been televised) is that she violated a deeply held black cultural taboo, which is that we shouldn't air our racial dirty linen in front of white folks.[24]

Guy-Sheftall offers context that helps explain the hearing "as part of a larger scenario which has been brewing for more than a decade." Starting in the late 1970s, despite having Black supporters, Black women authors like Ntozake Shange and Michele Wallace had been taken to task by some Black audiences and readers for speaking about abuse in the Black community. And Alice Walker was demonized for her 1982 acclaimed novel, *The Color Purple*, which race critics said portrayed Black men as violent and abusers. In *The New York Times*, Mel Watkins, a Black man, criticized Walker's lack of commitment to the Black community as a professional breach:

> Those black women writers who have chosen black men as a target have set themselves outside a tradition that is nearly as

old as black American literature itself. They have, in effect, put themselves at odds with what seems to be an unspoken but almost universally accepted covenant among black writers.[25]

And Tony Brown, another Black male journalist, shamed Walker for her involvement in the making of a movie based on her Pulitzer Prize–winning novel. Brown lambasted the movie as "the most racist depiction of Black men since *The Birth of a Nation* and the most anti-Black family film of the modern film era."[26] According to Brown, Walker's support of the film, which included sympathetic attention to Black women who suffered family violence, was evidence of her lack of personal commitment to Black people.

As she had been with the Thomas hearings, Guy-Sheftall was a counter-voice to this criticism. In 1997, Guy-Sheftall commented on a former student's first-person account of a rape she'd experienced at Spelman. The alleged assailants were Black men.[27] "There is an assumption that Black men are being targeted, or that there's actually some conspiracy to destroy Black men," Guy-Sheftall said. "I think that's the scenario around which these cases get framed and that it's very difficult to separate those notions." That frame is not invented. Guy-Sheftall, who grew up in Memphis, knows well the history of Black men being lynched as a result of false accusations of rape made by White women. But, she says, "In an ironic kind of way, when Black men get accused of rape, the Black woman almost gets put in the same category as White women who accuse Black men of rape, and she becomes the enemy, too."[28] This dynamic invalidates Black women's claims by conflating them with the false accusations used by White people as a tool for White supremacy. By doing so, we diminish Black women's experience with racism and open them up to gender violence, while also ignoring a history of harmful stereotypes historically used to target and victimize Black women. That history still haunts us.

A 2017 report by the Georgetown Center on Poverty and Inequality exposed the deep roots of everyday misogyny, misplaced notions of masculinity, and disparagement that Black women face. The title of the report, *Girlhood Interrupted: The Erasure of Black Girls' Childhood*, signals the center's conclusion that denigration of Black women starts with the negative and harmful beliefs that we project onto them as girls. The report details data showing that adults view Black girls as less innocent and more adultlike than their White peers, especially between the ages of five and fourteen. What does that mean? Compared with White girls of the same age, survey participants perceived the following:

- Black girls need less nurturing and protection.
- Black girls need to be supported and comforted less.
- Black girls are more independent and know more about adult topics, including sex.[29]

The report's authors concluded that these pernicious myths contribute to the disproportionate rates of punitive treatment of Black girls in the education and juvenile justice systems. These findings bring to mind Nelson's portrait of a Black girl holding the American flag. What challenges will she face? Will her fate be the same as Honestie Hodges? In 2017, eleven-year-old Hodges was handcuffed, frisked, and detained in the back of a police cruiser by Grand Rapids police officers who were searching her neighborhood for a forty-year-old stabbing suspect. What compels a person to ascribe the characteristics (criminality) and accountability of a forty-year-old suspect to a little girl who happens to be the same race and gender?

I see the repercussions reaching far beyond mere mistaken identities. This tendency to see Black girls as more culpable for their choices makes them less worthy of forgiveness. In schools as in the criminal justice system, Black girls' subjection to harsher punishment is a form of violence. Outside school, they are often seen as more savvy about sex than their peers of other races and are easily targeted for sexual exploitation. A Black girl may more easily become the object of the "she wanted it" rape myth because she wore certain clothes or agreed to ride in the car with an adult male. The perception of Black girls as less innocent and more adultlike ascribes to them a false sense of responsibility for risky "choices" that can have dangerous consequences. In her book *Pushout: The Criminalization of Black Girls in School*, for instance, Monique W. Morris describes a sexually trafficked fourteen-year-old named Diamond. Diamond refers to her twenty-five-year-old pimp as her boyfriend. In what Morris calls a game of control, he keeps her out of school, reinforcing the idea that her sexuality is her greatest asset.[30] The assignment of adult thinking to Black girls leads to less sympathetic or victim-blaming responses by adults or others they might reach out to for help. Why? Because "she should have known better" than to have put herself at risk.

Black boys have suffered from a similar kind of derogatory and dangerous labeling. The New York University law professor Kim Taylor-Thompson reminds us that twenty-five years ago a political scientist coined the term "superpredator" to describe Black urban youth. The depiction of Black children as violently and remorselessly animal-like stuck. And it is precisely these stereotypes that Black women are accused of perpetuating when they speak out about their abuse. But as is the case with Black girls, the criminalization of Black boys in courts and schools robbed them of "the protections of their childhood." We are just now coming to terms with the price the Black community has paid for a generation that was criminalized by a "lie that insists that Black children do not deserve the care we reflexively offer white children," a lie that rationalized our disparate treatment of them.[31]

The stereotyping of Black girls does not stop as they grow up. These perceptions feed into treatment of women in the adult justice system. Women of color who are suspects or prisoners are seen as less sympathetic, and this presumed proclivity toward violence based on race/gender myths impedes Black girls' and women's willingness to seek support for mental or other health-related issues or their getting help when they do seek it out. As with Native women, they're also unlikely to seek help from the legal system, because they know they may not be believed when they do reach out and could suffer even more indignity and harm. We are constantly flooded with the stereotypical media images, which Tia Tyree found in her research on the portrayal of Black women on television. In an article in *The Howard Journal of Communications* in 2011, Tyree analyzed ten reality television shows that aired in 2005 and 2008 and determined that at least one Black character in each show was portrayed as a racial and gendered stereotype, such as angry Black woman, hoochie, hood rat, homo thug, and Sambo.[32]

Hollywood writers did not dream all of this up on their own. That a political scientist was behind the spread of the notion of children as incorrigible "superpredators" explains the traction it gained among policy makers. The very idea was couched in language that spoke to them. Touting the Clinton administration's war on drugs, First Lady Hillary Clinton used the term to refer to gangs with ties to drug cartels. But what is so disturbing is that the idea took hold, embraced by politicians to promote tough-on-crime measures that lead to laws that permit middle schoolers to be tried as adults.[33] These measures along with racially discriminatory sentencing laws would eventually contribute to the mass incarceration that has politically disenfranchised a generation of young Black men and, increasingly, Black and Latinx women. In a particularly notorious case, on April 19, 1989, Donald Trump drew upon the ideas behind the label to call for the reinstatement of the death penalty in response to the five teenage boys who, as it turned out, were wrongly accused of gang-raping and nearly killing a White woman in New York City's Central Park. But the stickiness of the "superpredator" label was not serendipitous. Its deeper roots, like the stereotypes Tyree identified and those Native women confront, are centuries old.

While some may argue that there is no proof that these racist stereotypes are the cause for Black women's negative experiences, there is no doubt that they cast a shadow over public perception. The number of women in U.S. jails has increased fourteenfold since 1970, outpacing the growth in the men's prison population. The majority of those women are Black and Hispanic, mirroring demographic trends that cross gender lines. According to a MacArthur Foundation and Vera Institute of Justice report, at the heart of this stunning development are trauma, sexual violence, and mental health issues that are largely untreated and, in some cases, undetected or unacknowledged. Women in jail, the majority of whom are women of color, experience trauma at extraordinarily high rates both before and during their incarceration: 86 percent report having experienced sexual violence in their lifetimes, and women make up the majority of victims of staff-on-inmate sexual victimization. Black girls are more than three times as likely as their White peers to be incarcerated (94 per 100,000), and Native girls are more than four times as likely (123 per 100,000).[34]

And negative perceptions about Black women's worth have an impact on their experiences in places well beyond the criminal legal system. A 2017 report by the National Domestic Workers Alliance titled *The Status of Black Women in the United States* analyzes the broader experience of Black women in six categories—political participation, employment and earnings, work and family, poverty and opportunity, health and well-being, and violence and safety. The results are predictable to anyone aware of the level of disenfranchisement Black women experience. The report concludes by noting that "Black women are underinsured, more likely to be afflicted by preventable diseases, more likely to experience domestic partner violence than most other ethnic cohorts."[35] The conclusions of these two reports are grim and shocking. Gender and sexual identity provide an additional layer of disenfranchisement. In 2019, the American Medical Association described fatal anti-transgender violence in the United States as an epidemic.[36] A Human Rights Campaign report on violence against trans people in 2020 notes that of the thirty-nine trans women and men who were victims of violent deaths, nineteen were identified as Black.[37]

And then there are the lighter but nevertheless infuriating episodes we endure. For example, in 2017, the beauty blogger Vika Shapel promoted blackface as a beauty trend. (She called it the "chocolate challenge.") When called on it, Shapel admitted she "wasn't aware of the whole black-face concept before people began commenting on the photo." Around the same time, Madame Tussauds wax museum was being accused of lightening the complexion and shrinking the nose of its Beyoncé sculpture in its New York City location. So what? you might say. Black women are dealing with life and death, literally, some on a daily basis. Are internet fashion and beauty blogs, pop culture, and wax figures really worth fighting about?

The answer is yes. The gravity of some of Black women's challenges should not excuse the seemingly trivial ones. Moreover, media and pop culture portrayals have a tremendous impact on how children and adults define and see themselves. Equality means not only equal pay and equal rights and protection under the law; it means being able to express our outrage at the misrepresentations of Black women and girls and the under-calculation of their value, wherever they appear. In fact, what some call slights or microaggressions are often precursors to the macro physical and emotional aggression we experience.

In the early 1990s, at a presentation on sexual harassment on college campuses, I stayed away from discussing the Thomas hearing or in any way referring to my own experience with harassment, as was my practice at the time. The attendees were diversity and inclusion officers and staff from colleges throughout the Midwest and the South. The reception was cordial, no more and no less.

When it came time for questions, one Black man suggested that my talk was only an attempt to solve my personal "issues" and not anything this group should have to hear. I was used to the issue of sexual violence being minimized, and efforts to isolate me and my experience as irrelevant were common. Perhaps this questioner was angry with me because of my testimony against Thomas. But, even so, the comment was particularly jarring in a room filled with individuals whose jobs were to make college an inclusive experience for everyone. Was he alone, or did others in the room not make the connection between racial and gender hostility? Statistics show Black women are more likely to be assaulted by Black men than by men of other races. Likewise, White women are more likely to be assaulted by White men. Was he concerned that Black women's disclosure would shine a harsh light on Black men that, by virtue of their race, White men could avoid? One of the myths about sexual harassment was that it was an issue that concerned only White women. Orlando Patterson, a Black professor at Harvard, has argued that

Black women knew how to handle the issue and interpreted crude sexual come-ons as part of a Black down-home "courting" ritual that is a form of seduction.[38] Patterson's viewpoint is doubly troubling because it both romanticized and racialized aggressive sexual behavior.

Long-held racism and misogyny made a discussion of Black women's sexual mistreatment in this setting nearly impossible. At the time, it was clear that getting into a conversation about the audience member's motivation versus mine would not be fruitful. Instead, I tried to assure him that the issue of sexual harassment on campus was not just a personal issue, that it was prevalent, and that it interfered with women's access to educational opportunity. If I were to answer him today, I would acknowledge that I *was* trying to make sense of my own experience, but also that of countless others, and that when diversity and inclusion professionals ignore it or personalize it, they put all women, and especially women of color, at risk. Black people, whatever their gender identity, experience the world through both race and gender. Women of color on campuses face sexual misconduct at a higher rate than White women and are less likely to have their claims taken seriously by authorities if they speak up. We all need to do more to understand how and why Black women have been pioneers against sexual harassment and assault. It is because they, along with Native American women, bear the brunt of it. Black women like Paulette Barnes, who brought the early sexual harassment claims, no doubt knew from their daily experiences that in order to be truly equal, they would have to confront both racial and gender discrimination. Yet racial stereotypes combined with rape myths suggest that we are not worthy of the right to claim sexual abuse or that we do a disservice to our communities when the person we complain about is a person of color. To this day, I hear from Black students who find that they cannot speak out because they would have to implicate a "brother." Silencing victims won't eliminate a problem that is influenced by both gender and race, and our individual and community claim to equality remains at stake.

I also hear from young Black men who understand the danger of sexual abuse but fear that if they encourage women friends to break their silence, a rise in sexual assault claims will make them targets for false accusations. Given our country's history, their concern makes sense. Ava DuVernay's series *When They See Us*, which dramatizes the story of Kevin Richardson, Antron McCray, Raymond Santana, Korey Wise, and Yusef Salaam—five Black and Latinx teenage boys who were wrongly convicted and incarcerated for a rape they did not commit—reminds us how high the stakes truly are for our community. Donald Trump, then a private citizen living in New York, didn't wait for a conviction to condemn the boys. On May 1, 1989, just short of two weeks after the rape occurred, he placed an ad in local papers blaming the crime on the police department's overreaction to "public outcry about police brutality." The heading of the ad read "Bring Back the Death Penalty: Bring Back Our Police!" Ultimately, this cynical ploy of playing race against gender influenced public opinion against the teenagers, whom he called "roving thousands of wild criminals."[39]

Yet those concerns, which Black women as mothers, sisters, aunts, and community members share, cannot lead us, in the name of protecting the race, to deny Black women the right to speak out against any of their abusers or against men like the singer R. Kelly or the music producer Russell Simmons simply because they are among the few influential Black men. Our community's' shared burden of racism is at the heart of both the shaming of victims of color and the police violence that we decry. We cannot prevail against racism by silencing Black victims. But dealing with all the tensions within Black communities when it comes to gender-based violence is not simple. We have to come to an agreement that ending gender violence is in the best interests of our entire community, not just those who experience it directly.

What is missing in the discussion is the ability to come to terms with the dual impact of racism and sexism. There will be no complete elimination of gender-based violence until racism in its many forms is identified and addressed, but the reverse is also true. That does not mean that we must choose one fight over another; both struggles are valid and should be tackled concurrently. Black feminists like Beverly Guy-Sheftall, Evelynn Hammonds, and Johnnetta Betsch Cole have called for deeper conversations about this combination of subjugation both inside and outside our communities. Tarana Burke, author of the #MeToo movement, has launched a new effort, centered on Black survivors, called We, As Ourselves, picking up the mantle carried by Guy-Sheftall and Cole.

Guy-Sheftall has become an oracle, far ahead of the crowd in her willingness to be a bold voice for the rights of Black women and Black LGBTQ+ people in her words about sexual assault and partner violence. She and Cole co-authored a book urging that the health of the Black community depended on our ability to speak out about gender issues. In *Gender Talk*, Guy-Sheftall shared publicly her story of intimate partner abuse, which I discussed in chapter 7 of this book, for the first time as a rebuke to the idea that it is "irresponsible to air dirty linen in public for fear of perpetuating dangerous racial stereotypes."

Kimberlé Crenshaw, a law professor, has devoted a lifetime of study to the idea that a person's different identities can compound their experiences with discrimination, and she coined the term "intersectionality" to describe the phenomenon. The fact that today's Black Lives Matter movement is intentionally expansive, gender conscious, and affirming of "Black queer and trans folks, disabled folks, undocumented folks, folks with records, women, and all Black lives along the gender spectrum" is crucial to its mission of centering "those who have been marginalized within Black liberation movements" and gives me hope.

And as Crenshaw urged in a powerful TED talk on the "urgency of intersectionality," we all need to step up and do more:

> We have to be willing to bear witness to the often painful realities that we would rather not confront, the everyday violence and humiliation that many Black women have had to face, Black women across color, age, gender expression, sexuality, and ability.

MASK OF MASCULINITY

JUNE CLEAVER TO WARD CLEAVER: When you were young, if you had seen a boy pushing a baby carriage down the street, what would you have done?

WARD: What would I have done? Well, I would have clobbered him, of course. [Laugh track.]

JUNE: Eddie says he would probably get slaughtered.

—*LEAVE IT TO BEAVER*, "BEAVER'S DOLL BUGGY" (1961)[40]

In this fictional version of gender policing, June asks her question when she learns that her twelve-year-old son is bringing home a baby carriage in order to salvage its tires. Later, after being ridiculed by strangers, Beaver explains that he thought nothing of his actions until people on the street started mocking him.

Men have found their place as allies to women and nonbinary people who fight against gender-based violence. But to really understand the gender and antiwoman dimensions of the problem, we must consider how men are also victims of sexual and other physical gender-based violence. My generation grew up receiving the message that it's acceptable, even normal, to wallop boys for doing something that is considered feminine. In 1992, Robert L. Allen, who is an activist, a journalist, and a professor emeritus at the University of California, Berkeley, told me about his work with the Oakland Men's Project. Allen described OMP as a "multiracial organization of men and women devoted to community education around issues of male violence, sexism, racism, and homophobia." In one of its workshops, he explained, two facilitators play the roles of a father and his ten-year-old son. In the scene, the father berates the boy, who gets upset and starts to cry. What happens next is what Allen says really grabs the audience's attention, especially the boys. At the sight of the tears, the father grows angrier and yells, "Now what? You're crying? You little mama's boy! You sissy! You make me sick. When are you going to grow up and start acting like a man?" Boys in the audience silently suffer a moment of embarrassment as they recall being upbraided for displaying what is perceived as weak—not manly—emotions or behavior. When they do speak, they recall the names—sissy, wimp, nerd, fag, queer, mama's boy, punk, girl, loser, fairy—that have put them in fear of being identified with women or as gay.[41] When the facilitators asked the boys what they expected of girls, they said, "A girl should be polite and clean, she shouldn't argue, . . . fight or act too smart." When a girl is assertive or doesn't defer to boys, the boys often resort to name-calling—bitch, tomboy, dyke, whore, ball breaker, or cunt. In other words, she becomes an offensive sexual object who should be humiliated or intimidated into compliance with their expectations.

One might think we've moved beyond the thinking of 1960s "greatest generation" parents, as displayed by the Cleavers' exchange and the OMP dramatization. But there are plenty of examples today that show we haven't. According to OMP and other researchers, gendered role expectations can lead to their policing through aggression and violence, as indicated in the scene acted out by the OMP facilitators. This policing of appropriate expression of manliness is evident in the story that Mitt Romney's prep school classmates tell about his chasing down and then shearing another student's bleached-blond hair and the brutal haranguing that Seth Walsh took from his school peers for his clothes and hair. Think also of the scores of trans women and men who were killed in 2020. Cruel and violent behavior is a mechanism for enforcing a corrosive conceptualization of masculinity. And while the father in the OMP role play did not strike his son, his anger and aggression sent a powerful message about how men behave when they perceive weakness in their sons. Just the fear of getting "clobbered" for exhibiting "effeminate" traits can make it harder for victimized boys to talk about being forcibly "feminized" through rape or sexual abuse. Whether gay or straight, male victims who disclose are shamed or ridiculed for being queer, while gay victims carry the burden of painting their entire community as violent or deserving of violence if they tell their stories. Instead of being able to show their true selves, they are forced to deliberately mask any trait that might be taken as feminine and hide abuse.

Violence against men is one of many threads in the web of gender-based violence that must be acknowledged and eliminated. One in every six men will experience sexual assault, in most cases at the hands of another man. We talk a lot about the need to invite men into the #MeToo movement as allies. We also need to bring them in as survivors, and to do that, we need to change our attitudes about what being a man means and stop associating the notion with toxic behaviors under the guise of masculinity.

We've long acknowledged that men become abusers under the guise of masculinity. But we're now learning that men who suffer abuse are unlikely to disclose it because of ideas about appropriate behavior for men and boys. Earlier I talked about how false notions of masculinity allow the public to dismiss violent behavior as normal—just what men do. In this section I explore how ideas of "just what men do" under the pretext of manliness doubly binds some men—making them targets and then silencing them when they've been victimized.

Within days of the Thomas hearings back in 1991, an incest survivor called me to share how the Senate's response to me had echoes of his family's response to him when he attempted to disclose his abuse. The caller described the pain of trying to convince his family that he'd been sexually abused by a relative, only to be rejected in favor of his abuser. The caller was one of the brave incest survivors who have stepped forward. Other incest and sexual assault victims feel trapped and remain silent. Men who took part in a study of male victims of childhood abuse told researchers that telling would mean they "would just get hurt more" or that what happened was too "shameful." Typical responses also showed that the men were afraid of how it would hurt their relationships, afraid that their stories would be "too much" for people. Some were explicitly told to "keep it a secret."[42]

For men, the fears that force silence or create shame are compounded by myriad themes rooted in sex or gender—fear of being seen as gay or being outed as gay, feelings of isolation or shunning, fear of being seen as weak (or being told boys should not be victims), and fear of becoming an abuser themselves.[43] Our cultural discomfort with talking to boys about victimization means we do little or nothing to end gender-based violence, but it succeeds at keeping victims quiet and enabling systems that value silence over solutions.

The church is not the only institution used to cover abuses. One heartbreaking example of dissembling in connection with violence is that of the former congressman Dennis Hastert. But for his long-overdue plummet from grace, the story of Hastert's rise from a small-town high school wrestling coach to Speaker of the House would have gone down in history as a testament to our democracy. In 2015, Hastert was charged with banking violations and lying to the FBI about why he'd withdrawn large sums of money from his bank account. During an investigation, federal prosecutors discovered that the withdrawals were made to pay one of Hastert's victims as part of a settlement he had secretly agreed to. Despite a plea for leniency from Tom DeLay, the former House majority leader, Judge Thomas Durkin allowed Hastert's alleged victims to give statements at the sentencing hearing. And one by one Hastert confessed to molesting three boys on teams he coached from 1965 to 1981. But he described his repeated molestation of Stephen Reinboldt, who was gay, as "a different situation," leaving one to speculate whether Hastert considered the sex he had with the fourteen-year-old Reinboldt consensual.[44]

For decades Hastert's position as a beloved coach enabled his behavior. "Can you imagine the whispers, the finger-pointing, the sideways glances if you're a 14-year-old boy and you accuse the town hero of molesting you?" Durkin said before sentencing the former Speaker to fifteen months in prison.[45] But that statement only begins to tell how Hastert used his position to shield himself from scrutiny. It's no wonder that even after they graduated from high school and moved on from the wrestling team, none of the boys pressed charges against one of the most powerful men in U.S. government. "I felt intense pain, shame, and guilt," said one of his victims who never spoke about the abuse to his family or friends. "I've always felt that what Coach Hastert had done to me was my darkest secret."[46] Ultimately, it was the legal structure that protected Hastert. By the time of his prosecution for banking fraud, the statute of limitations for the sexual abuse that took place in the 1960s and 1970s had run out.

CULTURES AND SYSTEMS

"One in Four"

David McLoghlin

It has happened to a quarter of us
(us? Is that a community?)
twenty-five out of every one hundred
hung, hearts, spleen, and lungs
drawn, and everything is quartered,
memory split, hemisphered
like a dangerous rebel carcassed
and dispatched to the corners of the realm,
the Elizabethan, Cromwellian, Rome-subjugated
territory, so that no one will ever forget

or remember

. . .

twenty-five percent of this population
has been butchered.

The memories start to live back
through the limbic system
fragments of stained touch,
the flashbacks come
in the arms of real love.

Until it can be said,
until I can say, *me too*,
the crime will continue.
I join my voice to the silent chorus
to hold space for those who can't speak yet.
I speak, and I hold.
Hold the line.[47]

At eleven years old, David McLoghlin was sexually abused by a member of the clergy, an experience captured in his poem "One in Four," which speaks to the barriers to his ability to express himself and be fully heard even today as an adult. His poem reflects the deep impact the experience had on McLoghlin, which is mirrored in other victims' experiences. He describes the men who have endured sexual violence as having "been butchered" and addresses common post-traumatic stress symptoms exhibited by survivors, such as the "flashbacks" that come "in the arms of real love." Gender-based violence is as damaging and distressing for men who experience it as it is for women. Many women—particularly women of color—keep silent because they have little faith in any support from law enforcement. Men hide their own trauma for fear of suffering ridicule as a result of their revelation. As McLoghlin writes, "Until it can be said, / until I can say, *me too*, / the crime will continue." If we are going to persuade victims to come forward, we must rethink how manhood and womanhood are defined and how both definitions create unrealistic and unsafe demands on our behavior, starting when we're children. We must also know more about the feelings of shame and inadequacy associated with not meeting cultural expectations for manhood and how reporting systems embrace this culture in ways that keep men from recounting their abuse. In other words, some systems play the same role as the father in the OMP training program— in essence telling victims they should "man up."

THE MEN FROM MISSOULA

I recently came across a telegram in my files dated October 12, 1991. A man named Charles Sperry and thirty-five other men from Montana had sent it to me days after the Thomas hearing. In it, the men expressed their "full support and deepest respect" for me, adding that they "unequivocally" believed my testimony. They also acknowledged the role men had played in perpetuating systems of abuse and pledged to change their own behaviors and try to affect those of men in their communities.

It took me nearly thirty years to unearth the letter and finally read their pledge, which since 1991 had been misfiled with my teaching materials for a class I had long ago abandoned. It took only a few weeks to learn what was behind it. Charles "Chuck" Sperry ran a therapy group for men who had been victims of sexual violence. They ranged in age, social background, race, and ethnicity. The space Sperry offered was the one place where they could come together and speak freely about their pain.

Through trying to reach Sperry, I found a man named Scott, a member of the Confederated Salish and Kootenai Tribes and one of the pledge's signers, who shared with me the impact sexual abuse had on his life and generations of members of his tribe. Scott's uncle abused him, but he and other young victims had remained silent about the abuse in order to protect themselves, their abusers, and their community. He sees "how sexual violence perpetrated by men ran through my family, my tribe, and my reservation." In the following passage, Scott explains how the violence that he and his community experienced came to be.

> We (The Confederated Salish and Kootenai Tribes) were the first tribe in the Northwest to let the Catholic priests (and nuns) in. They ran boarding schools where many many children over generations were abused and sexually abused. My tribe was part of the second largest sexual abuse settlement and my family was at that boarding school. I attribute the sexual abuse that I received to that line from colonial violence to religious violence to violence against culture and children to my uncle and, ultimately, towards me.[48]

Investigating both his family and his tribal history over the years, Scott has learned that his uncle was a victim of abuse by an Ursuline Academy priest—like the victims who were part of the settlement mentioned before—and one of the "one in four" that McLoghlin writes about. In addition to the church's guilt here, Scott sees the role that colonization continued to play in the abuse of his uncle that was passed on to him and perhaps others in his generation. The subjugation of Native Americans from the outset of the country's founding set the stage for generations of ill treatment, sending the message that Native people are easy targets. And through institutional responses and perpetuated stereotypes, Scott sees the same message that Native women do—that somehow tribal members are deserving of abuse. As the Roman Catholic Church became a fixture in tribal life through both education and religion, it also became a system that silenced children like Scott well into adulthood.

MANLINESS

Our cultural complicity in gender stereotyping begins early and has a huge impact on how abuse is dealt with. In 2018, Common Sense Media did a meta-analysis of research on the impact of television programming on children and found that movies and television shows are "incredibly effective at teaching kids what the culture expects of boys and girls." With programming timed to children's development, television reinforces the idea that men are emotionally restrained, "aggressive and hostile," and that women are "submissive and weak" and overly concerned with their appearance. According to the report, programming that endorses traditional masculinity and the objectification of women can be tied to greater social acceptance and perpetration of sexual violence and aggression.

Boys and girls enact these cultural expectations at school, so it's not surprising that harassment, teasing, and bullying (more appropriately described as emotional torment) often define school culture, even to the point of toxicity. By the time they are young adults, men have absorbed ideas about masculinity and rape myths that convince them that "real men" know how to protect themselves from abuse. When it happens to them, the shame of not having been able to protect themselves will very likely keep them from disclosing it.

This behavior is called by different names, most of which disguise its violent nature with benign jargon. In Massachusetts, a hockey team called similar behavior "hazing." In Maryland, the term used for one football team's "initiation routine" was "brooming." South Carolina high school wrestlers dubbed their activities "trademarking." But these euphemisms only thinly veil the horrific cruelty of these rituals, which—make no mistake—*are* a form of gender-based violence, not because they are explicitly sexual, though some are, but because sex is used as a tool to enforce a gendered hierarchy. Still, as one sports journalist described it, hazing culture in sports has in some ways become "rape culture." Most assault stories within sports teams involve man-on-man assault, and hazing in college fraternities follows the same playbook. But statistics point to the underreporting of sexual assault, in particular among men and boys.

Few cases show the link between ideas of manliness and hostility toward behavior that is deemed feminine better than the sports headlines in stories covering the treatment of the Miami Dolphins tackle Jonathan Martin. In a 2013 incident that captured the attention of the public beyond sports fans, Richie Incognito was accused of harassing Martin. Incognito threatened to slap Martin's mother and taunted Martin by saying he was sleeping with Martin's girlfriend. A National Football League investigation into the team culture revealed the truly noxious gendered and homophobic nature of the harassment:

Incognito's "you're my bitch" comments added to name-calling that had begun in 2012, Martin's rookie season, when Incognito, [John] Jerry and [Mike] Pouncey began regularly calling Martin a "cunt," a "bitch," a "pussy" and a "faggot." Martin was not surprised to hear these words used by football players, but believed they were frequently hurled at him with demeaning intent. The evidence shows that these words—at least at times—were spoken to Martin in a cutting tone or with the intent to humiliate him. According to Martin, these types of taunts were a routine part of his life with the Dolphins.[49]

The investigation also included messages that Martin shared with his family about Incognito's behavior. Martin appears to have blamed himself for and internalized Incognito's and others' slurs that had been hurled at him throughout his lifetime:

I'm a push over, a people pleaser. I avoid confrontation whenever I can, I always want everyone to like me. I let people talk about me, say anything to my face, and I just take it, laugh it off, even when I know they are intentionally trying to disrespect me. I mostly blame the soft schools I went to, which fostered within me a feeling that I'm a huge pussy, as I never got into fights. I used to get verbally bullied every day in middle school and high school, by kids that are half my size. I would never fight back, just get sad & feel like no one wanted to be my friend, when in fact I was just being socially awkward. Most people in that situation are witty & quick with sarcastic replies, I never have been.[50]

At Incognito's urging, two other teammates participated in harassing Martin, but to a lesser extent. According to the league's report, the three taunted Martin "on a persistent basis with sexually explicit remarks about his sister and his mother and at times ridiculed with racial insults and other offensive comments." They also subjected another player to "homophobic name-calling and improper physical touching."[51]

Martin occasionally asked his teammates to stop making crude remarks but never filed a complaint with the team management. Instead, he announced he was leaving the team. His story emerged when the Dolphins' coach started looking into the reasons behind Martin's departure. Six years after the NFL's report, in an interview with *Sports Illustrated*, Incognito gave his side of the story:

> I fit the bill. Hey, racist, homophobic, whatnot. What I'm saying was, we were close, personal friends. It wasn't factored into, "Hey, this is guy talk, these are two alpha males talkin' to each other." Was some bad s—— said? Absolutely. But was this a case of bullying? Absolutely not.[52]

Incognito's response reflects the way in which ideas about masculinity have become internalized to the point of toxicity. Even six years later, he is in denial about the severity of his behavior, rather than viewing it as what it was: violent and abhorrent.

The internalization of gendered tropes and misguided ideas about what constitutes "guy talk"—as also demonstrated by Trump in his characterization of the *Access Hollywood* tape—perpetuates the idea that men know how to handle assault and therefore rarely experience it, which allows us to deny their stories and keep them from speaking out. And men who identify as gay have an additional layer of stigma and silencing to pass through in order to report their abuse. Statistics show members of the LGBTQ+ community are more likely to be raped and to experience other violence related to their sexual identity.[53] There is much more that we need to learn about how the experience is different for all genders, despite many shared emotional and systemic challenges.

We know that race can add another layer of stigma that prevents women from coming forward. The same is true of Black men who want to be heard above racist stereotypes. To date very few men have had the courage displayed by the actor Terry Crews in his testimony before the Senate Judiciary Committee in 2018. Crews powerfully addressed his charges of sexual assault by the talent agent Adam Venit at a Hollywood party in 2016. The California senator Dianne Feinstein asked Crews why he didn't physically retaliate during the assault, eliciting one of the more compelling aspects of Crews's testimony. The actor and former professional athlete spoke of how a violent response would have put him at greater risk as a Black man—including the risk of being imprisoned. Crews's testimony shows that sometimes the answer is not as simple as expecting victims to fight their abusers. Every person who is victimized by sexual violence is at some risk no matter how they respond. And many of their experiences receive little attention.

Recently, I was speaking to a group of church leaders who asked for my thoughts about how to end sexual abuse among the huge population of incarcerated people in this country. It was the first time in nearly thirty years of talking about gender-based violence that anyone had raised that topic with me. The U.S. Department of Justice estimates that between 149,200 and 209,400 incidents of sexual victimization occur annually in prisons and jails,[54] but it's unknown what percentage of these are reported. One can assume that because all sexual violence is underreported, male inmates may be less likely to complain about sexual violence than other men. In prison, men are kept silent by the volatility of their circumstances, as well as an understanding of how their crimes may color their future interactions with law enforcement. Many view people who are imprisoned as unworthy of protection, which raises the question of how people in and out of prison can negotiate systems to support victimized prisoners and get them the help they need. In part, what we need is for more men to talk about vulnerability. But without change to our prison systems and a cultural reassessment of the humanity of incarcerated persons, the population will remain at risk.

It seems odd in such an embattled environment, but poetry may provide the best portal to opening discussions of gendered violence against men. In eloquent prose, McLoghlin explains how and why he writes about abuse in his upcoming book, *Talking About It*:

> What I do in poems like "Disassociation" is to go back into the memory core to deal with volatile and toxic materials. The poem is both the hazmat suit and the ceramic form that contains and makes sense of fragmented, overwhelming experiences. . . . I'm writing about memories that were drowned and found a way to breathe underwater. So when they surface, it's inevitable for them to be strange and slightly misshapen in the light of day. What's crucial is the use of imagery and metaphor. . . . For me, fairy tales are a rich territory: probably because they've been carrying metaphors for trauma for centuries, as well as ways of healing, and ways of overcoming the enemy. And that is what this strand in my poetry aims to do.[55]

I now hear from men more than I have in the past. Recently, after a talk, a staffer at the event wrote to me and thanked me for merely mentioning men in the conversation. Physical abuse is not a measure of manliness, and these notions should not be lodged as an excuse for gendered aggression. Abuse of women, nonbinary adults, children, and other men is just that, abuse masked as masculinity. For those who identify as men, the liberty and license to talk about one's own experiences is at the root of ending gender-based violence for everyone. Violent or abusive behaviors are commonly viewed as an extension of masculinity and dismissed by the prevalence of a "boys will be boys" mentality and the social acceptance of "locker room talk" as banter that all men engage in. We are all complicit when we reinforce the spaces of silence by not challenging them.

The takeaways from Jonathan's, Terry's, Scott's, and David's stories are complex. But one thing is clear. Disarming abusers of the weapons they use to shame their victims is critical to ending abuse. This is true regardless of the victims' identity but is peculiarly important when the silencing takes place in the name of masculinity. And this effort can't wait until after the abuse occurs. Unfortunately, the connection between gender-based violence done to men and nonbinary people and violence to women is rarely made. But I am hopeful that the lessons learned from the elimination of violence against women—all women—will transcend gender and make the world safer for everyone.

FREEDOM FROM VIOLENCE

For all victims and survivors, regardless of identity, the ability to speak out without shame from outside groups or from within one's own tribe or community is key to self-sovereignty as well as equal rights in the United States.

The violence prevention advocate Brenda Hill (not related to the author) describes Native women's sovereignty this way:

> Sovereignty requires the respect and active support of others. Sovereignty is diminished by violence in all its forms. Silent witnessing or ignoring the violence of others is a form of violence in itself.

What this looks like can vary from community to community. When it comes to Native Americans, to borrow from Hill, gender justice means the "ability and authority to make decisions regarding all matters concerning the Tribe" and the community "without the approval or agreement of others."[56] Gender justice for all of us is the ability and authority to make decisions regarding all matters concerning ourselves without others' approval or agreement.

Of all the challenges of ending gender violence, expunging colonialism, slavery, false masculinity, and related misogyny from our cultures and systems feels like the biggest. Taking this on requires boiling the ocean—seeing complexities of the problem long overdue for solutions. For me this undertaking is deeply personal. When I see the girl on the cover of *The New Yorker*, I see myself. I also see the children in chapter 4 and the people of all ages and genders throughout this book. I see their despair and their promise. In their stories, so many of them heartbreaking, I see our hope for ending gender-based violence for future generations. And I believe that removing this scourge is possible.

NINE

Politics: Rage, Compromises, and Backlash

A mere month before the 2016 presidential election, Donald Trump was "caught on television" declaring that when he saw attractive women, he could "grab them by the pussy" and no one would do anything about it. Yet, immediately after the now-infamous *Access Hollywood* tape aired, a number of Republican senators stepped up to decry his statements. Senator Mitch McConnell called his words "repugnant and unacceptable under any circumstances."[1] Senator Mike Crapo, while touting Trump's two decades of "fighting against domestic violence," said the presidential candidate's comments were "inconsistent with protecting women" from abuse and withdrew his endorsement.[2] Senator John Thune called on Trump to apologize or drop out of the race and allow Mike Pence to become the nominee, while Senator Kelly Ayotte declared that she would not vote for him. But while they denounced the comments as demeaning to women, few actually renounced their support for Trump's candidacy altogether. And in a classic tit for tat, Trump went on the offensive, attacking Bill Clinton during his apology for the comments and later holding a press conference with Clinton's sexual assault accusers. Clinging to party allegiances, once Trump stood his ground, most demurely pledged to continue to support him as the nominee. After a brief fallout, Republicans rallied around their candidate in his campaign against Hillary Clinton. Even Crapo, earlier comments notwithstanding, capitulated.

Politicians talk a good game in the heat of a high-profile incident but then self-servingly turn around and support politicians or legislation that compromises women's authority over their bodies. Trump was not going to back down from his *Access Hollywood* comment. After his early critics equivocated and rallied around him, he had no reason to. He had secured his congressional support. Trump's primary ambition was to draw more male voters to his candidacy. He used misogynistic language to achieve his goal, taking a page from alt-right White supremacist organizations like A Voice for Men and Return of Kings. Both these groups and other men's rights organizations have grown their memberships by using extreme sexism often coupled with violence as a lure.[3]

By February 2018, Senator Crapo was all in for Trump. To help his own chances of reelection in Idaho, a right-leaning state where Trump was leading in the polls, he endorsed Trump's presidency.[4] Crapo applauded the "optimistic and ambitious agenda" Trump presented in his first State of the Union address and cited the "millions of workers," including Idahoans, who had "benefited from Trump's tax reform."

Crapo had previously described Trump as someone whose "repeated actions and comments toward women have been disrespectful, profane and demeaning."[5] But rather than risk his political future, Senator Crapo chose Trump as the person who best represented the country's interests, and spoke not another word about domestic violence or other gender violence.[6] And Crapo was far from alone. In time, Trump's early Republican critics, including the loudest ones like Ted Cruz and Lindsey Graham, lined up behind him and defended or ignored his attacks on women, including an insult about Cruz's wife's appearance. The slim chance that legislation aimed at eliminating gender violence would happen during a Trump presidency completely evaporated. When Trump nominated Brett Kavanaugh for the Supreme Court, it was clear before a single vote was cast that all Republican senators would confirm him even in the face of Christine Blasey Ford's charges of sexual assault.

It wasn't that politicians didn't care about violence against women; it was that ending gender-based violence mattered less than other political ambitions, like enlarging the party base and beating Clinton. In the end, a standard was set. Claiming impunity for sexually assaulting women was not enough to render a party's presidential candidate ineligible.

And Trump continued his rants against women.

Politicians' statements about abhorring violence against women rarely result in meaningful structural changes to address the problem. But could backlash against Trump's misogyny and the Republican's dismissive attitude toward it spark antiviolence political action?

RAGE AND RESISTANCE

Outside the Republican Party faithful, women seethed with anger over Trump's sexism. The election would be their opportunity to show their disgust. The morning after the November 8, 2016, election, people woke in disappointment and disbelief that women voters, with the majority of White women voting for Trump, had secured the election of a man who bragged about his entitlement to sexually assault women. But their despair quickly turned to anger, and soon they began organizing. Resistance had already started to build long before Trump stood in front of an inaugural audience on January 20, 2017, and, with his hand on the Lincoln Bible, took his oath to support the Constitution of the United States. But the day after the inauguration, that resistance poured out onto the streets, with massive women's marches around the globe and in Trump's backyard in the nation's capital. The rage boiled in every continent, including Antarctica, giving the world a sense of what women had been suppressing for generations. And the protesters weren't just marching for White, cisgendered "women's rights." Their grievances and agendas were as varied as the marchers themselves, encompassing LGBTQ+ rights, environmental issues, disability rights, and racial justice, to name a few. The *Access Hollywood* tape had jerked back into the public conversation the seeming dismissiveness of the problem of violence against women, placing it front and center.

Despite the enormous worldwide gathering of women who protested President-elect Trump's antiwomen conduct and statements in January 2017, and the #MeToo movement that followed, little action to end gender-based violence came out of Washington. But outside of the nation's capital, change was in the air. Over time, it took the form of

direct political action. On the heels of the Senate's wretched handling
of the Kavanaugh confirmation hearing, in November 2018 the determined women who had produced the Women's March joined forces
with other women around the country to elect midterm candidates who
were more likely to take up the cause of gender equity. Women ran for
offices at all levels and pushed candidates on the issues. One Senate
candidate, the Alabaman Doug Jones, was a beneficiary, defeating Roy
Moore, a Trump-supported candidate whom multiple women accused
of sexually assaulting them when they were teenagers; in another era, it
might well have been overlooked. Black women in Alabama were credited for Moore's defeat despite the president's endorsing him.

This cycle, from social rage to political resistance, isn't new, and neither is the backlash to the gains that come when women galvanize in
the face of political defeats. The virulent reactions to Trump's "grab
them by the pussy" callous pomposity are reminiscent of the fallout
from the Thomas hearings. And an exchange between readers in the
comments of a *New York Times* article by Susan Chira traced the 2018
rage at indifference to gender violence back to 1991.

Dec. 7, 2018

RICH: Just ponder the fact that we now have allegations of
sexual misconduct against two justices sitting on the United
States Supreme Court.

WALLY: Yes, and one has a really bad temper and hates democrats and the Clintons. Well, maybe make that two.

KIM: And a president who believes "he is entitled to be abusive to whomever he wants." It was only a matter of time
until a "regular citizen" used President Trump's behavior to
condone his own. These people are living examples of our

values in this country, and the fact that this behaviour is not only allowed, but condoned, and indeed lauded by putting these people in positions of power sends a horrible message to everyone who is not a straight, white male. I am a 52 year old professional white female, and I have encountered abhorrent behavior in literally every single job I have ever had. Every. Single. One. I have never reported any of it, and why? Because if it doesn't matter for Anita Hill or Dr. Ford when a Supreme Court Justiceship is at stake, why on earth would it matter in my situation? The fact that the same scenario played out 27 years later makes me want to cry, but the fact that it has played out in Fortune 500 corporations and law firms where I have worked for the past 30 makes me want to throw up AND cry.[7]

Trump and the Thomas and Kavanaugh hearings infuriated Rich, Wally, Kim, and many others across the country who looked back angrily at the state of the country in 2018. Rebecca Traister, a writer and columnist known for her acute political and social observations, has written about women's anger and how the "dissatisfactions and resentments of America's women have often ignited movements for social change and progress." Though in the United States, as in much of the world, women are taught to be compliant, Traister argues that getting mad has played a crucial role in "determining their political power" and bringing about "revolutionary social movements."[8] Perhaps this is precisely why women are sent the message, in more ways than one, to be silent and not use their voices.

But rage can serve many purposes. It can offer some clarity on issues that have perplexed and frustrated us. It can help us focus on what we feel passionate about and why. And it can also inspire us to join with others to act. In 1991, I received several letters from people directing their ire at the Senate and Clarence Thomas. A state representative from North Dakota wrote, "It is interesting to note that the central issues, (1) the U.S. Senate's ignoring the initial claim of sexual harassment, and (2) the administration's concerted defense of a sexual harasser, have been ignored—This <u>man</u> has just been appointed to the U.S. Supreme Court." Another writer who described himself as a White man who grew up "in a coal mining town in West Virginia" and who was "as old as my father" was more ardent. "Judge Thomas is confirmed: Today is a sad day for our nation. . . . I just wonder how many of the Keating Five will vote for confirmation. . . . I have seen <u>greed</u>, <u>dishonesty</u>, and <u>hatred</u> almost destroy our great nation. God help," he wrote. A self-described twenty-seven-year-old White woman from Oklahoma saw the hearing as a rallying cry. "I believe that the Senate vote to confirm Judge Thomas sends a strong message to the country that 'we don't care about women's issues.' Although sexual abuses of all ranges, childcare and civil liberties should be called by their correct name, 'society's issues,' this particular issue [sexual harassment] will finally galvanize people who have been politically silent for too long."[9]

All three writers were right about the political significance of the issues raised in the hearing. And my fellow Oklahoman's prediction about the animating effect of the hearing, written in a letter that was postmarked one day after the vote to confirm Thomas, was spot-on. Women were galvanized and ready for political, social, and legal changes. Excited about their ability to effect real change, in the 1992 election they were focused on better representation and better outcomes for women—at work, in education, and in society in general. They ran for public office, raised record amounts of money, and won; they worked to elect candidates who supported a "women's agenda" and succeeded in moving equal pay and reproductive freedom forward. And in record numbers they filed sexual harassment complaints with the Equal Employment Opportunity Commission.

With all this energy, why didn't we get the job done? Why didn't we eliminate the need for a #MeToo movement? Why didn't we raise public awareness of the significance of the range of "sexual abuses"? Why didn't we insist on electing a president whose words and actions reflected a belief that gender-based violence is intolerable? How did we vote into our nation's highest office a candidate whose words and behavior gave clear indication that he didn't believe in a woman's right to the sanctity of her own body? A simple answer to all of these questions is that we all underestimated the counter to our rage and our revolution. But my conversations with some of the pioneers in the work on gender-based violence showed me the answer is not so straightforward. To demonstrate why our collective fire subsided enough to allow for a Trump presidency demands that we turn a broader lens on gender politics in the 1990s and the first decade of the twenty-first century.

At the beginning of the 1990s, there was a period when society, politics, and law appeared to align to confront harassment in the workplace and recognize it as legitimate, dangerous, and unforgivable. A crucial change occurred in the law governing sexual harassment. Within months of Thomas's swearing-in ceremony, a civil rights bill that had been languishing in committees was resurrected. The proposed Civil Rights Act of 1991, which would lift the cap on the amount of money plaintiffs could recover once harassment was proven, was nearly identical to a bill that George H. W. Bush had vetoed the year prior. In April 1991, Bush denounced the proposed legislation and threatened another veto. That July, the month he nominated Thomas to a post on the Supreme Court, the president enjoyed a 74 percent approval rating. But by late October he was feeling the heat of the rage brought out by the Thomas confirmation hearing. Ignoring Bush's veto threat, Congress passed the 1991 version of the Civil Rights Act. It was the first major piece of civil rights legislation passed since the 1970s. No veto was forthcoming. Meanwhile, Bush's popularity was on the decline.

By July 1992, his approval rate had plummeted to 29 percent, opening the door for Governor Bill Clinton of Arkansas, a relative unknown on the national scene, to defeat him in the presidential election, usually won by the incumbent. Clinton's large margin of support by women was well documented.[10] And many female voters were open about the role that their anger with the Senate Judiciary Committee played in their getting behind Clinton, as were women politicians who ran on a pledge to change the way women were represented in Washington.[11]

In November 1992, before the dust settled from the Thomas hearing, people learned of sexual assault and harassment claims against the Republican senator Bob Packwood. In time, forty women spoke with the journalist Florence Graves about Packwood's alleged molestations. In 1992, Graves's *Washington Post* story about the allegations, supported by Packwood's own diaries, triggered the Senate Ethics Committee's formal investigation into his behavior. But much of what followed occurred behind the scenes, despite cries for a public hearing. Three years after the original complaint surfaced, Bob Packwood finally resigned under threat of expulsion. The hurdles the accusers had to clear showed how deeply the ethics process favored election officials, making it nearly impossible for "outsiders" like Packwood's accusers to be heard by the public. In the end, despite compelling testimony, Packwood was allowed to resign rather than be expelled from the Senate.[12]

Afterward, at public talks and in private conversations, people approached me hopeful that the downfall of Senator Packwood would open the door to a widespread reckoning on elected officials' misconduct. They were convinced that, this time, their demands for a collective reckoning would be met. Outside of Washington, holding elected officials politically accountable for apparently criminal behavior began to serve as a proxy for progress. For gender rights advocates Packwood's resignation and the increase in complaints filed with the EEOC signaled the dawn of a new day of consequences for Washington politicians, possibly into the future.

During the 1990s, a spate of sexual harassment claims gained national attention, and the U.S. Supreme Court decided a record number of sexual harassment cases, most ending in decisions for female plaintiffs. Thousands of others were decided without reaching the high court as complaints filed with the EEOC would, by 1993, double compared with the years before the Thomas hearing. For perhaps the first time, researchers and activists had solid proof that survivors' experiences were real, leading to a new social and legal consciousness around the issue.

But if we thought we had turned the corner on gender-based violence, we were mistaken. We underestimated the power of the existing culture of silence that stifled reports of prohibited school and workplace behaviors. We failed to foresee how organizations would put in place complex structures designed to undermine reporting and response efforts. Silence became part of a negotiated settlement. In 1991, the U.S. Supreme Court upheld the enforceability of mandatory arbitration in the case of *Gilmer v. Interstate/Johnson Lane Corp.* At the time of the ruling, only 2 percent of the non-union work population had mandated arbitration in their employment contracts. The *Gilmer* decision opened the door to mandated arbitration for employers. Employers' demands that workers sign nondisclosure and mandatory arbitration agreements, which require employees to settle directly with the employer rather than through the courts, became the norm and escalated over the next decade.

COMPROMISE

Throughout the early years of the 1990s, women's advocates continued warning leaders about the problem of gender violence. But revelations about Bill Clinton's affair with Monica Lewinsky, which began in 1995, shortly after the twenty-one-year-old became a White House intern, dealt a serious blow to the efforts. Clinton's subsequent impeachment made it even harder for anti–gender-violence appeals to gain political traction. Throughout the 1990s, the affair hung like a dark cloud over the heads of liberal-leaning women advocating against gender-based violence. Whether the affair amounted to an impeachable act didn't matter. Conservative women accused feminists who failed to demand that Clinton resign or be removed from office of turning their backs on victims. And women who had protested Thomas's appointment to the Court were labeled hypocrites for supporting Bill Clinton. Their silence and certainly open support for Clinton were interpreted as a statement that sexual misconduct, even in the Oval Office, brought no serious consequences and was unworthy of punishment.

Clinton's affair with Lewinsky wasn't the only thing that compromised his authority to propose a gender-rights agenda. His dishonesty about the affair became an acceptable alternative to accountability for both public policy and private behavior. In his book *The Naughty Nineties*, the writer David Friend wrote that the Clinton era's "rejection of a common, fundamental value system . . . allowed the ethically ambiguous individual—it allowed the president himself—to play fast and

loose with the truth. It allowed him to waffle in his public pronounce-
ments and private behavior, and then to recalibrate, reboot, and be
redeemed."[13] Clinton apologized on multiple occasions for his behavior, including at a breakfast for religious leaders in which he claimed
"genuine repentence" and redemption.[14]

Chances of a public reckoning on gender-based violence all but fiz-
zled with Clinton's impeachment hearing in 1998 and acquittal in 1999,
and Hillary Clinton would play a conflicted role in the public discussion. She had already become a political and cultural icon of gender
equality, owing in part to her well-received speech at the World Conference on Women in Beijing in 1995. "Women's rights are human rights,"
a line from her talk, became a mantra for women's advocates around
the globe. But, according to Emma Coleman Jordan, a Georgetown University law professor, Hillary's failure to step up and denounce Bill's
behavior contributed to women's challenges in pushing the government
toward a progressive women's agenda. Jordan, a former White House
fellow, helped form my legal team in 1991 and has an astute understanding of Washington political messaging. She observed how Hillary's position muddled the liberal women's anti–gender-violence message and
caused ambivalence and confusion among the public about whether issues like harassment and sexual assault were important to the Clintons.
Patricia Ireland, as president of the National Organization for Women,
was put on the hot seat numerous times to explain Bill Clinton's behavior. Speaking to the press, Ireland said she and other leaders were
"attacked on both sides of the issue—there were hard-core Democrats
who thought NOW should not criticize a president perceived as 'good'
on women's issues. And there were many Republicans, as well as long-
time feminists, who argued that NOW's reaction—and that of most

women's groups—to Clinton/Paula Jones/Lewinsky/et al. was too little, too late."[15]

Multiple accusers would come forward about Bill Clinton's alleged
abuse, allegations that included a charge of sexual assault.[16] Ireland was
quick to say that Bill Clinton was not the organization's "dream candidate" and that the behavior with Lewinsky was "indefensible," but that
part of her message never got through. The public instead latched on
to her statement that "women tend to vote on the issues, which is why
Clinton can behave as a dog as a husband and a father and still have
women's support."[17] The messaging attempted to draw a line between
Bill's personal behavior and his political positions in order to salvage
the latter. But Jordan told me Ireland's message never satisfied the public. And Hillary's decision to pursue a political strategy based on protecting Bill exposed the "rots in the planks" on which the political
agenda was built.[18] Another case of political ambition or expediency
trumping justice and equity.

Critics took full advantage of the inability of Clinton supporters to
deflect charges of complicity and hypocrisy. Statements that some observers interpreted as feminists' tacit collective acceptance of Clinton's
lie about Lewinsky in 1998 were weaponized against all of us. The episode weakened the movement and began to pave the way for putting a
man who was caught on tape bragging about committing acts of sexual
assault into the Oval Office. And when scores of women came forward
with complaints of rape and other misconduct against Trump, though
some voters were appalled, many seemed to simply shrug while Trump's
ardent supporters used our country's reelection of Clinton as a classic
"whataboutist" cover. But in Jordan's view, "The anger never went away
entirely. It continued to exist underground."[19]

In part, that smoldering anger was kindled by the dismissive and disparaging commentary about Title IX and Title VII sexual harassment and assault claims and the people who filed them. Though in the wake of the Thomas hearing many employers adopted policies prohibiting sexual harassment, in many places nothing changed. Those same employers often chose symbolic compliance with their own policies rather than robust plans to change the culture and climate of workplaces that had accommodated misconduct. In addition to the structural devices that blocked full disclosure of formal complaints of abuse, social backlash against antiharassment advocates erupted. Beginning in the 1990s, women were placed squarely in the crosshairs of the culture wars as claims about sexual assault and harassment were denied as "feminist hysteria" and compared to "witch hunts" by critics of Title IX. The political criticism culminated in the second decade of the twenty-first century with George Will's unsubstantiated claim that college campus sexual assault figures were inflated.[20] Outrage from politicians over George Will's suggestion that women lied about being raped was swift and intense. Four senators excoriated Will for trivializing "the scourge of sexual assault" and legitimizing dangerous myths about sexual assault.[21] A number of papers dropped Will's columns.

When record numbers of women filed complaints with the EEOC between 1991 and 1994, legal options appeared to be our path to eliminating abuses that were occurring in the workplace. But lawsuits are costly, and litigation and settlement processes can be grinding, lasting beyond the working lives of complainants. Far too often, cases produce little long-term relief for women who come after the original litigants.

Sexual harassment is only one form of gender-based aggression, but tracking the history of one notorious sexual harassment case from the 1990s sheds light on the disappointing reaction to all forms of gender-related harassment. In 1999, Ford Motor Company settled a suit brought by nineteen Latinx, Black, and White women whose sexual and racial harassment complaints dated back to 1996. The $8 million settlement was the fourth largest ever in the Equal Employment Opportunity Commission's history.[22] The women complained that bosses and fellow laborers treated them as property or prey. Men crudely commented on their breasts and buttocks; graffiti of penises was carved into tables, spray-painted onto floors, and scribbled onto walls. They groped women, pressed against them, simulated sex acts, or masturbated in front of them. Supervisors traded better assignments for sex and punished those who refused.[23]

One could assume that having to pay out such a sizable settlement might push a company to significantly alter the way it handled sexual assault claims. It might also initiate interventions aimed at changing company culture. But more than twenty years later, at the height of the #MeToo movement, women in the same Ford plant in the Chicago area complained of the same hostile work environment, prompting a new lawsuit. The 1999 settlement, though record setting, had not resulted in substantive change for the women who followed decades later. Neither the company's human resources offices, the women's unions, the opinions of a federal agency and then a federal judge, nor "independent monitors policing the factory floors for several years," which were mandated under the settlement, offered the assembly-line workers relief from persistent torment.[24] Understandably, by 2017, Sharon Dunn, who sued Ford back in the 1990s, was disheartened and angry. "For all the good that was supposed to come out of what happened to us, it seems like Ford did nothing," she said. "If I had that choice today, I wouldn't say a damn word."[25]

Dunn's anger and fatigue are understandable. Far too often victims who complain get worn down by abusive behavior and the structural denials of the hurt they've suffered. In the meantime, no one is held accountable, and cultures remain the same for a new generation of workers. A few people are willing to come forward and invest the energy to complain. When possible, they look for a better environment, but otherwise victims "choose" to suffer in silence or maybe convince themselves that it's not so bad.

There were comparable frustrations with the efficacy of Title IX, meant to protect people from sexual assault in educational settings. With guidance from Catharine MacKinnon, students at Yale University in 1980 were among the first to win a suit requiring a university to provide better protection against sexual harassment and assault. That year, a court ordered the school to establish antiharassment processes as part of the institution's responsibility under Title IX. But in 2011, as I noted in chapter 5, women students complained that harassment persisted as part of Yale culture. An article in the school's alumni magazine spelled out some of the behavior that had become ritualized and that students objected to:

> Every year since at least 2005, an incident of shockingly blatant misogyny at Yale has made news on campus—and sometimes in the national media. Last fall, fraternity pledges stood on Old Campus and chanted "No means yes, yes means anal." The year before, athletic teams and fraternities circulated an anonymous e-mail with photos of incoming freshman women, ranked by how drunk the writer would need to be to sleep with them. In 2008, a group of fraternity pledges photographed themselves standing outside the Women's Center holding a sign that read, "We love Yale sluts." The list goes on.[26]

In a 2010 complaint filed with the U.S. Department of Education, twelve women and four men, all Yale students or recent alumni, contended that the Ivy League school's failure to respond to individual experiences of sexual assault and the open misogyny on the school's campus violated Title IX's protections. The Department of Education's investigation, which closed in 2012, found, among other things, that Yale underreported incidents of sexual harassment and violence "for a very long time" and failed to meet its obligation to keep adequate records of complaints filed on the campus.[27] Alexandra Brodsky, one of the students in the group of sixteen complainants, charged Yale with silencing her when she reported being raped by a fellow student. Brodsky was satisfied with neither the Education Department's report nor the school's response to it. A year after its release, still rankled, she took part in a protest in front of the department's offices in Washington, D.C. In a statement about the rally, Brodsky's dissatisfaction with Yale's and the government's responses was clear: "I was betrayed by my friend, then my school, then my government. Not enough has changed at Yale. . . . We're left with little more than empty promises."[28]

Those "empty promises" became policy—but with the opposite intent—during the Trump administration's oversight of the Department of Education. Secretary of Education Betsy DeVos took office promising an overhaul of the Title IX regulations of sexual harassment and assault that was meant to balance the rights of accusers and the accused.[29] Rather than move the cause forward, the new rules undermined victims' protections, and gender equality advocates and many universities pushed back. Fatima Goss Graves, the president and CEO of the National Women's Law Center, said, "If this rule goes into effect, survivors will be denied their civil rights and will get the message loud and clear that there is no point in reporting assault."[30] But with no power to change DeVos's regulations, schools scrambled instead to implement the new rules, which heightened survivors' burden of proof in assault cases, thereby treating sexual harassment claims different from other claims of discrimination covered by civil rights laws.[31]

As far as victims are concerned, the failure of corporations like the Ford Motor Company and universities like Yale to address the gender-based violence within their organizations amounts to a separate wrong-doing, even beyond their initial grievances. The psychology professor Jennifer Freyd has coined the term "institutional betrayal" to refer to the "failure to prevent or respond supportively" to complaints of sexual assault and harassment committed by other individuals within the institution. It's not just the gender-based violence that fuels women's anger; it's the failure to provide an adequate response or an effort to get to the truth of a matter. Or in some cases, as with the Senate Judiciary Committee hearings, rage arises because of the openly hostile response to the very idea of a claim of sexual misconduct.

Institutional and public counter to Title IX and Title VII claims point to the limitations of these legislations as the primary legal frames for protecting against gender violence. Both laws allowed for interpretations that enabled institutions to protect their interests, often at the expense of finding the truth. This has over the years come to be known as "check the box" compliance with the law. Sure, one can pass laws to regulate people's behavior, but resistance to change will continue until broader understanding and acceptance of gender violence is achieved. Ultimately, one cannot legislate morality, but laws should reflect our aspirations for equality. The struggle to get there must be waged on multiple fronts, including social, cultural, political, and legal.

Resistance to assuring women's safety was present in pundits' and critics' negative reaction to a reenergized interest in addressing sexual harassment. Evidence of the pervasive existence of gender-based violence continued to mount, but political bodies failed to respond in a constructive way. The back-and-forth on gender-equity issues in the first part of the century and the outspoken and tacit resistance to the idea that sexual assault and harassment were significant social and political problems help explain Trump's election.

In 2017, the simmering ire boiled over. When #MeToo revelations hit the mainstream and sparked a new conversation, it gave hope that the overt and covert ways that victims were silenced were about to end. Accused power moguls hired the best defense lawyers, but this time the fight was out in the open, with an energized and angered public demanding accountability. Governors in California and New York signed bills into law that prohibited the use of nondisclosure agreements in sexual harassment settlements. The federal government signaled that it would adopt similar measures. Survivors in the United States dared to believe that our political leaders would take up the challenge to recognize and confront gender violence as the antithesis of gender equality.

On September 27, 2018, people across the country held their collective breath in anticipation of testimony in a hearing that many hoped would clarify how far our awareness of gender violence had evolved. When Christine Blasey Ford faced yet another Senate Judiciary Committee considering yet another Supreme Court nominee, Brett Kavanaugh, whom she accused of sexual assault, many were hopeful that the nearly three decades of consciousness-raising about sexual violence would yield a victory of some sort for women. But that hope was quickly dashed.

Louise Fitzgerald wasn't surprised. A professor emerita of gender and women's studies and psychology at the University of Illinois, Fitzgerald has studied the issue of sexual harassment in the workplace and its impact on women and men for four decades. Her research in the field is now considered groundbreaking, and Fitzgerald has supervised and mentored dozens of researchers on the topic. But when she started her work, people questioned why she would want to study sexual harassment. They failed to see the significance of an age-old problem that a large swath of working women experienced and many viewed as connatural.

In October 1991, Fitzgerald was on Capitol Hill during the Thomas confirmation hearing. She waited in the wing, having volunteered to testify as an expert witness. The Senate Judiciary Committee declined to call her. In an email she wrote to me in 2020, her frustration with the lack of progress we've made since then was palpable:

> I have spent almost 30 years trying to figure it out. When the MeToo movement began, I had tons of journalists coming around acting so shocked and surprised and saying "This CANT be true. She must be making it up. Maybe it was a misunderstanding—maybe they [the accused men] need training," and ALWAYS, ALWAYS asking me "why women don't report" (I wish I had a nickel . . .) and I would just look at them and say "Where have you been for the last 25 years?" "Why are you so surprised?" The reporting question is perennial (perhaps eternal), because it places the responsibility in exactly the wrong place and most people are happy to have it that way.

From the absence of a clear reporting option to the flawed investigation, the Senate Judiciary Committee's process in the Kavanaugh hearing was designed to create a "he said/she said" scenario and to avoid the work of getting to the truth about Ford's complaint. Absent a change in the procedures, one can only assume that the committee is content for an accuser who steps up in the future to shoulder what should be the committee's responsibility—bringing the facts to light.

BACKLASH

The author Susan Faludi warned women of the mounting "backlash" against gender equality in the 1980s in her 1991 bestselling book of the same name. After the Thomas confirmation hearing and the passage of the Civil Rights Act of 1991, the counterattack manifested itself through broad vocal cultural pushback as well as reduced legal protections that aided the institutionalization of policies and tactics proposed as pro-business but that disadvantaged women workers, just as their numbers were increasing. Commenting in 2020 for an interview published in *Signs*, Faludi compared the 1980s tone of backlash that she described in her book with more recent antifeminist expressions. "The backlash of the eighties was far more subtle, undercover in some respects," she wrote. "Its central tool was the propagation of the myth that it was *feminism* itself that was making women unhappy—that women's newfound feminist independence and liberation was cheating them of love, marriage, children, mental health. Looking back at the introduction of *Backlash*, I see that I wrote, 'The force and furor of the backlash churn beneath the surface, largely invisible to the public eye.' Not anymore. The gloves are off now. Which at least makes the backlash easier to see, if no less painful."[32]

And the blowback, gaslighting, and silencing of survivors and victims injure all women and deliberately negate our value to society. On

March 8, 2019, International Women's Day, Gallup reported that "a record-low 59% of all Americans in 2018 said women in their country are treated with respect and dignity, but less than half (48%) of those who identified as women currently feel they are treated with respect." The study found that feeling respected is tied to women's feelings of being safe in their communities, which is intrinsically tied to gender equity.[33] All too easily, that disrespect turns into physical peril, as well as social and political vulnerability.

Ironically, the same internet technology that facilitated organizing and publicizing the 2017 social movement against gender violence is being used to undermine that very movement. Social media has become a tool for harassing and bullying—a weapon of resistance to gender advancements. The growth in online assaults when women make gains or show their disagreement with gender inequalities suggests that online behavior is a counterattack to progress. The ubiquity and convenience of technology in our lives give it a certain cover that to date has made it difficult to regulate. Some platforms ensure bullies anonymity and the freedom to act outside normal social constraints and norms with impunity, and the instant amplification of a derogatory message can be devastating to its target; "going viral" can be as toxic as its name implies. Cyberbullying of youth by other youth is a growing problem. Inappropriate behavior that began in chat rooms in the early years of the twenty-first century has expanded as young people are drawn to social media and video sharing. Nearly 34 percent of middle and high schoolers say they have been cyberbullied, including instances of stalking, blackmail, and sexual extortion. Middle and high school girls are often the targets of sexual harassment in the form of cyberbullying, and LGBTQ+ students are at a higher risk of cyberbullying and harassment because of their gender or sexual identity.[34] The technology that enables abuse also makes it hard and in many cases impossible to trace it to its source, which hampers intervention. And the lack of consequences fuels use of the technology and more abuse.

Technology-enabled abuse is not limited to schools. The digital revolution has made its way into the workplace, where computers are common equipment, and pornographic images, including privately produced revenge porn and commercially produced porn, are regularly shared with co-workers, individually and in groups. Experts estimate that 60 percent of employees have viewed pornography during daytime business hours. And though employers have recently started investing in programs aimed at retaining and developing talented women, that investment may be lost if women who are recruited leave because their managers or others routinely make them uncomfortable by consuming pornography in offices and other business settings.[35]

Outside the workplace, the internet is used to target and troll women and incite others to pile on. Just five months after the #MeToo awakening, according to Amnesty International, the freedoms women have gained are being undermined by online, often anonymous harassment. The human rights organization noted the enormity of the harassment that women experience on Twitter.[36] One in every fifteen tweets directed at women are abusive and include threats of doxing, hacking, and violent rape. And race plays a role as well. Black women are 84 percent more likely to receive abuse than White women, while Asian women are 70 percent more likely to be the target of racist or ethnic slurs.[37]

Like other forms of gender violence, internet violence is not entirely about a single comment or tweet; it's about how the persistent, intentional torment many women experience online diminishes, angers, and threatens their sense of security. This environment leads some women to leave social media altogether, fearing that sharing details about their lives or views might make them increasingly vulnerable to slurs or threats of physical and sexual violence. Take, for example, Gamergate, best described as a barrage of vicious online attacks, including rape and death threats, waged largely against women and people of color who argued for greater inclusion in the gaming industry. Set off in 2014 as a hashtag campaign, Gamergate posts continued for months. In 2016, the actress Leslie Jones took a hiatus from Twitter after experiencing relentless racist and sexist trolling. In an interview on National Public Radio's *All Things Considered*, Tanya O'Carroll, director of Amnesty Tech, summed up the risk to women's equality this way: "Really, anytime a woman has the audacity to hold an opinion and express it in a proud or confident way online, they may become victim to a backlash and potentially an orchestrated backlash. . . . When we talk about this issue and think about the freedom of expression consequences, it's really important to realize whose freedom of expression are we prioritizing."[38]

SUSTAINING

For all the excitement in 2017 that the issue was finally on the agenda and for all the gains in the number and diversity of women elected in 2018, even with the record-high number of women candidates who ran for president a year later, the 2020 presidential election campaigns were, to the disappointment of many, practically devoid of any serious candidate attention to the #MeToo reckoning. Tara Reade's charge that the presumptive Democratic presidential nominee, Joe Biden, assaulted her spotlights the fact that failing to fully reckon with accusations of sexual assault can have consequences even decades later, for both the accusers and those accused. Reade's options for filing a complaint in 1993, when she says the attack occurred, were limited. Without a reliable and trustworthy system for reporting claims of sexual assault against men in powerful positions, the public is left to figure out the truth on its own. This was the case with the charges Reade raised against Biden, and it was true in 2018 when Ford charged Kavanaugh with sexually assaulting her when they were teenagers. We can't go back in time with either case. But given the significance of the moment in deciding the leadership of our country and the seriousness of her allegations, an investigation into Reade's charges was called for. We shouldn't wait until there is another claim against a candidate or a nominee to think through how they should be handled. And the proliferation of false and unsubstantiated information on the internet makes reliable, formal channels for reporting abuse more important than ever.

Inquiry into charges should have been neutral, thorough, and evenly applied to outstanding claims of sexual misconduct against both Biden and Trump. Had there been such an investigation, the findings should have been made available to the public. Because a complete inquiry that included a documented complaint process and full investigation never took place, uncertainty about whom to believe and whether it matters has continued. In the future, when claims against a candidate arise, how we proceed comes down to whether we take allegations of sexual violations seriously enough to insist that public institutions have fair procedures in place to protect the rights both of individuals to come forward and of the accused to defend themselves. Transparency in the process would boost public knowledge and enable us to make informed decisions about the men—because, so far, it's always been men—we elect to lead our country. Waiting until the next claim of this nature arises risks putting the parties involved through hastily designed procedures and the country through the uncertainty of speculation about who is telling the truth. Our failure to put structures in place is a signal to the public that we don't take the claims seriously.

The problem of nonexistent or inadequate ways to raise complaints isn't limited to the presidential race or to public institutions. Bolstered by the Supreme Court in cases like *Vance v. Ball State* (discussed in chapter 3) and the *Gilmer* decision, employers have developed tactics to resist accountability for a range of workplace abuses. In 1991 mandated arbitration was rarely included in employment contracts. Today 56 percent of all employees are required to settle claims against their employers through arbitration procedures that a 2018 Economic Policy Institute report finds "overwhelmingly favor employers."[39]

Today, the use of nondisclosure agreements as an offensive weapon is well established and well-known. Actresses who accused the media producer Harvey Weinstein of sexual assault and received settlements were bound by NDAs. Settlements allow victims to avoid the public attacks that typically occur when women openly complain about sexual assault and harassment. However, NDAs force them to remain silent or forfeit the settlements even when the behavior that occurred was serious enough to warrant a criminal charge. By allowing individual claims to be hidden, such agreements enable serial abuse and undermine public safety. And, with victims sworn to secrecy, we can never know for certain just how many offenders and offenses have occurred. These agreements, along with the limitations on class-action lawsuits established by the Supreme Court's decision in *Wal-Mart Stores Inc. v. Dukes*, make it more difficult, time-consuming, and costly to address systemic problems within organizations.

It's hard to imagine policy makers taking a tough stance on private sector abuses when they ignore the problems of gender violence and its prevalence within the government. Accountability in Washington is the only way to shore up the integrity of our democracy. So our political leaders must clean their own houses even as they pursue the aggressive measures needed to protect victims and survivors throughout our country's workforces.

And we should never underestimate the coalition, fueled by ex-president Trump, whose venomous antiwoman ideology has not been denounced by Republican leaders. I am certain that behind the plot to kidnap the Michigan governor Gretchen Whitmer was antagonism to women's leadership. Not only is the governor a woman, but so are the state's secretary of state and attorney general. The insurgent attempt to undermine the election results is an indication of just how far White nationalists, neo-Nazis, and others who dangle gender violence as a lure will go to achieve their vision of what makes the United States great. We have yet to learn what pull they will have on policy makers who rely on their outlandish vocal support and energy. As we wake up to the very real threat we face, my hope is that organizers, advocates, and elected officials will hone their anger toward passing legislation aimed at ending gender-based violence, as well as increasing women's power to change policy.

Will our leaders continue to deny our political value and ignore the challenges to it? Despite the lack of sustained progress and even in the face of the harsh backlash Faludi described, Fitzgerald is philosophical about the past three decades. But that doesn't temper her rage. Reflecting on the past thirty years, from when she tried to educate the Senate Judiciary Committee at the Thomas hearings to today, she admits that she still does not know all the answers. But her rage has provided her with clarity about the solutions necessary to end sexual harassment. As Fitzgerald explained in an email to me,

The Civil Rights Act of 1991 let Congress off the hook for doing anything meaningful; women had better opportunities to pursue individual remedies but there was no sustained government or policy initiatives at the societal level, no "official" office that was responsible for ongoing education and progress. It was treated as an individual problem—not a social issue . . . the distinction Mill [the nineteenth-century philosopher and ethicist John Stuart Mill] makes between a private trouble and a public issue . . . and that will never be effective. As long as harassment is an individual problem, then society has no responsibility to prevent or solve it. It's like getting run over by a truck—bad luck, true, tragic even—but essentially a private event. To this day people do not understand that this is a systemic issue involving power, privilege, and vulnerability—we still treat it as if it's just some dirty old man indulging his salacious interests.

And of course, those with the power and privilege have an interest, conscious or implicit, to privatize the problem and the solution, rather than institutionalizing women's voices and interests.

In 1991, Cindi Leive was an editorial assistant at *Glamour* magazine, rising through the publishing ranks under the tutelage of *Glamour*'s legendary editor in chief Ruth Whitney, who revolutionized the magazine by publishing articles about women's sexuality and political power. In 1968, Ruth was the first fashion magazine editor to put a Black model on the cover. In 2001, when Leive took on the job as *Glamour*'s editor in chief, she followed in Whitney's footsteps and then some, growing the magazine's circulation and doubling down on the publication's focus on women's significant contributions to the world. When I asked Leive why progress stalled, she pointed to male dominance as the reason the road to eliminating gender violence has been tortuous and incremental:

Bias toward masculinity is such a huge sprawling system built all around us (and, alas, within us) that no one incident or moment—no matter how powerful or enraging—could possibly take it down. The hearings illuminated the problem, vividly and unforgettably. But they happened at a moment when women were still so vastly outnumbered in positions of power—despite a vague public impression that we'd come a long way, baby—that the structural changes needed to make change stick were impossible to come by fast. How are you going to rebuild a whole house just by shining a flashlight into one dirty corner, especially when the contractors on the job are the guys who built it wrong in the first place?

Though Leive's question is rhetorical, it begs for an answer. In fact, sustainable change for a systemic problem is possible only when you shine a light on the variants of the problem and the colossal number of systems it infests. Doing so gives reasonable people a reason to be angry. And we *should* be enraged by our culture and systems that pass gender-based violence onto our children like some cruel inheritance. That our leaders, in public and private institutions, fail to see the personal and systemic harm of gender-based violence should infuriate us. The seeming indifference to passing the problem of gender violence from generation to generation is maddening, as is our continued devaluation of women that serves as an excuse for why little can be— but should be—done to end the violence and achieve gender equity. And our rage must also be directed to the racism and false masculinity that layer onto misogyny and justify violence.

Is the anger that lingers enough to support the revolution that Rebecca Traister imagines? Will the "dissatisfactions and resentments of

America's women" ignite a reinvigorated and sustained movement demanding progress and social change? In 2019, Cecile Richards, the former president of Planned Parenthood and a founder of a PAC that seeks to tap into women's political power, expressed concern that the political energy from the 2017 Women's March on Washington might not last. "My nightmare would be waking up 10 years from now and going, 'That march, that was so great, but you know, like, what happened?'"[40] What Richards pointed out is the difference between resistance and a purposeful use of resistant energy.

Will the anger be galvanizing? Will embracing it "help us build the world we want to see," as Brittney Cooper urges?[41] How do we evolve systems built on a mentality that gender-based violence is "not so bad" to systems that demand that gender-based violence end? Ad hoc anger alone won't suffice. Our attention to the problem must be unceasing. Progress depends on our combined outrage, clear thinking, willingness to demand more, and hard work to achieve it.

To borrow from the civil rights leader Ella Baker: we who believe in freedom and equality and justice cannot rest until they come. But as an unrepentant believer in our right to live without gender violence who has benefited from the wisdom of others who are like-minded, I know that leaders in politics, business, education, and culture must also believe that a world free from gender violence is worth pursuing. With leadership comes the responsibility to fix problems. If the United States is to continue to claim its existence as a country founded on freedom, equality, and justice, our political leaders must squarely address gender-based violence, one of our country's biggest problems.

TEN

Accountability

W hat presidential candidate will best address the question of sexual harassment against women?"

During the presidential primary season in 1992, at the end of a program, the organizer handed me a note card with this question written on it. I never saw who wrote the note or had the chance to respond. But the writer's awareness that we need a president to lead the fight against sexual harassment stuck with me. Bill Clinton became the nominee and won the election that year. And given the fallout from the Thomas hearings, many who voted for him assumed that he would take a stand against sexual harassment. Indeed, two years after being elected, Clinton signed the Violence Against Women Act into law. But in time, stories about his sexual behavior in the past and during his time as president emerged and led to his impeachment. Clinton squandered any credibility he had to lead the fight against harassment and sexual assault. Today, after filling the White House with men who did nothing or not nearly enough to address gender-based violence and one who made it seem insignificant, we're still waiting for a president who will lead an anti–gender-violence agenda. What does the job require? At the very least it takes someone who is willing to do difficult, often politically courageous work to identify abusers; who will take action to hold offenders accountable; and who will commit to preventing the violence from reoccurring. But these steps only begin the job of altering noxious behavior. In fact, challenging the culture that underpins gender-based violence and overhauling systems that have bias baked into them is the hard work.

In March 2019, I sat in a hotel room in Houston, Texas, waiting for a conversation that was nearly twenty-eight years in the making. The apology that in December 2017 Joe Biden told a journalist he owed me was about to happen—maybe. For more than a year, as other journalists asked Biden whether he had reached out to me, Chuck and I played a game. Each time the doorbell rang unexpectedly at our home in Massachusetts, we would race each other to be the first to ask, "Could that be Joe Biden coming to apologize in person?" It was our way of making light of what had become an absurd standoff. In December 2017, he could have immediately said "I'm sorry" rather than wait until weeks before announcing that he was running for president. He could have spared us both months of drama.

From my twenty-fourth-floor room, as my eyes stretched across the Houston skyline, my expectations were pretty low. I was anxious and wanted a witness, but Chuck had stepped out of the room. The phone finally rang, and for thirty minutes the former vice president and I spoke. Mostly Biden talked and I listened. He shared his regret for what I'd gone through and expressed his admiration for what I'd done to change the culture around sexual harassment in this country. His words were carefully couched, though seemed sincere. But one thing struck me. He never mentioned what the *country* went through with the hearing. Yes, I suffered threats and insults during the hearing and immediately after I returned home. To this day I remain numb to offensive voice-mail messages left on my office phone. Yes, I live with the occasional misogynist, racist rant even today. I have come to expect them. But I'm not the only one who suffered from the hearing that Biden chaired in 1991. I daresay millions agonized as they viewed it. For thirty years in public and private, women have come to me in tears recalling that debacle. Men have expressed the disillusionment they felt for themselves and on behalf of their sisters, daughters, and wives. Surely, he had heard from people whose spirits and faith in our democracy were broken as they watched. They too were entitled to some expression of Biden's remorse.

Biden had started to remind me about his work to address gender violence when Chuck entered the room. The former vice president considered the Violence Against Women Act one of his signature legislative achievements. He spoke with pride about his work with the White House Council on Women and Girls. Near the end of his time in the Obama administration, Biden was front and center in the It's on Us campaign to end sexual assault on college campuses. In an op-ed carried by campus newspapers across the country, he wrote, "It is abundantly clear that we still live in a culture in which violence against women is allowed—even encouraged—to persist."[1] All are noteworthy efforts that have empowered victims and survivors and ultimately made them safer. But as we spoke, both Biden and I knew that the Supreme Court's effective gutting of VAWA's protections had gone unaddressed and that the number of assaults on campuses had continued to climb.

"More work is needed," I said. "Your past work uniquely positions you to make a difference." Though I encouraged him to see ending gender-based violence as his calling, I'm not sure he heard me.

Fortunately, I wasn't emotionally invested in a Biden apology. Women are often told to accept an apology for bad and even brutal behavior for their own healing. For twenty-eight years, I went through a process of repairing the harm done to me by the hearing. I did so by learning about sexual harassment and reflecting on the Judiciary Committee's hostility to my testimony. Understanding that the problem was bigger than sexual harassment and much bigger than me gave me purpose and also helped me heal. Looking back on it, a line from a gospel song I heard many times as a child stands out: "I wouldn't take nothing for my journey now." For three decades, I've had the benefit of learning from advocates who are championing the causes of gender-violence victims through nearly impermeable criminal and civil court processes or workplace, educational, housing, social service, and financial systems. I've heard from people in red states and blue states about the importance of laws and resources where they live that center on victims' needs. Researchers and activists remind me that for meaningful solutions we need more information about each of the behaviors involved in gender violence to help us understand the complexity of the whole. Most important, I've had the privilege of hearing from survivors who have somehow found their way through agonizing abuse and failed response structures, and I've heard from victims, still struggling, who would be survivors if they could just get the empathetic support they need. I am so very sorry for the pain that the hearing put my family, friends, and many others through, and that I cannot assist all the people who come to me for help. I show my remorse by trying to prevent others from becoming victims. But I would not change my decision to testify. For the past thirty years, this has been my journey, and I expect it to continue in some fashion for the rest of my life.

The public has come to expect politicians to apologize for their blunders, but very rarely are we satisfied with what they say, in part because the "apologies" don't provide any fixes for the troubles they cause. When behavior, intentional or not, has negative, life-changing consequences for masses of people, mere words are not enough. I was very serious when I suggested that Biden take up the cause of solving the problem. We should expect the people in power to do all they can to ensure that the behavior doesn't recur. I hold myself and my actions to this standard. Any candidate for president of the United States needed to come up with a plan to address the crisis of gender-based violence. I wanted leadership and accountability—someone who would pledge to confront gender-based violence as an enormous existential threat to the health and social, political, and economic well-being of its victims and the country.

I have always remembered the question posed to me in 1992, but it has expanded in my mind to include all forms of violence toward women. Every four years, I will ask, "What presidential candidate will best address gender-based violence?" The answer lies, in part, in a candidate who understands and communicates how gender violence does irreparable damage to individuals and their families and how it burdens communities. The best candidate is the one who believes so much in equality that he or she is willing to take bold action to tackle a complex scourge that is deeply embedded in our culture and systems. I want someone who is ready to say, "Because I believe in equality, I'm willing to stake my political career on ending gender-based violence and commit to putting together the plan for doing just that." The question doesn't change and neither do the qualifications.

When Biden left office at the end of the Obama administration, he took on the challenge of curing cancer. He announced his candidacy for president with the pledge that if he was elected, America "was gonna cure cancer." Understandably, some cancer researchers were incredulous. After all, curing cancer is not that simple. Cancer is more than one disease, they said, so a claim to cure all cancer could not be credible. But in August 2020, when I told CNN's Gloria Borger that I would vote for Biden for president, I wasn't simply voting against Trump. I was thinking about Biden's pledge to end cancer. It was a bold promise and gave me hope that he would see gender-based violence as a similar crisis worthy of a similar commitment from the most powerful man in the country and, some might argue, the world.

DUTY—AND DANGER

Gender-based violence is a public crisis and a national embarrassment that has cast a dark shadow over our government.

Three of the past five U.S. presidents have been accused of behavior ranging from rape to sexual assault and unwanted touching. To date there is no clear resolution of the charges against any of them because of failed systems for investigating and adjudicating complaints that would apply to sitting presidents or candidates. And with no clear independent processes in place, deciding the fate of the person who is likely to be the nation's leader too often comes down to politics.

Two current Supreme Court justices accused of sexual assault and harassment were seated following shockingly inept confirmation hearings. A substantial number believe that both justices lied under oath and that getting justice in the highest court in the country has been compromised. The proceedings themselves were a stain on the judiciary in this country, which prides itself on fairness in the way our trials and hearings are conducted.

From 1995 to 2018, congressional staff and visitors have filed an unknown number of complaints against U.S. congressmen and senators, some that have resulted in the finding of violations. But we may never know exactly who or how many or what they cost the taxpayer because the system that policy makers voted for in 1995 that was supposed to hold elected officials accountable for sexual misconduct kept the payments away from the prying eyes of the public that was footing the bill. The reforms to the 1995 law put into place in 2018 didn't provide adequate protections against retaliation to ensure that people will come forward.

Military scandals involving sexual harassment and assault, intimate partner violence, rape, and death—the latest of which involve deaths of uniformed service members at Fort Hood—happen with such frequency that they are all but predictable. Military leaders concede that the systems in place across the Defense Department are inadequate. Yet reforms don't improve the situation. These atrocities deplete troops' morale, thereby threatening our national security and discouraging new enlistments.

And the U.S. Commission on Civil Rights' grim findings about sexual harassment in federal agencies are disheartening but telling. In 2020 the commission majority found the following:

- widely prevalent workplace sexual harassment in the federal government (a federal survey estimated one in seven federal employees experienced sexually harassing behaviors at work between 2016 and 2018);

- structural power imbalances and gender disparities that are strongly predictive of workplace sexual harassment;
- a dearth of publicly available data on the frequency of harassment;
- a widespread fear of retaliation among victims of sexual harassment for reporting misconduct;
- fewer workplace protections for federal employees compared with private sector workers due to antiquated laws; and
- lower caps on monetary damages in sexual harassment lawsuits for federal employees, which can discourage victims from risking their careers and reputations to seek redress and deter attorneys from taking their cases.[2]

A number of federal agencies collect important data on various forms of gender violence, but as the Commission on Civil Rights reports, gaps in information exist within the federal workforce. Our count of the abuses that exist in the country's K–12 schools are incomplete, as is information on how abusive behavior affects learning. We do know that in elementary and secondary schools across the country a range of gender-based violence is happening, including bullying, sexual assault, rape, sexual harassment, unwanted sexting, and sex trafficking. Just how much happens and how much damage it causes are unknowns that need to be addressed in order to fix accountability.

The government at every level and every branch has a massive amount of work to do in order to set the tone for the millions of workers affected by gender-based violence, including those in the private sector and individuals in schools and communities throughout the country, and especially those who engage local law enforcement to report gender-based violence.

The evidence of systemic failures is reflected in the countless civil complaint filings by survivors of all ages and racial, sexual, ethnic, and economic identities that drag on for decades before being resolved in the courts. And even when a case is closed, sometimes the behavior persists and is passed on to the next generation of workers, notwithstanding court orders to eliminate clear violations of the law.

The magnitude of gender-motivated violence is reflected in the stacks of memoirs, newspaper and magazine articles, and social media posts about bullying, harassment, assault, gender policing, rape, and murder happening in public and private spaces, including in homes, in schools, in workplaces, and on streets. Recent high-profile trafficking and assault prosecutions of individuals who have engaged in violent, abusive behavior for decades suggest how easily trafficking can continue under the radar.

Meanwhile, gender-based violence imperils our country's health, safety, economic security, housing, transportation, and educational opportunities. It puts at risk our national security, as well as our social and political standing within this country and around the globe, and it reduces our ability to credibly advocate for human rights and gender equality.

DELIBERATE AND INTENTIONAL ACTION

A few years after I arrived in Boston and settled into my position at Brandeis, I knew I needed to know more than the law if I wanted to effect change. My focus at the time was on race discrimination and the role that federal funding played in locking in the disadvantages that arose from racism, such as funding roads and transportation systems

that benefited suburbs where homeowners and real estate agents practiced overt and covert racial discrimination. I wrote a short paper on
an idea that I called "racial impact analysis," which proposed a requirement that locally based federally funded projects be analyzed for their
impact on underrepresented groups and/or communities of color before the funding commitment could be secured. The analysis required
gathering social and economic data on what the funding would provide
for the locations and who demographically would benefit from it in
terms of housing, jobs, and other services. By requiring that the impact
analysis reports be made available to the public, my approach also called
for more transparency in how projects were funded. I presented the idea
to a colleague (now a former colleague) who I naively thought would
be sympathetic to the proposal. His reaction stunned me. He argued
that such an idea would succeed only if I removed any reference to
race in the plan. He explained his belief that "a race-neutral approach
is the only way to address racism."

I continued to pursue the idea. I spoke with Alan Jenkins about it.
He had worked in the Clinton administration with the federal government and was at the Ford Foundation, which had started to ask its grant
applicants for information about demographics to make sure the benefits were shared equitably across identities. A few years passed, and
our conversations continued after Jenkins left Ford to become the executive director of the Opportunity Agenda, an organization dedicated
to driving lasting policy and culture change through communication
strategies and community engagement.[3] Jenkins worked on the Opportunity Agenda's version of the concept, which the Department of Housing and Urban Development adopted during the Obama administration.
The Opportunity Agenda was also training others outside its organization to do the analysis. The process showed how collecting informa-

tion that illustrates inequalities and applying it to correct practices and policies built on racist misinformation and disinformation can lead to systemic change.

I put my own impact analysis on hold to focus on other projects but never gave up on it. Today, as I look back on the cool reception I got for the idea, in addition to being struck by my colleague's eagerness for a race-neutral solution to remedy racism, I also realize the root of my instinct to resist his thinking. His was a simple approach to a complex problem. Eliminating race from the analysis equation was his way of avoiding dealing with the messy problem of racism—pretending that race didn't matter, that only class mattered. In doing so, he was also making it easier for racism to continue.

After the senseless and brutal deaths of Breonna Taylor and George Floyd in the first half of 2020, the Black Lives Matter movement finally forced us to open our eyes to the fact that individual claims of not being racist are not enough. To prevent the violence that ended Taylor's and Floyd's lives, we must understand that racism has been built into our perceptions, culture, and systems. In order to eliminate it, we must act in ways that are deliberately antiracist, an approach developed by Ibram X. Kendi that has generated new thinking about racism and how to end it. We've learned that the need to become antiracist is especially urgent as a way to end violence supported by state action whether from our police, the courts, or legislators. All of these systems must perform in ways that are intentionally antiracist.

This is also true for gender-based violence. It's not enough to say that we don't discriminate against women. We must dig deeper and become *anti*-gender-based violence. No longer is it acceptable to say we don't know the facts, but we're going to make decisions without them, or throw up our hands in surrender to the old "he said, she said" excuse for doing nothing. Now I think of how impact analysis can address gender-based violence. Collecting information about how gender-based violence is experienced and analyzing it with the goal of ending it are not only possible; they are indispensable to solving the problem. Moreover, ignoring the biased, misogynist, and antiwoman roots of the problem will only provide cover for the abuse. In her dissent in the *Vance* case, Justice Ginsburg exposed how her colleagues' focus on the "gender neutral" question of what constituted a supervisor made it possible for egregious workplace abuses and lax corporate accountability to continue. The decision can be corrected by legislation, which seems to be the only way to stop the Court's conservative majority from proceeding with the "immoderate and unrestrained course to corral Title VII" that Ginsburg warned of. But only legislation that is fact based and intentionally opposed to gender-based violence will correct that course. Yet it's not too much to imagine a time when the dissent becomes the majority and the miserly approach to protecting against harassment is reversed, when we will have judges, like Spottswood Robinson, who believe that the purpose of civil rights laws is to expand protections against workplace rules that arise from misogyny and prejudice.

In the same vein, Congress should pass legislation to amend the Violence Against Women Act to correct the mistakes of *United States v. Morrison*. The idea that violence against women has no impact on the commerce and the health of this nation has no basis in reality. Framing and passing a law that would essentially overturn the Supreme Court's decision may be a heavier lift, but it has the potential for monumental impact. And having a federal right to be free from crimes of violence motivated by gender as the law intended should be fundamental to our thinking about what equality means.

We are now in a period of reckoning about gender-based violence.

It hasn't penetrated our political or legal systems, but I believe that, like never before, the public is poised to embrace it. We should not let this moment pass. A true reckoning will force us to face the inconvenient truth about how we have coddled and encouraged gender violence. As a society, we need a sea change in our thinking about this persistent problem. It isn't the "not so bad" behavior that's happening to someone else. It's happening to our family members, friends, coworkers, and neighbors. It's happening to our children and not because "boys will be boys" but because in many cases we haven't taken the problem seriously enough to see the harm. Even when strangers are its victims, gender violence hurts all of us. The harm is not something that we can leave to our intuition to resolve. Many of our instincts about the problem are tainted by misogyny and our historic subjugation of women and attenuation of women's worth. Our public processes and legal proceedings as well as policies within workplaces and schools should be grounded in facts used to define the depth of the problem, solutions to it, and consequences for the violations, not "he said, she said" dismissals. We need to understand that a political agenda that relies on the suppression of more than half of the population is a threat to our democracy, no matter whose political career is at stake.

But most of all, we need to collectively hear and see victims and survivors as central to any solutions we imagine. That means we must consider that not all victims are the same and that there is no "perfect" victim. In order to find victim-centered solutions to gender-based violence, we will need to address racism, including the vestiges of colonialism and slavery, along with homophobia, misogyny, and gender bias. There must be accountability for harm whether found in transitional or transformative justice or through a reformed criminal justice system. For this, I ask myself and others, as a country where nearly one out of every one hundred persons is in federal, state, or local jails, is putting more people in jail the sole solution to gender-based violence? The answer is no. But I believe that a reformed legal system must honor victims' decisions to file criminal complaints and we must honor the right of the accused to due process, both of which we have failed to do in far too many cases, especially involving people of color. The above are difficult but critical challenges we as a society must confront to achieve a systemic solution to gender-based violence. But we can start by believing that a systemic, cultural reckoning is called for and that victims and survivors and the rest of society will be better off for it.

Finally, we must hold ourselves accountable as individuals. And as individuals we have choices. We can and should choose not to engage in abusive behavior, whether bullying or rape or all the behaviors in between. Each of us must believe that our behavior matters and that we can bring about measurable change, small and large.

One of the most gratifying experiences on my journey happened in 2020. A group of sexual violence survivors convened to develop the Survivors' Agenda, a community-driven guide toward the survivor justice that "those who have navigated sexual abuse and other forms of sexual violence" deserve. They asserted that ignoring or erasing the fact of gender violence from victims' and survivors' experiences denied their inherent power and resilience. They called for the passage of specific policies and an approach to systemic change that is survivor centered and led. They have experienced the toll that limited economic and employment opportunities can take on their lives, making them more vulnerable to harassment in the workplace and to physical violence and financial exploitation at home. They've seen and lived with housing, transportation, and educational insecurity as well as homelessness as the result of intimate partner violence. Gender identity, ethnicity, sexual identity, immigration status, and race have increased survivors' and victims' risk of gender-based violence and threatened the well-being of their communities. To solve gender-based violence as they see it, all of these factors and more must be incorporated into new laws and considered when money gets funneled to housing, education, transportation, and employment systems and support.

For any of this to be possible, we need leadership that holds itself accountable to end gender-based violence. On January 20, 2021, Biden issued a memorandum to the heads of executive departments and agencies with direction that the goal of regulatory reviews in his administration will be to promote "public health and safety, economic growth, social welfare, racial justice, environmental stewardship, human dignity, equity, and the interests of future generations." Ending gender-based violence should be included on the list. Biden has also issued an executive order to advance racial justice and equity for underserved communities. And key to the well-being of underserved communities are the concerns of trans and nonbinary people and women of color to be free from gender-based violence. All of the factors listed in these two executive actions are known to be imperiled by gender violence. And eliminating gender-based violence can contribute to all the public interests on Biden's lists. But in addition to an anti-gender-based violence approach to reviewing policies and existing initiatives, Biden should be demanding that departments and agencies engage survivors or victims and their advocates to develop new initiatives deliberately aimed at ending violence or healing the harm it causes.

Finally, to show his intentionality, the president should elevate the urgency of this issue to the status it deserves by appointing a coordinator to work with the departments and the public and to report directly to him. We need a president and leaders throughout the country who believe it's possible to end gender-based violence and who act in ways that reflect that belief. Biden might be tempted to appoint a gender violence czar or perhaps czarina. But I hope he resists this approach. Titles matter. More than force, this job demands equal amounts of compassion, depth of wisdom, knowledge about culture, and the power and patience to engineer systemic change. The job title should match this description.

As for me, my journey has brought me to the point of believing unequivocally that victims are truthful; that their lives have value; that ending gender-based violence is the only way to achieve true equality, across all identities; that each of us has a role to play in making our world safe for everyone; and that together we can end gender violence.

ACKNOWLEDGMENTS

I thank my agent, Wes Neff, of the Leigh Bureau, who was the first to believe that I could capture the story of gender-motivated violence in America. Wes patiently stuck with me as I worked to get the ideas behind the book right and has since championed *Believing* at each step of its development. Thank you to Joy Johannessen for her thoughtful and skillful treatment of my unpolished proposal for *Believing*. Joy's editing helped me imagine the potential for the book and find the right language to express that potential.

I am grateful to the team at Viking for believing that America is ready for a conversation about the whole of gender-based violence and for believing that I could make a meaningful contribution to it. My gifted editor, Wendy Wolf, was a model of wisdom and patience. Her skillful guidance enabled me to shape the many, varied reasons that I see gender violence as a public crisis into a book that addresses it. I'm grateful to Wendy for bringing together a creative group of people to work on *Believing*. Many thanks to Terezia Cicel, Jason Ramirez, Claire Vaccaro, and Ingrid Sterner for their exceptional contributions.

Concepción de León's careful reading of the manuscript, her smart edits, and her calls for clarity along with her awareness about the ways her generation sees gender violence were invaluable.

I thank all of the brave souls who have shared their stories of abuse publicly and privately. For each victim and survivor, those who have spoken and those who remain silent, I hope this book affirms and comforts you.

The wisdom of many thought leaders and thought partners rings in my ears every time I feel the enormity of the issues we face in the world or I am frustrated by the lack of progress toward equity. I benefited greatly from their astute, challenging, and, when needed, calming perceptions, whether about how to improve the book or the state of the world.

I cannot say enough about the friends and colleagues who generously volunteered to read and comment on drafts of *Believing*. I am deeply indebted to each for their thoughtfully nuanced and shrewd insights, their suggested edits, and their belief in the cause, all of which greatly improved the manuscript structure and encouraged me to be a better communicator.

Thank you to my colleagues at Brandeis for supporting my work for more than two decades and who remind me of academia's responsibility to do work that speaks to the lives of those whom systems, processes, and policies have left unprotected from violence. Without the Brandeis community's encouragement of my untraditional career path, I could never have imagined *Believing*. The Ford Foundation and the Collective Future Fund have enabled engagement with my colleagues and students at Brandeis and with other scholars and advocates that have richly informed this book. Thank you to the leaders and staff of these organizations for your support and guidance. A number of fellow women law professors, former colleagues at the University of Oklahoma, and academics in other disciplines have reached out to me over the years with their support for my work and when I've faced public criticism. Through the years, my students at Brandeis and the University of Oklahoma have kept me connected to the insights and energy of Generations X through Z. And I salute Zeta Phi Beta Sorority, Incorporated, for welcoming me into a sisterhood that is dedicated to improving communities around the globe.

I am deeply appreciative of the team at the Hollywood Commission for the extraordinary work they do every day to make sure entertainment workers are safe and valued. They are resourceful, creative, and committed beyond imagination.

Several friends' belief in me made my journey to becoming an advocate for equality possible. For decades our relationships have endured through good times and bad. I owe you a special debt.

My sincere gratitude to all of the ministers and congregations who have offered me spiritual guidance throughout the years and reminded me of the higher calling of work that promotes social justice and ends human suffering.

I thank you all for the joy you've brought to my life!

NOTES

INTRODUCTION: BOILING THE OCEAN

1. U.S. Department of Health and Human Services, Family and Youth Services Bureau, Mission Statement, www.acf.hhs.gov/fysb/fact-sheet/domestic-violence-and-homeless ness-statistics-2016; Eleanor Lyon, Shannon Lane, and Anne Menard, *Meeting Survivors' Needs: A Multi-State Study of Domestic Violence Shelter Experiences*, National Institute of Justice, Oct. 2008, vawnet.org/sites/default/files/materials/files/2016-08/MeetingSurvi vorsNeeds-FullReport.pdf.
2. Study of the Secretary-General, "Ending Violence Against Women: From Words to Action," United Nations, Oct. 9, 2006, www.un.org/womenwatch/daw/vaw/launch/english /v.a.w-consequenceE-use.pdf.

CHAPTER 1: OUR STATE OF DENIAL

1. John Eligon, "Black Doctor Dies of Covid-19 After Complaining of Racist Treatment," *New York Times*, Dec. 23, 2020, www.nytimes.com/2020/12/23/us/susan-moore-black -doctor-indiana.html.
2. Dennis M. Murphy, "Directly Addressing the Issue of Racial Equity in Our Facilities," press release, Indiana University Health, Dec. 23, 2020, https://iuhealth.org/for-media /press-releases/directly-addressing-the-issue-of-racial-equity-in-our-facilities.
3. Claire Safran, "What Men Do to Women on the Job: A Shocking Look at Sexual Harassment," *Redbook*, Nov. 1976.
4. Claire Safran, "The Joint Redbook–Harvard Business Review Report: A Survey of 2,000 Executives: What Women at Work Say About Sex at Work," *Redbook*, March 1981.

5. Safran, "Joint Redbook–Harvard Business Review Report."

6. Marina Angel, "Sexual Harassment by Judges," *University of Miami Law Review* 45, no. 4 (1991): 817.

7. Angel, "Sexual Harassment by Judges."

8. "Federal Judge William Frey, 59, Settled Arizona Busing Dispute," *New York Times*, Feb. 19, 1979, timemachine.nytimes.com/timemachine/1979/02/18/112855315.html?page Number=40.

9. Shirley A. Wiegand, "Deception and Artifice: Thelma, Louise, and the Legal Hermeneutic," *Oklahoma City University Law Review* 22 (1997): 25.

10. Roxane Gay, *Not That Bad: Dispatches from Rape Culture* (New York: HarperCollins, 2018).

11. Angel, "Sexual Harassment by Judges."

12. Jane Mayer, "What Joe Biden Hasn't Owned Up to About Anita Hill," *New Yorker*, April 27, 2019, www.newyorker.com/news/news-desk/what-joe-biden-hasnt-owned-up-to-about-anita-hill.

CHAPTER 2: FROZEN

1. Joe Perticone, "Republicans Are Floating a Conspiracy That Chuck Schumer Plotted the Entire Kavanaugh Saga," *Business Insider*, Oct. 10, 2018, https://www.businessinsider.com/chuck-schumer-brett-kavanaugh-christine-ford-allegations-2018-10.

2. Mollie Hemingway and Carrie Severino, "The Left Savaged a Man's Reputation and America's Institutions—and Paid No Price for Its Indecency," July 14, 2019, *Wall Street Journal*, https://www.wsj.com/articles/kavanaugh-fight-was-no-win-11563136659.

3. Dahlia Lithwick, "In the Room Where It Happened," in *Believe Me: How Trusting Women Can Change the World*, edited by Jessica Valenti and Jaclyn Friedman (New York: Seal Press, 2020).

CHAPTER 3: A "RECURRENT FEATURE OF OUR SOCIAL EXPERIENCE"

1. U.S. Commission on Civil Rights, Briefing Report, *Federal #MeToo: Examining Sexual Harassment in Government Workplaces*, April 2020, www.usccr.gov/pubs/2020/04-01-Federal-Me-Too.pdf.

2. Nancy Gertner, "Sexual Harassment and the Bench," *Stanford Law Review Online* 71 (2018): 88, 96.

3. *Vance v. Ball State University*, 570 U.S. 421 (2013) (Ginsburg, J., dissenting).

4. Corey Rayburn Yung, "How to Lie with Rape Statistics: America's Hidden Rape Crisis," *Iowa Law Review* 99 (2014): 1197.

5. James Griffith, "The Sexual Harassment–Suicide Connection in the U.S. Military: Contextual Effects of Hostile Work Environment and Trusted Unit Leaders," *Suicide and Life-Threatening Behavior* 49, no. 1 (2019): 41–53.

6. Erika Beras, "Poll: Nearly Half of the Women Who Experienced Sexual Harassment Leave Their Jobs or Switch Careers," *Marketplace*, March 9, 2018, www.marketplace.org/2018/03/09/business/new-numbers-reflect-lasting-effects-workplace-harassment-women/.

7. Gillibrand et al. to Gene L. Dodaro, May 29, 2018, www.gillibrand.senate.gov/imo/media/doc/GAO%20Letter%205.29.18.pdf.

CHAPTER 4: THE MYTH OF THE WOKE GENERATION

1. Kim Parker, "Generation Z Looks a Lot Like Millennials on Key Social and Political Issues: Among Republicans, Gen Z Stands Out in Views on Race, Climate, and the Role of Government," Pew Research Center, Jan. 17, 2019, www.pewresearch.org/social-trends /2019/01/17/generation-z-looks-a-lot-like-millennials-on-key-social-and-political-issues/.

2. Barnes & Noble College Insights, "Conversations with Gen Z: Values & Beliefs," Oct. 11, 2018, next.bncollege.com/gen-z-students-values-beliefs/.

3. Holly Schroth, "Are You Ready for the Gen Z Workplace?," *California Management Review* 61, no. 3 (2019): 5–18, cmr.berkeley.edu/assets/documents/sample-articles/61-3-schroth .pdf.

4. Justin Patchin, "Tween Cyberbullying in the United States," Cyberbullying Research Center, Oct. 7, 2020, cyberbullying.org/tween-cyberbullying-in-the-united-states.

5. Sameer Hinduja, "Bullying, Cyberbullying, and Suicide Among U.S. Youth: Our Updated Research Findings," Cyberbullying Research Center, Aug. 27, 2018, cyberbullying.org /bullying-cyberbullying-suicide-among-us-youth.

6. Common Sense, "Social Lifesocial Media: 2018 Teens Reveal Their Experiences," p. 6, https://www.commonsensemedia.org/sites/default/files/uploads/research/2018_cs_social mediasociallife_fullreport-final-release_2_lowres.pdf.

7. Jo, May 1, 2008, comment on Tara Parker-Pope, "Sexual Harassment at School," *Well* (blog), *New York Times*, May 1, 2008, well.blogs.nytimes.com/2008/05/01/sexual-harass ment-at-school/.

8. "How Today's High School Cliques Compare to Yesterday's," *Science Daily*, www.science daily.com/releases/2019/01/190108125424.htm; Rowena Crabbe et al., *Journal of Adolescent Research* 34, no. 5 (Sept. 1, 2019): 563–96, published online Dec. 25, 2018; "High School Cliques Now Fall into 12 Categories, Study Shows," *Men's Health*, Jan. 9, 2019, www .menshealth.com/health/a25834640/12-types-of-high-school-cliques-new-study-finds/.

9. Jason Horowitz, "Mitt Romney's Prep School Classmates Recall Pranks, but also Troubling Incidents," *Washington Post*, May 12, 2012, www.washingtonpost.com/politics/mitt -romneys-prep-school-classmates-recall-pranks-but-also-troubling-incidents/2012/05 /10/gIQA3WOKFU_story.html.

10. Philip Rucker, "Mitt Romney Apologizes for High School Pranks That 'Might Have Gone Too Far,'" *Washington Post*, May 10, 2012, www.washingtonpost.com/politics/2012 /05/10/gIQAC3JhFU_story.html.

11. Bessel van der Kolk, *The Body Keeps the Score: Brain, Mind, and Body in the Healing of Trauma* (New York: Viking, 2014).

12. Dorothy L. Espelage et al., "Understanding Types, Locations, and Perpetrators of Peer-to-Peer Sexual Harassment in U.S. Middle Schools: A Focus on Sex, Racial, and Grade Differences," *Children and Youth Services Review* 71 (Dec. 2016): 174–83.

13. *Hill v. Cundiff*, 787 F.3d 948, 969 (11th Cir. 2015).

14. Email from Catherine Lhamon on file with author, Dec. 23, 2020.

15. Carrie Goldberg, *Nobody's Victim: Fighting Psychos, Stalkers, Pervs, and Trolls* (New York: Plume, 2019).

16. Email from Lhamon on file with author.

17. Van der Kolk, *The Body Keeps the Score: Brain, Mind, and Body in the Healing of Trauma*, p 2.

18. U.S. Department of Justice, Consent Decree, U.S. District Court for the State of Minnesota, *Jane Doe et al. and U.S. v. Anoka-Hennepin School District No. 11*, www.clearinghouse.net /chDocs/public/ED-MN-0001-0002.pdf.

19. Peter Eglin and Stephen Hester, "'You're All a Bunch of Feminists': Categorization and the Politics of Terror in the Montreal Massacre," *Human Studies* 22 (1999): 253–72, doi:10.1023/A:1005444602547.

20. Jess Bidgood, "Owen Labrie Gets Year in Jail for St. Paul's School Assault," *New York Times*, Oct. 29, 2015, www.nytimes.com/2015/10/30/us/owen-labrie-st-pauls-school-sen tencing.html.

CHAPTER 5: INSTITUTIONAL NEGLECT

1. Greg Garber, "It's Not All Fun and Games," ESPN, www.espn.com/otl/hazing/wednes day.html.

2. Tommy Beer, "NCAA Athletes Could Make $2 Million a Year if Paid Equitably, Study Suggests," *Forbes*, Sept. 1, 2020, www.forbes.com/sites/tommybeer/2020/09/01/ncaa-ath letes-could-make-2-million-a-year-if-paid-equitably-study-suggests/?sh=ba755675499f.

3. Beer, "NCAA Athletes Could Make $2 Million a Year if Paid Equitably."

4. *Report of the Independent Investigation, Sexual Abuse Commited by Dr. Richard Strauss at Ohio State University*, May 15, 2019, https://presspage-production-content.s3.amazonaws.com/up loads/2170/finalredactedstraussinvestigationreport-471531.pdf?10000.

5. Maddie Ellis, "UNC Suspends Recognition of Fraternities Named in Federal Drug Trafficking Investigation," *Daily Tar Heel*, Dec. 17, 2020, www.dailytarheel.com/article/2020 /12/unc-fraternities-named-in-connection-with-federal-drug-trafficking-investigation.

6. Nick Papandreou, "Papandreou: Committing to Change in the IFC," *Daily Northwestern*, Jan. 13, 2021, dailynorthwestern.com/2021/01/12/opinion/papandreou-committing-to -change-in-the-ifc/.

7. Tracy Connor and Sarah Fitzpatrick, "Gymnastics Scandal: 8 Times Larry Nassar Could Have Been Stopped," NBC News, Jan. 25, 2018, www.nbcnews.com/news/us-news/gym nastics-scandal-8-times-larry-nassar-could-have-been-stopped-n841091.

8. Tracy Connor and Rehema Ellis, "Michigan Police Department Apologizes for Doubting 2004 Larry Nassar Accuser," NBC News, Jan. 31, 2018, www.nbcnews.com/news/us -news/michigan-police-department-apologize-doubting-larry-nassar-accuser-n843126.

9. Connor and Fitzpatrick, "Gymnastics Scandal."

10. Joan McPhee and James P. Dowden, *Report of the Independent Investigation: The Constellation of Factors Underlying Larry Nassar's Abuse of Athletes*, Ropes & Gray, Dec. 10, 2018, Ropes-Gray -Full-Report.pdf.

11. McPhee and Dowden, *Report of the Independent Investigation*.

12. "President Simon Announces Resignation from MSU," Jan. 24, 2018, https://msu.edu/is sues-statements/2018-01-24-simon-resignation.

13. Anne E. Simon, "A Brief History of Alexander v. Yale," *Directions in Sexual Harassment Law*, edited by Catharine A. MacKinnon and Reva B. Siegel (New Haven, CT: Yale University Press, 2004).

14. Judith Lichtman, interview by Jana Singer, April 10 and 17 and May 5, 2006, and March 18, 2010, purl.stanford.edu/xy513yg7477.

15. Email from Philip Hart on file with author, October 13, 2014.

16. Molly Hite, "Sexual Harassment in the University Community, Initiatives; Special Issue: Sexual Harassment (Part 2)," *Journal of NAWADC* 52, no. 4, 1990.

17. Roger Ebert, review of *Oleanna*, RogerEbert.com, Nov. 4, 1994, www.rogerebert.com /reviews/oleanna-1994.

18. Peter Chiaramonte, "Power Play: The Dynamics of Power and Interpersonal Communication in Higher Education as Reflected in David Mamet's *Oleanna*," *Canadian Journal of Higher Education* 4, no. 1 (2014): 38–51.

19. Richard Badenhausen, "The Modern Academy Raging in the Dark: Misreading Mamet's Political Incorrectness in *Oleanna*," *College Literature* 25, no. 3 (Fall 1998): 1–19.

20. Joyce Kulhawik, "New Rep's 'Oleanna' Shows How Much Conversation on Sexual Harassment Hasn't Changed," WBUR, Oct. 23, 2017, www.wbur.org/artery/2017/10/23/new -rep-oleanna-review.

21. Kulhawik, "New Rep's 'Oleanna' Shows How Much Conversation on Sexual Harassment Hasn't Changed."

22. Email from Philip Hart on file with author, October 13, 2014.

23. Gray to Board of Governors, Information Theory Society, IEEE, June 12, 2018, ee.stanford.edu/~gray/ITS_BOG_letter.txt.

24. U. S. District Court for the District of New Jersey, Complaint and Jury Demand, *Verdu v. The Trustees of Princeton University*, https://law.justia.com/cases/federal/district-courts /new-jersey/njdce/3:2019cv12484/407298/31/

CHAPTER 6: THE MILLENNIAL WORKPLACE

1. Barbara J. Risman, "Good News! Attitudes Moving Toward Gender Equality," *Psychology Today*, Dec. 17, 2018, www.psychologytoday.com/us/blog/gender-questions/201812 /good-news-attitudes-moving-toward-gender-equality.

2. Risman, "Good News!"

3. Morley Safer, "The 'Millennials' Are Coming," *60 Minutes*, Nov. 8, 2007, www.cbsnews .com/news/the-millennials-are-coming/.

4. Kayla Patrick, Meika Berlan, and Morgan Harwood, "Low-Wage Jobs Held Primarily by Women Will Grow the Most over the Next Decade," National Women's Law Center, Aug. 2018, wlc.org/resources/jobs-largest-projected-growth-2012-2022-almost-half-are-low -wage-nearly-two-thirds-are-female-dominated/.

5. Ziati Meyer, "Amid McDonald's Strike, Fast-Food Workers Often Vulnerable to Sexual Harassment," *USA Today*, Sept. 8, 2018, www.usatoday.com/story/money/2018/09/18/age -few-options-make-fast-food-staff-vulnerable-sexual-harassment/1307263002/.

6. Brett Anderson, "John Besh Restaurants Fostered Culture of Sexual Harassment, 25 Women Say," *New Orleans Times-Picayune*, Oct. 21, 2017, www.nola.com/news/business /article_2b0d2515-ea21-5afd-92c1-5717ef7b81a8.html.

7. Yuki Noguchi, "Protests over Sexual Harassment at McDonald's Grow as Shareholders Meet," *All Things Considered*, NPR, May 23, 2019, www.npr.org/2019/05/23/726071587 /mcdonalds-protests-over-sexual-harassment-grow-as-shareholders-meet.

8. National Women's Law Center, "TIME'S UP Legal Defense Fund Provides Financial Support for Low-Wage Women Workers Filing Sexual Harassment Charges Against

McDonald's," press release, May 22, 2018, nwlc.org/press-releases/times-up-legal-defense-fund-provides-financial-support-for-low-wage-women-workers-filing-sexual-harassment-charges-against-mcdonalds/.

9. Katie Johnston, "Sexual Harassment Prevalent Among Tipped Workers in Boston," *Boston Globe*, Nov. 13, 2016.

10. Jaya Saxena, "Is There a Place for Hooters in 2018?," *GQ*, June 19, 2018, www.gq.com/story/is-there-a-place-for-hooters-in-2018.

11. "700,000 Female Farmworkers Say They Stand with Hollywood Actors Against Sexual Assault," *Time*, Nov. 10, 2017, time.com/5018813/farmworkers-solidarity-hollywood-sexual-assault/.

12. *Rape on the Night Shift*, FRONTLINE, PBS, June 23, 2015, www.pbs.org/wgbh/frontline/film/rape-on-the-night-shift/#video-2.

13. Sasha Khokha, "'Rape on the Night Shift' Investigation Helps Change California Law," KQED, Sept. 20, 2016, www.kqed.org/news/11090957/rape-on-the-night-shift-investigation-helps-change-california-law.

14. Richard Blanco et al., *Grabbed: Poets and Writers on Sexual Assault, Empowerment, and Healing* (Boston: Beacon Press, 2020).

15. Michelle L. Estes and Gretchen R. Webber, "'More Closeted Than Gayness Itself': The Depiction of Same-Sex Couple Violence in Newspaper Media," *Journal of Interpersonal Violence* 36, no. 1–2 (2021).

16. Peter Gosselin and Ariana Tobin, "Inside IBM's Purge of Thousands of Workers Who Have One Thing in Common," *Mother Jones*, March 22, 2018, www.motherjones.com/crime-justice/2018/03/ibm-propublica-gray-hairs-old-heads/.

17. Kenneth Terrell, "IBM Faces Age Discrimination Lawsuit, Company Believes Layoffs Were 'Valid and Lawful,'" AARP, April 3, 2019, www.aarp.org/work/working-at-50-plus/info-2019/ibm-age-discrimination-case.html.

18. Viet Thanh Nguyen, "Asian Americans Are Still Caught in the Trap of the 'Model Minority' Stereotype. And It Creates Inequality for All," *Time*, June 26, 2020, time.com/5859206/anti-asian-racism-america/.

19. Ginny Fahs, "Silicon Valley's Toxic Culture Requires a Legal Fix," *Atlantic*, Sept. 8, 2019, www.theatlantic.com/ideas/archive/2019/09/change-harassment-silicon-valley-change-law/597373/.

20. Fahs, "Silicon Valley's Toxic Culture Requires a Legal Fix."

21. Theodore Schleifer, "Here's How 20 Different Venture Capital Firms Are Policing Sexual Harassment," Recode, March 10, 2018, www.vox.com/2018/3/10/17102940/venture-capital-sexual-harassment-policies.

22. Cat Zakrzewski, "LPs Move to Curb Sexual Harassment in VC Industry," *Wall Street Journal*, Feb. 9, 2018, www.wsj.com/articles/lps-move-to-curb-sexual-harassment-in-vc-industry-1518179432.

23. Aarti Shahani, "The Investor Who Took On Uber, and Silicon Valley," *All Tech Considered*, NPR, June 15, 2017, www.npr.org/sections/alltechconsidered/2017/06/15/532973451/the-investor-who-took-on-uber-and-silicon-valley.

24. Type Investigations (@typeinvestigate), "Two years after the dawn of #MeToo," Twitter, Oct. 7, 2019, https://twitter.com/typeinvestigate/status/1181231002108215297.

25. Sara Ashley O'Brien, "One Year After the Google Walkout, Key Organizers Reflect on the Risk to Their Careers," CNN, Jan. 9, 2020, www.cnn.com/2019/11/01/tech/google -walkout-one-year-later-risk-takers/index.html.

26. Jeff Green, "Sexual Harassment Training Now Required for 20% of U.S. Workers," Bloomberg, Oct. 10, 2019, www.bloomberg.com/news/articles/2019-10-10/sexual-harass ment-training-now-required-for-20-of-u-s-workers.

27. Frank Dobbin and Alexandra Kalev, "Why Sexual Harassment Programs Backfire and What to Do About It," *Harvard Business Review*, May–June 2020, scholar.harvard.edu/files /dobbin/files/hbr_2020_dobbin_kalev.pdf.

28. Email from Mary Rowe on file with author, Feb. 7, 2021.

CHAPTER 7: A WOMAN'S WORTH: REPRESENTATION, VIOLENCE, AND EQUALITY

1. TIME'S UP, "We Have Her Back," timesupnow.org/work/we-have-her-back/.

2. Southern Poverty Law Center, "Male Supremacy," www.splcenter.org/fighting-hate /extremist-files/ideology/male-supremacy.

3. Anti-Defamation League, "When Women Are the Enemy: The Intersection of Misogyny and White Supremacy," www.adl.org/resources/reports/when-women-are-the-enemy -the-intersection-of-misogyny-and-white-supremacy#white-men-adopt-a-victimhood -narrative.

4. "Senator Kirsten Gillibrand on Sexism," *Overheard with Evan Smith*, posted May 14, 2019, www.youtube.com/watch?v=Xa2CpJihf1Q.

5. "Defense Department Whistleblowers Say Military's Sexual Assault Program Is Failing Survivors," Yahoo News, Nov. 19, 2020; Thomas J. Brennan, "Gag Order: How Marine Corps Culture Silenced a Victim of Sexual Assault," Military.com, Dec. 1, 2020, www .military.com/daily-news/2020/12/01/gag-order-how-marine-corps-culture-silenced -victim-of-sexual-assault.html; Norah O'Donnell et al., "Pentagon Whistleblowers Say They Were Fired or Suspended for Reporting Sexual Assault Cover-Ups: 'People Are Afraid,'" CBS News, Nov. 19, 2020, www.cbsnews.com/news/pentagon-military-whistle blowers-fired-for-reporting-sexual-assault-coverup/; Lisa Carrington Firmin, "A Call to Action: Sexual Assault and Harassment in the Military," *Military Times*, Dec. 2, 2020, www.militarytimes.com/opinion/commentary/2020/12/02/a-call-to-action-sexual -assault-and-harassment-in-the-military/.

6. Maggie Astor, "Kamala Harris and the 'Double Bind' of Racism and Sexism," *New York Times*, Oct. 9, 2020, www.nytimes.com/2020/10/09/us/politics/kamala-harris-racism -sexism.html.

7. Institute for Women's Policy Research, "Same Gap, Different Year. The Gender Wage Gap: 2019 Earnings Differences by Gender, Race, and Ethnicity," Sept. 2020, iwpr.org /iwpr-issues/employment-and-earnings/same-gap-different-year-the-gender-wage -gap-2019-earnings-differences-by-gender-race-and-ethnicity/.

8. "A Proclamation on National Equal Pay Day," 2021 Presidential Actions, The White House, March 24, 2021, www.whitehouse.gov/briefing-room/presidential-actions/2021 /03/24/a-proclamation-on-national-equal-pay-day-2021/.

9. Jen Christensen, "Rape and Domestic Violence Could Be Pre-existing Conditions," CNN, May 4, 2017, www.cnn.com/2017/05/04/health/pre-existing-condition-rape-do mestic-violence-insurance/index.html.

10. Estelle B. Freedman, *Redefining Rape: Sexual Violence in the Era of Suffrage and Segregation* (Cambridge, MA: Harvard University Press, 2013).

11. Catherine Woodiwiss, "#WhyIStayed and #WhyILeft Show the Many Faces of Abuse," *Sojourners*, Sept. 9, 2014, sojo.net/articles/whyistayed-and-whyileft-show-many-faces-abuse.

12. Survivors' Agenda, Sept. 24, 2020, live-survivorsagendaorg.pantheonsite.io/wp-content /uploads/2020/09/2020-09-19_SurvAgenda_English-1.pdf.

13. Johnnetta Betsch Cole and Beverly Guy-Sheftall, *Gender Talk: The Struggle for Women's Equality in African American Communities* (New York: Ballantine Books, 2003).

14. Adonica W. Franklin, "Promotion of a Community Resource Guide for Homeless Women Who Are Victims of Intimate Partner Violence," College of Health Professions, Wilmington University, April 2018.

15. World Health Organization, "Intimate Partner Violence and Alcohol Fact Sheet" 2004, www .who.int/violence_injury_prevention/violence/world_report/factsheets/ft_intimate.pdf.

16. Jill Tiefenthaler, Amy Farmer, and Amandine Sambira, "Services and Intimate Partner Violence in the United States: A County-Level Analysis," *Journal of Marriage and Family* 67, no. 3 (Aug. 2005): 565–78, www.jstor.org/stable/3600189.

17. Deepa Mahajan et al., "Don't Let the Pandemic Set Back Gender Equality," *Harvard Business Review*, Sept. 16, 2020, https://hbr.org/2020/09/dont-let-the-pandemic-set-back-gen der-equality.

18. Schaefer Edwards, "Houston Shelters Are Still Providing Refuge Despite the Pandemic," *Houston Press*, Aug. 20, 2020, www.houstonpress.com/news/houston-shelters-continue-their -work-despite-covid-19-11489701.

19. Michael Roberts, "COVID-19: How Abusers Are Using the Virus Against Victims," *Westword*, April 14, 2020, www.westword.com/news/covid-19-denver-and-abusers-using-virus -against-victims-11687545.

20. Lisa Backus, "As Pandemic Grinds On, Domestic Violence Shelters Grapple with Budget Gaps and Growing Needs," *C-HIT* (blog), Oct. 13, 2020, http://c-hit.org/2020/10/13/as -pandemic-grinds-on-domestic-violence-shelters-grapple-with-budgets-gaps-and-grow ing-needs/.

21. Julie M. Kafka et al., "Fatalities Related to Intimate Partner Violence: Towards a Comprehensive Perspective," *Injury Prevention* 27, no. 2 (2021): 137–44, doi:10.1136/injuryprev -2020-043704.

22. Sharon G. Smith, Katherine A. Fowler, and Phyllis H. Niolon, "Intimate Partner Homicide and Corollary Victims in 16 States: National Violent Death Reporting System, 2003–2009," *American Journal of Public Health* 104, no. 3 (2014): 461–66.

23. United States Department of Justice, Office of the Solicitor General, *U.S. v. Morrison* Brief, www.justice.gov/osg/brief/united-states-v-morrison-brief-merits.

24. Mahajan et al., "Don't Let the Pandemic Set Back Gender Equality."

25. "The Power of Parity: How Advancing Women's Equality Can Add $12 Trillion to Global Growth," McKinsey Global Institute, September 2015, www.mckinsey.com/featured-in sights/employment-and-growth/how-advancing-womens-equality-can-add-12-trillion-to -global-growth#.

26. Lyndsey Gilpin, "The National Park Service Has a Big Sexual Harassment Problem," *Atlantic*, Dec. 15, 2016, www.theatlantic.com/science/archive/2016/12/park-service-ha rassment/510680/.

27. Nidhi Subbaraman, "39% of National Park Employees Say They've Faced Sexual Harassment or Discrimination," *BuzzFeed News*, Oct. 13, 2017, www.buzzfeednews.com/article /nidhisubbaraman/national-parks-harassment-survey.

28. Shannon O'Hara, "Monsters, Playboys, Virgins and Whores: Rape Myths in the News Media's Coverage of Sexual Violence," *Language and Literature: International Journal of Stylistics* 21, no. 3, July 24, 2012.

29. Zachery Cohen, "From Fellow Soldier to 'Monster' in Uniform: #MeToo in the Military," CNN, February 7, 2018, www.cnn.com/2018/02/07/politics/us-military-sexual-assault -investigations/index.html.

30. *United States v. Morrison*, May 15, 2000 (Souter, J., dissenting), www.law.cornell.edu/supct /pdf/99-5P.ZD.

31. Office of Attorney General Maura Healey, "AG Healey Issues Statement in Response to Atlanta Shootings, Rise in Anti-Asian Violence," press statement, www.mass.gov/news /ag-healey-issues-statement-in-response-to-atlanta-shootings-rise-in-anti-asian -violence March 18, 2021.

CHAPTER 8: VICTIM SHAMING

1. Françoise Mouly, "Kadir Nelson's 'Election Results,'" *New Yorker*, Nov. 16, 2020, www .newyorker.com/culture/cover-story/cover-story-2020-11-23.

2. White House Council on Women and Girls, *Rape and Sexual Assault: A Renewed Call to Action*, Jan. 2014, web.archive.org/web/20140127132602/http://www.whitehouse.gov/sites /default/files/docs/sexual_assault_report_1-21-14.pdf.

3. Emiko Petrosky et al., "Racial and Ethnic Differences in Homicides of Adult Women and the Role of Intimate Partner Violence—United States, 2003–2014," *Morbidity and Mortality Weekly Report*, July 21, 2017, 741–46.

4. Melissa Harris-Perry, *Sister Citizen: Shame, Stereotypes, and Black Women in America* (New Haven, CT: Yale University Press, 2011).

5. Sarah Deer and Mary Kathryn Nagle, *McGirt v. Oklahoma*, Brief of Amici Curiae National Indigenous Women's Resource Center, Tribal Nations, and Additional Advocacy Organizations for Survivors of Domestic Violence and Assault in Support of Petitioner, www .supremecourt.gov/DocketPDF/18/18-9526/132692/20200211164034368_189526 %20NIWRC%20McGirt%20Amicus%20Brief.pdf.

6. André B. Rosay, *Violence Against American Indian and Alaska Native Women and Men: 2010 Findings from the National Intimate Partner and Sexual Violence Survey*, National Institute of Justice Research Report, May 2016, www.ncjrs.gov/pdffiles1/nij/249736.pdf.

7. Urban Indian Health Institute, "Our Bodies, Our Stories," www.uihi.org/projects/our -bodies-our-stories/.

8. Deborah Krol, "Identifying, Tracking, and Preventing Human Trafficking in Indian Country," *Navajo-Hopi Observer*, March 19, 2019, www.nhonews.com/news/2019/mar/19 /identifying-tracking-and-preventing-human-traffick/.

9. National Congress of American Indians Policy Research Center, "Human & Sex Trafficking: Trends and Responses Across Indian Country," *Tribal Insights Brief* (Spring 2016), www.ncai.org/policy-research-center/research-data/prc-publications/TraffickingBrief .pdf.

10. Abigail Echo-Hawk, Adrian Dominguez, and Leal Echo-Hawk, *MMIWG: We Demand More*, Urban Indian Health Institute, Sept. 20, 2019, uihi.org/resources/mmiwg-we-demand-more/.

11. Andrea Smith, *Conquest: Sexual Violence and American Indian Genocide* (Durham, NC: Duke University Press, 2015).

12. Sarah Deer et al., eds., *Sharing Our Stories of Survival: Native Women Surviving Violence* (Lanham, MD: AltaMira Press, 2007).

13. J. Kēhaulani Kauanui, ed., *Speaking of Indigenous Politics: Conversations with Activists, Scholars, and Tribal Leaders* (Minneapolis: University of Minnesota Press, 2018).

14. Phil Ferolito, "Family History Helps Fuel Tamaki's Passion for Justice," *Yakima Herald*, Jan. 9, 2018, www.yakimaherald.com/news/local/family-history-helps-fuel-tamakis-pas sion-for-justice/article_9f332064-f5d3-11e7-92c6-43feaa0e17e7.html.

15. B. L. Azure, "Sexual, Physical, and Emotional Abuse Suit Filed," *Char-Koosta News* (Pablo, MT), Oct. 6, 2011, 8–9, www.charkoosta.com/news/sexual-physical-and-emotional-abuse -suit-filed/article_144dbea6-7552-548a-90c0-ec148d77b732.html.

16. Azure, "Sexual, Physical, and Emotional Abuse Suit Filed."

17. Jane Gargas, "Nuns Agree to Pay $4.45M to Settle Abuse Claims, Including from Yakima Plaintiff," Knight-Ridder/Tribune Business News, Feb. 4, 2015.

18. Dan Cook, "Northwest Jesuits Reach $166 Million Sex Abuse Settlement," Reuters, March 25, 2011, www.reuters.com/article/us-jesuits-sexabuse/northwest-jesuits-reach-166 -million-sex-abuse-settlement-idUSTRE72O67S20110325.

19. Ferolito, "Family History Helps Fuel Tamaki's Passion for Justice."

20. Azure, "Sexual, Physical, and Emotional Abuse Suit Filed."

21. Bonnie Clairmont, "Overview of Sexual Violence Perpetrated by Purported Indian Medicine Men," in Deer et al., *Sharing Our Stories of Survival*, 226.

22. White House Council on Women and Girls, *Rape and Sexual Assault*.

23. Mary Kathryn Nagle and Sarah Deer, "*McGirt v. Oklahoma*: A Victory for Native Women," *George Washington Law Review*, July 20, 2020, www.gwlr.org/mcgirt-v-oklahoma-a-victory -for-native-women/.

24. Beverly Guy-Sheftall, "Breaking the Silence: A Black Feminist Response to the Thomas/ Hill Hearings (for Audre Lorde)," in "The Clarence Thomas Confirmation: The Black Community Responds," special issue, *Black Scholar* 22, no. 1/2 (Winter 1991–Spring 1992).

25. Mel Watkins, "Sexism, Racism, and Black Women Writers," *New York Times Book Review*, June 15, 1986, 3.

26. Jacqueline Bobo, "Sifting Through the Controversy: Reading *The Color Purple*," *Callaloo*, no. 39 (Spring 1989): 332–42.

27. Lori S. Robinson, "I Was Raped," *Emerge*, May 1997.

28. Evelynn M. Hammonds, "Whither Black Women's Studies: Interview," *differences: A Journal of Feminist Cultural Studies* 9, no. 3 (1997).

29. Rebecca Epstein, Jamilia J. Blake, and Thalia González, *Girlhood Interrupted: The Erasure of Black Girls' Childhood*, Center on Poverty and Inequality, Georgetown Law (2017), www

.law.georgetown.edu/poverty-inequality-center/wp-content/uploads/sites/14/2017/08
/girlhood-interrupted.pdf.

30. Monique W. Morris, *Pushout: The Criminalization of Black Girls in Schools* (New York: New Press, 2016).

31. Kim Taylor-Thompson, "Why America Is Still Living with the Damage Done by the 'Superpredator' Lie," *Los Angeles Times*, Nov. 27, 2020, www.latimes.com/opinion/story /2020-11-27/racism-criminal-justice-superpredators.

32. Tia Tyree, "African American Stereotypes in Reality Television," *Howard Journal of Communications* 22, no. 4 (2011): 394–413, www.tandfonline.com/doi/abs/10.1080/10646175 .2011.617217?journalCode=uhjc20.

33. Taylor-Thompson, "Why America Is Still Living with the Damage Done by the 'Super-predator' Lie."

34. Sentencing Project, "Incarcerated Women and Girls," Nov. 24, 2020, www.sentencing project.org/publications/incarcerated-women-and-girls/.

35. Asha DuMonthier, Chandra Childers, and Jessica Milli, *The Status of Black Women in the United States*, Institute for Women's Policy Research (2017), www.domesticworkers.org /sites/default/files/SOBW_report2017_compressed.pdf.

36. Julie Euber, "American Medical Association: Transgender Deaths Are an Epidemic," *NPQ: Nonprofit Quarterly*, Oct. 2, 2019, nonprofitquarterly.org/american-medical-associa tion-transgender-deaths-are-an-epidemic/.

37. Human Rights Campaign, "Fatal Violence Against the Transgender and Gender Non-conforming Community in 2020," www.hrc.org/resources/violence-against-the-trans-and -gender-non-conforming-community-in-2020.

38. Orlando Patterson, "Race, Gender, and Liberal Fallacies," *New York Times*, Oct. 20, 1991, www.nytimes.com/1991/10/20/opinion/op-ed-race-gender-and-liberal-fallacies.html.

39. Olivia B. Waxman, "President Trump Played a Key Role in the Central Park Five Case. Here's the Real History Behind *When They See Us*," *Time*, May 31, 2019, time.com/5597843 /central-park-five-trump-history/.

40. *Leave It to Beaver*, season 4, episode 38, "Beaver's Doll Buggy," aired June 17, 1961, diytube .video/video/leave-it-to-beaver-s04-e38-beavers-doll-buggy.

41. Anita Faye Hill and Emma Coleman Jordan, *Race, Gender, and Power in America* (Oxford: Oxford University Press, 1995).

42. Lynn Sorsoli, Maryam Kia-Keating, and Frances K. Grossman, "'I Keep That Hush-Hush': Male Survivors of Sexual Abuse and the Challenges of Disclosure," *Journal of Counseling Psychology* 55, no. 3 (2008): 333–45.

43. Ramona Alaggia, "Disclosing the Trauma of Child Sexual Abuse: A Gender Analysis," *Journal of Loss and Trauma* 10, no. 5 (2005): 453–70.

44. Monica Davey, Julie Bosman, and Mitch Smith, "Dennis Hastert Sentenced to 15 Months, and Apologizes for Sex Abuse," *New York Times*, April 27, 2016.

45. Davey, Bosman, and Smith, "Dennis Hastert Sentenced to 15 Months."

46. Davey, Bosman, and Smith, "Dennis Hastert Sentenced to 15 Months."

47. Richard Blanco et al., *Grabbed: Poets and Writers on Sexual Assault, Empowerment, and Healing* (Boston: Beacon Press, 2020).

48. Email from Scott in author's personal file, Nov. 24, 2020.

49. Theodore V. Wells Jr. et al., *Report to the National Football League Concerning Issues of Workplace Conduct at the Miami Dolphins*, Feb. 14, 2014, nfldolphinsreport.com/wp-content/uploads/2020/11/PaulWeissReport.pdf.

50. Wells et al., *Report to the National Football League.*

51. Wells et al., *Report to the National Football League.*

52. Scooby Axson, "Incognito Denies Bullying Incident; Says Funeral Home Arrest Fueled by Drugs, Alcohol," *Sports Illustrated*, Sept. 25, 2019, www.si.com/nfl/2019/09/25/richie-incognito-jonathan-martin-bullying-hbo-interview.

53. Elizabeth A. Armstrong, "Silence, Power, and Inequality: An Intersectional Approach to Sexual Violence," *Annual Review of Sociology* 44 (2018).

54. Sheryl Pimlott Kubiak et al., "Reporting Sexual Victimization During Incarceration: Using Ecological Theory as a Framework to Inform and Guide Future Research," *Trauma, Violence, and Abuse* 19, no. 1 (2018).

55. Contributor Spotlight: David McLoghlin, *Hayden's Ferry Review*, June 19, 2014, haydensferryreview.com/haydensferryreview/2014/06/contributor-spotlight-david-mcloghlin.html.

56. Brenda Hill, *From the Roots Up: Ending Violence Against Native Women* (Rapid City, SD: Sacred Circle, National Resource Center to End Violence Against Native Women, 2009), www.niwrc.org/sites/default/files/documents/Resources/From_the_Roots_Up.pdf.

CHAPTER 9: POLITICS: RAGE, COMPROMISES, AND BACKLASH

1. "Trump's *Access Hollywood* Tape: The 48-Hour Fallout," *Politico*, July 9, 2019, www.youtube.com/watch?v=cNJGbUWPwe4.

2. "Trump's *Access Hollywood* Tape."

3. Anti-Defamation League, "When Women Are the Enemy: The Intersection of Misogyny and White Supremacy," www.adl.org/resources/reports/when-women-are-the-enemy-the-intersection-of-misogyny-and-white-supremacy#white-men-adopt-a-victimhood-narrative; Aja Romano, "How the Alt-Right's Sexism Lures Men into White Supremacy," *Vox*, April 26, 2018, www.vox.com/culture/2016/12/14/13576192/alt-right-sexism-recruitment.

4. Chuck Malloy, "Trump Has Idaho Pols Dancing with the Stars," Associated Press, Feb. 7, 2018, apnews.com/article/a2f19c3beaa1400ca35ccfee2f644982.

5. Josh Friesen, "Sen. Crapo Says He Will Vote Trump for President," *Idaho State Journal*, Oct. 21, 2016, www.idahostatejournal.com/members/sen-crapo-says-he-will-vote-trump-for-president/article_ceb047bd-5479-55d5-9595-25178f5b145d.html.

6. Malloy, "Trump Has Idaho Pols Dancing with the Stars."

7. Susan Chira, "'Clearly the Tide Has Not Turned': A Q&A with Anita Hill," *New York Times*, Dec. 6, 2018, www.nytimes.com/2018/12/06/us/anita-hill-sexual-harassment-metoo.html.

8. Rebecca Traister, *Good and Mad: The Revolutionary Power of Women's Anger* (New York: Simon & Schuster, 2018).

9. All three letters are on file with the author.

10. *NOW*, PBS, Oct. 10, 2004, www.pbs.org/now/politics/gendergap.html; Thomas B. Edsall and Terry M. Neal, "Strains in a Key Constituency; Some Women Reassess Clinton in Light of Willey Accusations," *Washington Post*, March 17, 1998, A06.

11. U.S. Senate, "Year of the Woman," Nov. 3, 1992, www.senate.gov/artandhistory/history/minute/year_of_the_woman.htm.

12. Florence George Graves, "Going Public About Packwood," *Washington Post*, Sept. 10, 1995, www.washingtonpost.com/archive/opinions/1995/09/10/going-public-about-packwood/219aed13-2795-4bcb-91bd-c8c9ae05da6d/.

13. David Friend, *The Naughty Nineties: The Triumph of the American Libido* (New York: Twelve, 2017), 211.

14. "Clinton Speaks to Prayer Breakfast," transcript, CNN, Sept. 11, 1998, www.cnn.com/ALLPOLITICS/stories/1998/09/11/transcripts/clinton.prayer.html.

15. Alina Tugend, "For Patricia Ireland, a World of Feminism; the Outgoing NOW President Led Through the Treacherous '90s. Her Successor Will Have New Challenges," *Los Angeles Times*, June 28, 2001.

16. Susan Schmidt, "Starr Probing Willey Allegations," *Washington Post*, Nov. 1, 1998.

17. Jennifer Frey, "Then and NOW; Patricia Ireland Reflects on Her Years Leading the Crusade for Women's Rights," *Washington Post*, July 19, 2001.

18. Emma Coleman Jordan, interview with author, Dec. 2020.

19. Jordan, interview with author.

20. George F. Will, "Colleges Become the Victims of Progressivism," *Washington Post*, June 6, 2014, www.washingtonpost.com/opinions/george-will-college-become-the-victims-of-progressivism/2014/06/06/e90e73b4-eb50-11e3-9f5c-9075d5508f0a_story.html.

21. Steve Elbow, "Tammy Baldwin, Other Senators Rip George Will for Column on Campus Rape," *Capital Times* (Madison, WI), June 11, 2014, madison.com/news/local/writers/steven_elbow/tammy-baldwin-other-senators-rip-george-will-for-column-on/article_192252ac-3fdb-56f3-b4b4-aef4507348fd.html.

22. "U.S. and Ford Settle Harassment Case," *New York Times*, Sept. 8, 1999, www.nytimes.com/1999/09/08/us/us-and-ford-settle-harassment-case.html?searchResultPosition=3.

23. Susan Chira and Catrin Einhorn, "How Tough Is It to Change a Culture of Harassment? Ask Women at Ford," *New York Times*, Dec. 19, 2017, www.nytimes.com/interactive/2017/12/19/us/ford-chicago-sexual-harassment.html.

24. Chira and Einhorn, "How Tough Is It to Change a Culture of Harassment?"

25. Chira and Einhorn, "How Tough Is It to Change a Culture of Harassment?"

26. Nicole Allan, "Title IX Investigation into Climate for Women at Yale," *Yale Alumni Magazine*, May/June 2011, yalealumnimagazine.com/articles/3147-span-title-ix-investigation-into-climate-for-women-at-yale-span.

27. Gavan Gideon and Caroline Tan, "Department of Education Ends Title IX Investigation," *Yale Daily News*, June 15, 2012, yaledailynews.com/blog/2012/06/15/department-of-education-ends-title-ix-investigation/.

28. Carole Bass, "Alexandra Brodsky '12, '16JD: 'My School Betrayed Me,'" *Yale Alumni Magazine*, July 13, 2013, yalealumnimagazine.com/blog_posts/1517-alexandra-brodsky-12-16jd-br-my-school-betrayed-me.

29. Sophia Tatum, "Education Dept. Unveils New Protections for Those Accused of Sexual Misconduct on Campuses," CNN, Nov. 16, 2018, www.cnn.com/2018/11/16/politics/education-department-betsy-devos-sexual-misconduct/index.html.

30. Annie Grayer and Veronica Stracqualursi, "DeVos Finalizes Regulations That Give More Rights to Those Accused of Sexual Assault on College Campuses," CNN, May 6, 2020,

www.cnn.com/2020/05/06/politics/education-secretary-betsy-devos-title-ix-re
gulations/index.html.

31. Grayer and Stracqualursi, "DeVos Finalizes Regulations."

32. "A Conversation with Susan Faludi on Backlash, Trumpism, and #MeToo," *Signs* 45, no. 2 (Winter 2020), www-journals-uchicago-edu.eu1.proxy.openathens.net/doi/full/10.1086 /704988.

33. Julie Ray, "Respect for U.S. Women Hit New Low Before Midterms," Gallup, March 8, 2019, news.gallup.com/poll/247211/respect-women-hit-new-low-midterms.aspx.

34. Justin Patchin, "Summary of Our Cyberbullying Research (2007–2019)," Cyberbully- ing Research Center, July 10, 2019, cyberbullying.org/summary-of-our-cyberbullying -research.

35. Nathan W. Mecham et al., "The Effects of Pornography on Unethical Behavior in Busi- ness," *Journal of Business Ethics*, June 14, 2019, link.springer.com/article/10.1007/s10551 -019-04230-8.

36. Amnesty International, "#ToxicTwitter and the Silencing of Women Online," Violence Against Women Online in 2018, www.amnesty.org/en/latest/research/2018/12/rights -today-2018-violence-against-women-online/.

37. "Troll Watch: Online Harassment Toward Women," *All Things Considered*, NPR, Jan. 6, 2019, www.npr.org/2019/01/06/682714973/troll-watch-online-harassment-toward-women.

38. "Troll Watch: Online Harassment Toward Women."

39. Alexander J. S. Colvin, "The Growing Use of Mandatory Arbitration," Economic Policy Institute, April 6, 2018, www.epi.org/publication/the-growing-use-of-mandatory-arbitra tion-access-to-the-courts-is-now-barred-for-more-than-60-million-american-workers/.

40. Lisa Lerer, "For Democrats, the Future Is Female," *New York Times*, Sept. 16, 2019, www .nytimes.com/2019/09/16/us/politics/on-politics-supermajority.html.

41. Brittney Cooper, *Eloquent Rage: A Black Feminist Discovers Her Superpower* (New York: St. Martin's Press, 2018), 273.

CHAPTER 10: ACCOUNTABILITY

1. White House, Office of the Vice President, "Vice President Joe Biden Op-Ed: It's on Us to Stop Campus Sexual Assault," Nov. 9, 2015, obamawhitehouse.archives.gov/the-press -office/2015/11/09/vice-president-joe-biden-op-ed-its-us-stop-campus-sexual-assault.

2. U.S. Commission on Civil Rights, Briefing Report, *Federal #MeToo: Examining Sexual Ha- rassment in Government Workplaces*, April 2020, www.usccr.gov/pubs/2020/04-01-Federal -Me-Too.pdf.

3. Opportunity Agenda, About, www.opportunityagenda.org/about.

INDEX

"1,600 Men for Anita Hill & Christine Blasey
	Ford" initiative, 51–52
A Voice for Men (AVFM), 167, 262
Access Hollywood, 56, 83, 214, 256, 261–64, 273
affirmative consent policies, 134
Affordable Care Act, 173
African American Women in Defense of
	Ourselves, 51–52
African Americans, 9, 13–14, 50–51, 98, 149, 230–32
Alabama, 89, 92, 265
Alexander, Ronni, 122
Alexander v. Yale University, 21, 121–23, 130
Allen, Robert L., 245
Allentown School District, 100
Alphabet, 200–201
Amazon, 152, 157
Amnesty Tech, 284
Anderson, Brittany, 148
Angel, Marina, 22, 104–5
Anita: Speaking Truth to Power (film), xiv
anti–gender-based violence, 206–10, 301–2
antiharassment
	efforts, 143, 196, 274
	policies/laws, 154–55, 157, 276
	training, 134–35, 137, 149, 153, 156, 158,
		163–64, 217
Antilla, Susan, 155–57
Antioch College, 134
Asian women, 153, 165, 174, 221–22, 283
Atlanta, xi–xii, 186, 221–22
Ayotte, Kelly, 262

baby boomers, 76–77, 80–81, 108, 145, 150,
	155, 160
Backlash (Faludi), 281
Bank of America, 24–26
Barnes, Paulette, 28–30, 241
Barnes v. Costle, 28–30
Bausch and Lomb, 23–24
Belton, Sharon Sayles, 230
Besh, John, 146–48
Besh Restaurant Group, 146–47
Bhargava, Anurima, 92–93
bias, 32, 132, 161, 220
	and antibias training, 163–64
	cultural, 142, 195
	gender, 28–29, 302–3
	racial, 28–29, 77, 144
	and sexual assault, 17, 67
	systemic, 222, 292
Biden, Joseph, 12, 190, 217, 296
	accused of sexual assault, 207, 284–85
	apologizes to Anita Hill, 292–95
	chairs Thomas hearing, 35, 42–43, 233
	executive actions of, 305–6
	and gender-based violence, 206, 293, 305–6
	recognizes Equal Pay Day, 172–73
Big Mouth (Netflix series), 163
Birdsall, Sarah, 123–24
Black children, 91, 149, 235–38, 240, 242
Black Lives Matter, 144, 162, 243–44, 301
Black Lives Matter Global Network
	Foundation, 51–52

Black men, 41, 108–10, 160, 230–34, 238, 240–42, 257
Black women, xii, 69, 109, 165, 172, 185, 214, 288
  fast-food workers, 146
  and gender violence claims, 230–37, 240–44, 275
  at higher risk of assault, 29–30, 220–21, 238, 241, 283
  and intimate partner violence, 178–81
  and politics, 239, 265
  and right to vote, 174–76
  stereotypes about, 232, 234–43
  unacknowledged abuse of, 51–52, 110
blaming, of victims, 32, 45, 94–95, 130, 176–77, 184, 188, 236
Blanco, Richard, 149–50
Booker, Cory, 58
Boren, David, xiii
Boston, 21–22, 80, 99–100, 203, 299
Bowdler, Michelle, 67–68
"boys will be boys," 23, 103–4, 107–8, 259, 303
Bradford, Janice, 109
Bradford, Mark, 108–11
Bradley, Joseph, 198–99
Bradwell, Myra, 198–99
Bradwell v. State of Illinois, 198–99
Brandeis University, xiii–xiv, 299
Brett Kavanaugh confirmation hearing, 66, 69–70
  confirms Kavanaugh, 58–59, 263
  Ford's testimony in, 47–62, 86, 210, 279
  forms of denial at, 45, 55–56
  "he said/she said" scenario of, 280–81
  Kavanaugh's testimony in, 55, 210
  outrage/activism after, 56–57, 60–62, 265–66
Breyer, Stephen, 210
"bro culture," 144, 146, 151–52, 154
Brodsky, Alexandra, 277
Brown, Elsa Barkley, 51–52
Brown, Tony, 234
Brown v. Board of Education, 26–28
bullying, 7, 91, 218, 304
  by children, 81–86, 88, 100, 106, 253
  and LGBTQ+ individuals, 90, 144
  prevalence of, 298–99
  in sports, 254–56
  tragic outcomes of, 88, 92, 95
  See also cyberbullying
Burke, Tarana, 149, 243
Bush, George H. W., 268–69
bystander training, 159, 163–64

California, 149, 154, 279
Catholic church/clergy, 11, 226–28, 248–53
Catholic schools, 80–81, 226–28
Center for American Women and Politics (Rutgers), 60–61
Centers for Disease Control and Prevention (CDC), 51, 87

Chang, Emily, 144, 151
Chicago, 147, 178, 275
children, xvi, 7, 13, 32, 40, 88, 91, 207
  carry behavior into adulthood, 81, 100, 247
  denials by, 89–90
  disciplining of, 99–100
  experience gender violence, 73, 76–79, 82–86, 144
  gender-based violence passed on to, 289
  intergenerational commitment to, 107–10
  and intimate partner violence, 179–85, 187, 189
  "normal" sexual harassment by, 101–4, 108
  sexual harassment by seen as "normal," 101–4, 108
  sexual/physical abuse of, 194, 206, 221, 223, 226–28, 246–53, 259
  vulnerable to future abuse, 112
  See also school shootings; schools
Chira, Susan, 265–66
Chronicle of Higher Education, The, 135, 139
citizenship, 61, 173–75, 195–202, 209–10, 219, 223, 228
civil rights, 90, 207
  laws, 11, 26–29, 277–78, 302
  movement, xi–xii, 160–61
  protections, 115, 197, 216, 302
  violations, 24–26, 28, 30–31, 143, 195, 197, 200
Civil Rights Act of 1964, 21–22, 29, 197
Civil Rights Act of 1991, 268–69, 281, 288
Civil Rights Amendments of 1972, 101
Clairmont, Bonnie, 228
Clarence Thomas confirmation hearing, xi, 66, 280, 287, 289
  chaired by Biden, 35, 42–43, 233, 292–94
  confirms Thomas, xiii, 46, 267–69, 271
  damage done by, 61–62, 69–70
  forms of denial at, 33–43, 45–46
  Hill judged/shamed for testifying at, 2–4, 232–33, 240, 293–94
  and issues of race, 41, 51, 231–33
  judiciary committee for, 50–51
  legacy of, xiv–xv, 2–4
  outrage/activism follows, 60, 63, 75, 195, 265–71, 291
  political significance of, 210, 267
  senators' dismissive/hostile during, 40–41, 45–46, 180, 247, 294
  supporters of Hill's testimony, 3–4, 51, 251
  witnesses not called for, 33, 42, 232–33, 280
class-action lawsuits, 147, 156, 286
class/classism, 9, 11, 118, 144–45, 150, 161, 223
Clery Act, 134
climate change, 145, 164, 209
Clinton, Bill, 262, 265, 269, 271–73, 291–92, 300
Clinton, Hillary, 161, 165–66, 237, 262–63, 265, 272–73
Cole, Johnnetta Betsch, xi–xii, 243

college administrations, 123, 155, 208
  fail to live up to responsibility, 136–39
  and gender wage gap, 171–72
  lose lawsuits/claims, 276–78
  protect faculty/institution, 115, 124–29, 136, 161
college campuses, 88, 293
  assaults/harassment on, 10–11, 111–39, 143, 161, 223, 241, 274
  hierarchies/structures in, 125–33, 136–37, 144, 139, 254
  protests on, 144–45
  "rape culture" of, 134, 136, 143, 164
  rapes on, 113–14, 120–21, 133–34, 210–11, 234, 277
  See also hazing culture/rituals; *Oleanna* (Mamet)
college sports, 114–17, 119–21, 123, 276
Collins, Susan, 47, 57–58
colonization, 9, 224–26, 252–53, 260, 303
Color Purple, The, 233–34
commerce, interstate, 197–201, 211, 302
Common Sense Media, 79, 253
Confederated Salish and Kootenai Tribes, 252–53
Congress Leads by Example Act (2020), 72
Congressional Accountability Act (1995), 72
Corne, Jane, 23–24
Corne v. Bausch and Lomb, 23–24, 26
Cornell University, 21, 126
corporations, 71, 150–57, 195, 266, 275, 278, 302
Cosby, Bill, 216
Cotton, Tom, 58–59
courts, xvii, 4, 196, 211, 294, 299, 301
  and child harassment suits, 87, 91, 99–104
  early sexual harassment cases in, 21–33, 108
  limitations on filing claims, 64–65
  rise of sexual harassment/assault cases in, 5, 63, 66–67
COVID-19, xv, xvii–xviii, 219
  Biden's recovery plan for, 206
  and gender-based violence, xvi, 187–88
  and intimate partner violence, 189–90, 194
  and racial discrimination, 16–17
  women's economic setbacks in, xvi, 172–73, 199–200
Cranbrook prep school, 83–86, 106, 246
Crapo, Mike, 261–63
Crenshaw, Kimberlé, xiv, 243–44
Crews, Terry, 257, 259
criminal justice system, 42, 67, 70, 183, 189, 195, 202–5, 235–37, 294, 303–4
criminal sexual assault convictions, 5, 67, 102–3, 134
cyberbullying, 78–79, 282–84

dating violence, xvi, 87, 169, 229
Davis, Aurelia, 102–3
Davis, LaShonda, 101–4, 111
Davis, Saundra, 65–66

Davis v. Monroe County Board of Education, 101–4
Declaration of Sentiments, 173–75
DeConcini, Dennis, 24, 45–46
Deer, Sarah, 225–26, 229
DEI Advisory Council, 201
Democrats, 58–61, 85, 172, 206–10, 272
denial, 51, 63, 81, 222
  cost of, 68–73
  examples of, 18–20, 71, 89–90
  having the power to, 33–43
  individual, 40–42, 55–56, 256–57
  institutional, 40, 41–43, 55–56, 58, 70, 72
  societal, 3–4, 9, 15, 32–33, 40, 70
  structural, 42–43, 55–56, 70, 72, 276
  and women's health, 15–17
Detroit, 177–83, 187–88, 194
DeVane, Geneva, 23–24
DeVos, Betsy, 277–78
disabled persons, 90, 207, 243–44, 264
Disclosure (film), 162–63
disenfranchisement, 9, 60–61, 174–75, 224, 238–39
District of Columbia, 27, 72
diversity, 144, 155, 159, 171, 201, 218
Doerr, John, 153
domestic violence, 4, 7–8, 143, 168–69, 175, 229
  Democrats' platform on, 207–8
  and economic hardship, 173, 179, 188
  politics of, 189–90
  sufferers of, 70–71
  See also intimate partner violence; shelters
Dowden, James P., 120
Dunn, Sharon, 275–76
Durkin, Thomas, 248
DuVernay, Ava, 242

Easterbrook, Steve, 148
Ebert, Roger, 129
economic
  abuse of women, 10, 177, 209, 304
  hardships of women, 172–74, 179, 184–85, 195, 199–200
  impact of gender violence, 67–73, 205, 295, 299
  impact of intimate partner violence, 189–90
  impact of sexual harassment, 7–8, 64, 155, 195, 216
  security/insecurity, 8, 145–46, 304–5
  worth of women, 169–73, 176, 195, 198–99, 205
Economic Policy Institute, 286
education, 7, 13, 241, 298–99, 305
Elam, Paul, 167
emotional abuse, 34, 177, 253–54
entertainment industry, 200, 215–19, 222, 286
Environmental Protection Agency, 29
Epstein, Jeffrey, 11
Equal Employment Opportunity Commission (EEOC), 2, 19, 65, 72, 157, 201–2, 268, 270, 274–75
Equal Pay Day, 172

Equal Rights Amendment (ERA), 99
Espelage, Dorothy, 87–88
ethnicity, 12, 78, 142, 147, 218, 221–22, 305

Fahs, Ginny, 154
Faludi, Susan, 281, 287
Farley, Lin, 21
farmworkers, 148–49, 201–2
fast-food workers, 146–48
FBI, 41, 46–47, 56, 210, 248
Federalist Society, 49
Feinstein, Dianne, 68–69, 210, 257
feminism, xiv–xv, 109, 142–43, 160, 169, 281
feminists, 50–53, 104, 131, 143, 174, 185, 205, 243,
    271–74, 281
finance industry, 150–57, 159, 169
First Amendment, 79
Fitzgerald, Louise, 279–80, 287–88
Flathead Indian Reservation (Montana), 227
Fletcher, Bettina, 114, 116
Floyd, George, xvi, 230, 301
food industry, 145–50, 159, 164, 201
Ford, Christine Blasey
    on memories of trauma, 54, 86
    questioned by prosecutor, 53, 55, 58
    seeks accountability, 59–60
    senators' "he said/she said" scenario,
        280–81
    senators' responses to, 47, 58–59, 210
    supporters of, 51–52, 266
    testimony of, 48–61, 104, 263, 279, 285
Ford Motor Company, 275, 278
foundations, 127–28, 139, 300
Fowler, Susan, 151, 155, 157
fraternities, 114, 117–19, 254, 276
Freud, Anna, 32, 69
Freud, Sigmund, 32–33
Frey, William C., 23–24, 26, 28, 34
Freyd, Jennifer, 278
Friend, David, 271–72
funding, 169, 171–72, 299–300, 305

Garber, Greg, 116
Garza, Alicia, 51–52
Gay, Roxane, 39
gays, 108–10, 243–48. See also LGBTQ+
    individuals
Gen Xers, 108, 141, 143–44, 160–61
Gen Yers. See millennials
Gen Zers, 77–80, 108, 143–44
gender
    bias, 28–29, 77, 144, 151, 164, 169, 171–73
    conformity, 223, 245–46
    discrimination, 6–7, 57, 90, 151–59, 169–71, 195,
        198, 241–42
    diversity, 58, 60, 159
    hierarchy, 8, 118, 144, 254
    hostility, 98–99, 150–55, 159, 240

identity, xvii, 6–7, 12, 91, 97–98, 184, 211,
    239, 305
inequities, xvi, 156–57, 199, 205, 209, 214
policing, 244–47, 299
gender-based violence
    collecting data about, 300–302
    costs of, 12, 73, 177–78, 297
    culture of, 292–93
    discounting of, 61–62, 69, 241, 264
    generation to generation, 9, 80, 252–53, 289,
        299
    how to end it, 301–6
    intergenerational commitment to, 76–80,
        107–10, 161, 163
    a national crisis, 7, 9–10, 12, 295–99
    patterns of, 100, 159
    as personal matter, 196, 210, 241, 288
    seen as "normal" behavior, 143–45, 247
    surges in, 9, 12, 189–91, 211
    See also sexual assault/harassment
gendered role expectations, 244–47
General Social Survey, 142
Georgetown University Law Center, xiv–xv
Gertner, Nancy, 64–65
Gillibrand, Kirsten, 68–69, 167–68, 176,
    206–7, 209
Gilmer v. Interstate / Johnson Lane Corp., 270–71, 286
Ginsburg, Ruth Bader, 65–66, 73, 210, 302
Glamour magazine, 288
global economy, 200
Goddess, Rha, xv
Goldberg, Carrie, 91
Golden, Andrew, 105
Google, 152, 157–58, 200–201
Gorsuch, Neil, 229
Government Accountability Office (GAO), 68–69
Grace Hopper Celebration of Women in
    Computing, 48, 55–57
Grassley, Charles, 46–47, 50, 53, 55, 57, 61
Graves, Fatima Gross, 277
Graves, Florence, 269
Gray, Bob, 138
Great Migration, 178–79
Great Recession, 190–92, 194
Greenberg, Jack, 27–28
Grimké, Sarah, 174–75, 205
guns/gun violence, 169, 191–93, 207–9
Guy-Sheftall, Beverly, xv, 185–87, 232–34, 243

Haberman, Maggie, 84–85
Hamilton, Mary, 175–76
Hammonds, Evelynn, 243
Harris, Kamala, 51, 165, 168, 213, 217
Harris, Meena, 51–52
Harris-Perry, Melissa, xv, 220–21
Hart, Philip, 125–26, 132–33, 143
Hastert, Dennis, 248–49
Hatch, Orrin, 46–47, 61

hate crimes, 85, 167, 211, 221–23
hazing culture/rituals, 114–18, 254
Healey, Maura, 211
health, 196
   crises of, 188–90
   gender gap in, 15–17, 70, 80
   and gender violence, 7–8, 10, 51, 68, 205,
      295, 299
   and women of color, 237, 239
Helena, Montana, 226–28
Herman, Debra, 124
Higginbotham, A. Leon, Jr., 229–30
Hill, Brenda, 260
Hill v. Cundiff, 89–90
Hite, Molly, 126–29
Hodges, Honestie, 235
Hollywood, 75, 148–49, 162–63, 215–19, 237,
   257, 286
Hollywood Commission, 215–19
homicides, 104–6, 191–95, 208, 299
homelessness, 7, 305
homophobia, xvii, 12, 78–79, 81, 87, 118, 161, 163,
   220, 245, 303
homophobic slurs, 90, 93–95, 97–99, 254–56
Hooters waitresses, 148
"hostile environment sexual harassment," 22
housing, 7–8, 208, 299–300, 305
Houston, Charles Hamilton, 26–27
Howard University School of Law, 26–27
Hudson, Keith, 41
Hudson Union Society, 37–38
Hudson v. McMillan, 41
human rights, 21, 161, 201, 272, 283, 299
Human Rights Campaign, 90, 239
Hunter College, xiv–xv

I May Destroy You (HBO show), 69
IBM, 150
Illinois, 198–99
Im, Yeohee, 137–38
incest, 3, 8, 247
Incognito, Richie, 254–56
Indian Citizenship Act (1924), 175
Indiana University Health North Hospital,
   16–17
"institutional betrayal," 278
International Women's Day, 282
internet, 78–79, 282–85
"intersectionality," 243–44
intimate partner violence, 3–4, 6, 15, 77, 113, 164,
   205, 305
   Black women and, 178–81, 220, 239, 243
   children and, 179–84
   costs of, 12, 177, 184–85, 188–90
   and leaving vs. staying, 180–85, 187–88
   in the military, 297
   and Native American women, 224, 228–29
   and politics, 176–77

a shared responsibility, 189–96
   See also shelters
Ireland, Patricia, 272–73
It's on Us campaign, 293

Jacobsen Middle School, 92–97
jail, 237–38, 257–58, 304
Jenkins, Alan, 300
Jesuit missionaries, 227–28
jewelry store chains, 200
Jim Crow South, 13, 26, 178–79
job loss, xvi, 8, 18, 20–25, 28–32, 68,
   189–90
Johnson, Lyndon B., 27
Johnson, Mitchell, 105
Johnson, Paula, 135–36
Jones, Doug, 265
Jordan, Emma Coleman, xv, 272–73
judges, 15, 22–31, 61, 64, 71–72, 175, 195. *See also*
   U.S. Supreme Court; *specific names*

Katzenbach, Nicholas, 197
Kavanaugh, Brett, 45, 49–62, 104, 210, 285, 296.
   See also Brett Kavanaugh confirmation
   hearing
Kendi, Ibram X., 301
Kennedy, Anthony, 49, 101, 103–4
Kennedy, Kathleen, 215, 217
Kent, Sandra, 179–80
Khan, Shamus, 107
Kimball, Ed, 124–25
King, Deborah, 51–52
King, Martin Luther, Jr., xii, 160
Klein, Freada Kapor, 21–22, 155, 217
Klein, Jessie, 105
Kleiner Perkins Caufield & Byers,
   151–54
Klobuchar, Amy, 58
Know My Name (Miller), 67–68
Kreisberg, Andrew, 216
Kroll, Nick, 163

Labrie, Owen, 106–7
Larkin, Deborah Slaner, xiv–xv
Latinx, 82, 146, 173, 238, 242, 275
Lauber, John, 83–86, 111
Lauer, Matt, 165
law enforcement, xvi, 5, 208, 258, 298
   and getting convictions, 67
   and intimate partner violence, 183–84, 187,
      193–94
   prosecute the accused, 102–3
   rape cases and, 4, 203
   and women/girls of color, 91, 225–26, 250
law practice, 5, 22, 198–99
leadership, accountability of, 12, 72,
   218–19, 290–92, 295–96, 305–6.
   See also politicians

legal system, 11, 61–62, 304
  bias against rape victims, 67
  and intimate partner violence, 183, 187
  lock in gender-based disadvantages, 195
  protects abusers, 248–49
  women of color and, 237–38
  and workplace harassment, 274–75
Lehman College (New York), 105
Leive, Cindi, 288–89
Lépine, Marc, 104
Lewinsky, Monica, 271–73
Lewis, John, xii, xvi
Lewis, Lillian Miles, xii
LGBTQ+ individuals, 7, 60, 77, 214, 243
  bullying of, 144, 282
  at higher risk of assault, 6, 90, 149, 257
  and intimate partner violence, 184
  marches/protests of, 264
  and #MeToo movement, 149–50
  rights for, 207
  self-silencing of, 221
Lhamon, Catherine, 89–91, 110
Lichtman, Judith, 124–25
"locker room talk" defense, 56–57, 259
low-wage workers, 145–49, 157–58, 162–63, 275

MacArthur Foundation/Vera Institute of Justice
    report, 238
MacKinnon, Catharine, 21–23, 25, 32, 121–22, 276
Mamet, David, 129–32
mandatory arbitration, 270–71, 286
Mann, Jessica, 202–3
Marshall, Thurgood, 27–28
Martin, Jonathan, 254–56, 259
masculinity
  abuse masked as, 244–49, 259, 289
  cultural expectations of, 251–54
  notions of, 222–23, 235, 244–49, 256–60
Massachusetts, xiii–xiv, xvi, 83, 203, 211, 254, 292
Maxwell, Phillip, 84
May, Emily, xv
McBride, Sarah, 90
McClung, Ollie, 197
McDonald's, 146–48
McGirt v. Oklahoma, 229
McKinsey Global Institute report, 199–200
McLoghlin, David, 249–52, 258–59
McPhee, Joan, 120
men
  claim power over women, 9, 142–43, 223–24
  entitlement of, 28–29, 56–57, 106–7, 117, 205–6
  sexual/physical assault of, 3, 6–7, 223, 245–54,
    257–59
  who testify on behalf of women, 157
mental health, xvi, 7–8, 68, 128, 225, 237–38, 281
Merchant, Nilofer, 8, 68
Meridian Township Police Department, 119–20
Meritor Savings Bank v. Vinson, 30–31

#MeToo movement, 131, 208, 268, 284
  and antiharassment efforts, 143, 158
  demands systemic change, 162
  founding of, 49, 149, 243, 264, 280
  men as allies for, 246
  prioritizes antiharassment efforts, 143, 158
  reckoning brought about by, 200
  revelations of, 76, 142–43, 217, 279
  sparks activism, 137–38, 148–49, 275
  stories of, 6, 54, 75–76, 124, 149–50
  undermined online, 283
Miami Dolphins, 254–56
Michigan State University, 119–20
midterm elections, 60–61, 265
military, 6, 168, 204, 297
millennials, 158
  accept sexual harassment/assault, 143–44
  call for reforms/change, 134, 164
  and gender wage gap, 170–71
  progressive views of, 77–81, 108, 141–45, 164
  workplaces of, 144–45, 150–51
Miller, Chanel, 67–68, 134
Miller, Margaret, 24–26
Miller v. Bank of America, 24–26
Minnesota, 31, 97, 162–63, 230
misogyny, xvii, 81, 260, 293
  and Black women, 235, 241
  and gender-based violence, 9, 12, 164, 302–3
  plagues the world, 103, 144
  and racism, 221–23, 241, 289
  of Trump, 56–57, 261–65, 268
  and women candidates, 166–67
  at Yale University, 276–77
Missoula, Montana, 251–53
Mitchell, Rachel, 53, 55, 58
Mock, Freida, xiv
Moonves, Les, 216
Moore, Roy, 265
Moore, Susan, 16–17
Morris, Monique W., 236
Morris, Oklahoma, 98–99
Mott, Lucretia, 173–74
Murray, Patty, 68–69, 206
Mvskoke Nation, 229

NAACP Legal Defense Fund (LDF), 27–28
Nagle, Mary Kathryn, 229
Nassar, Larry, 119–20
National Academies of Sciences, Engineering,
    and Medicine's Committee on the
    Impacts of Sexual Harassment in
    Academia, 126, 135–37, 139
National Domestic Workers Alliance, 239
National Indigenous Women's Resource
    Center, 224
National Organization for Women (NOW), 272–73
National Park Service employees, 201
National Women's Law Center, 145, 147, 277

Native American women, 237–38, 253
　abused by Catholic clergy, 226–28
　at higher risk of assault, 220–21, 224, 226, 241
　protections for, 207, 226–29
　rape of, 9, 223–26
　rights of, 174–75, 225
　self-silencing of, 220–22, 224–25
　sovereignty of, 228–29, 259–60
Nelson, Kadir, 213, 219, 235
New Orleans, 146–47
New York, 11, 99–100, 168, 175–76, 238–39, 242, 279
New York City Commission on Human Rights, 21
New York Times, The, 51–52, 60, 81, 84, 219, 233–34, 265–66
New Yorker, The, 213, 235, 260
Newman, Katherine S., 105–6
Nineteenth Amendment, 175–76, 206
Nixon, Richard, 23–26
nonbinary people, 6–7, 56, 83, 97, 112, 189, 245, 259, 305
nondisclosure agreements, 196, 220, 270–71, 279, 286
Norman, Oklahoma, 179–80
North Country (film), 31, 162–63
Northwestern University, 118
Norton, Eleanor Holmes, 21, 72
Not That Bad: Dispatches from Rape Culture (Gay), 39

Oakland Men's Project (OMP), 245–46, 251
Obama, Barack, 190–91, 214, 224, 228–29, 293, 296, 300
O'Carroll, Tanya, 284
Occupy Wall Street, 144, 164
O'Connor, Sandra Day, 101, 104
Oklahoma, xii–xiii, xv–xvii, 2, 36–37, 178, 203, 229, 267
Oleanna (Mamet), 129–32, 162–63
Olivarius, Ann, 123
"One in Four" (McLoghlin), 249–50, 252
Opportunity Agenda, 300–301
Oral Roberts University, 38, 160

Packwood, Bob, 269–70
Pao, Ellen, 151–55
Papandreou, Nick, 118, 133
Parker-Pope, Tara, 81
Parks, Rosa, 232
Patterson, Orlando, 240–41
pay equity/inequity, 156, 168–73, 195, 268
Paycheck Fairness Act, 169
PBS FRONTLINE, 148–49
Peay, Kathleen, 114–17, 121
Pelchat, Zachary, 92–93
Pence, Mike, 168, 261
Peratis, Kathleen, xiv–xv
"perfect victim" myth, 67, 149, 204, 220, 303

performance reviews, 19, 69, 153
Phenomenal Woman Action Campaign, 51–52
physical assault/harassment, 7, 10, 23–24, 34, 87, 95, 180–81, 194
Plymouth State, 126
Pogrebin, Letty Cottin, xiv–xv
police, 175–76, 180, 183–87, 192, 204, 225–28, 235, 242, 301
political power, of women, 265–66, 287–88, 290
politicians, xvii, 15, 49, 55
　accountability of, 271–72, 286–87, 297
　deny sexual harassment problem, 33–35, 70
　failure of, 261–64, 279, 284–87
　responsibility of, 194–95, 209, 290, 295
　sexual misconduct by, 248–49, 265, 269–73, 284–85, 291–92, 296–97
　women, 4, 165–69, 175, 205, 209, 265–69, 284, 287
politics, 10–11, 168, 199–200, 206–11, 279, 295–96, 303
Poo, Ai-Jen, xv
pop culture, 73, 162, 239–40
pornography, xvi, 35–36, 66, 152, 221, 283
post-traumatic stress, 7, 116, 250
poverty, xvi, 10, 76, 145–46, 193–94, 239
power
　dynamics of, 162, 188
　hierarchies of, 117–18, 130–33, 136–37
　imbalance of, 58, 65–66, 147, 154, 298
　male-dominance of, 288–89
　structural balance of, 125–33
　violators in positions of, 144, 266, 279, 285
presidential elections, 165–68, 190, 207, 213, 261–64, 267–69, 284–86, 291–92, 295–96
Pressley, Ayanna, 206
Price, Leon, 23–24
Price, Pamela, 122–23
Princeton University, 137–38
Project Include, 155
protections, 4, 11–12, 28, 70, 72, 101, 103, 196, 200, 220, 277–78, 281. See also Violence Against Women Act
Prout, Chessy, 106–7

quid pro quo harassment, 22, 24–26, 29–30, 200

R. Kelly, 221, 242
racial
　diversity, 58, 78, 142, 159
　equality, 144–45, 228
　harassment case, 65–66
　identity, 11–12, 108
　justice, 207, 264, 305
　privileges, 29, 223
　slurs, 65, 90, 256, 293
　stereotypes, 220, 225, 237–43, 257
　tropes, 167
　violence, 41, 65, 197

racial discrimination, 13, 25–30, 118, 197, 218,
    241–42, 299–302
racism, 76, 103, 145, 161, 163, 242, 245
    and bullying, 98–99
    children less tolerant of, 77
    and Clarence Thomas hearing, 41, 51
    elimination of, 178, 301
    federal funding and, 299–300
    and gender-based violence, xvii, 6, 9, 220–22,
        228, 303
    and gender violence claims, 230–34
    and LGBTQ+ individuals, 90
    and misogyny, 221–23, 241, 289
    online, 79, 284
    and sexism, 17, 243
    in the South, 26–27
"Racism, Sexism, and Power" (talk), 230–32
Ramirez, Deborah, 57
Ramirez, Monica, 148
Randall-Gay, Brianne, 119
Ransby, Barbara, 51–52
rape, 4, 8, 31, 38–39, 68, 79, 162, 304
    false accusations of, 234, 238, 242
    and justice system, 186, 202–5
    lack of convictions for, 168, 175–76, 204
    law professor and, 124–25
    legalization of, 167
    myths about, 236, 241, 254, 274
    PBS documentary on, 148–49
    prevalence of, 66–67, 298–99
    "rape bait" case, 89–90, 101
    rape kits and, 67, 204, 208
    those at higher risk of, 201–2, 236, 257
    See also college campuses; military; Native
        American women
Rape and Sexual Assault: A Renewed Call to Action, 214
Rape on the Night Shift (film), 148–49
Reade, Tara, 207, 284–85
Redbook survey, 17–20, 42, 70
Rehnquist, William, 196–99
Reifler, Margery, 123
Reinboldt, Stephen, 248
Republicans, 49–50, 53–55, 58–61, 206–10,
    261–64, 269–73, 287
Return of Kings (ROK), 167, 262
"revenge porn," 208, 283
Richards, Cecile, 290
Robinson, Spottswood, III, 26–31, 33–34,
    195–96, 302
Romney, Mitt, 83–86, 106, 246
Rowe, Mary, 163–64
Rutgers University, 60–61

Safer, Morley, 144–45
Safran, Claire, 18
school shootings, 100, 104–7
schools, xvii, 40, 164, 208
    and Black children, 236–37

"cliques" in, 82–83, 86, 88, 96
culture in, 82–83, 90–91, 96–97, 106–7, 111
gender-based violence in, 8, 10–11, 76–77,
    80–86, 107–8, 111–12, 144
and gender cultural expectations, 253–54
indifferent to harassment claims, 89–91, 94–95,
    99–103
policies/reforms for, 95–96, 195
responsibility defined by court, 101–4
sexual assault/harassment in, 4, 81–82, 87–101,
    196, 298
sexual conquest ritual in, 106–7
Schumer, Chuck, 58–59
science field, 171–72, 201
Seed, David, 86
Seneca Falls, New York, 173–76
sex
    banter, 35–36, 256, 259, 275
    discrimination, 21–23, 25, 28–30, 32
    traded for jobs/benefits, 19, 200, 275
    trafficking, 11, 205–6, 224, 236, 298–99
    workers, 208
sexism, 145, 161, 163, 245, 262, 264
    and Clarence Thomas hearing, 51
    and #MeToo movement, 75
    online, 78–79, 284
    passed generation to generation, 81
    and racism, 17, 243
    and women candidates, 165–69, 175
    and women's economic worth, 169–71
sexual extortion, 18, 20–21, 24, 28, 66, 72, 132,
    154, 195, 201, 218, 282
sexual assault/harassment
    acceptance of, 217
    biological inevitability of, 23–25, 28–29
    definition of/types of, 18, 20–22, 32
    discounting of, 61, 69–71, 147
    intragenerational dissonance and, 142–45
    institutionalized, 125–33
    lack of system for reporting claims, 285–86
    legal concept of, 195
    prevalence of, 4, 57, 298–99
    putting end to, 49, 158–59, 195
    seen as "normal" behavior, 101–4, 133
    and system for reporting claims, 285–86
    women arrested for, 183
sexual identity, 9, 11–12, 83, 91–99, 108, 204, 305.
    See also LGBTQ+ individuals
Shange, Ntozake, 233
Shapel, Vika, 239
Shaw, Nina, 215, 217
"she said, he said," 56, 131, 203, 280–81, 301–3
Shelby, Nigel, 92, 108, 111
shelters, xvi, 7, 177–90
Simon, Anne, 121–22
Simon, Lou Anna, 120
Simpson, Alan, 40, 46
Simpson, June Ann, 89

slavery, 13, 41, 174, 178, 229–30, 260, 303
Smith Barney, 155–57
Smith, JoAnne, xv
Snyder, Rachel Louise, 184
social media, 76–79, 91, 181, 200, 215, 282–84, 299
social stigmas, 90, 177, 184, 188, 230–34, 257
Souter, David, 210–11
Southern Poverty Law Center, 167
Specter, Arlen, 34–40, 53
Spelman College, xi–xii, 185, 232, 234
Sperry, Charles "Chuck," 251–52
St. Paul's School (New Hampshire), 106–7
Stanford University, 67, 134
Stanton, Elizabeth Cady, 173–76
Stapleton, Claire, 157–58
Status of Black Women in the United States, The, 239
Steinem, Gloria, 143
stereotypes, 220, 225, 230, 232–42, 253–54, 257
Stern, Herbert Jay, 21
Stone, Lisa, 122
Strauss, Richard, 117, 223
street harassment, 6, 66, 164, 175, 299
suicide, 7, 68, 79, 86, 88, 90, 92, 95, 102–3
"superpredators," 236–38
survivor justice, 206, 208, 219–20, 223, 228, 303–5
Survivors' Agenda, 304–5
systemic violence xvii, 9, 80, 110, 119–120, 203, 216, 247, 251–53, 288–90, 295

Tab, The, 78–79
Tales from the Boom-Boom Room: Women vs. Wall Street (Antilla), 155–57
Tamaki, Blaine, 226–27
Taylor, Breonna, xvi, 301
technology, xvi, 48, 55, 78–79, 172, 282–84
technology industry, 144–45, 150–59, 162, 169, 200–201
Tehachapi, California, 92–97
television programs, 253–54
Thomas, Clarence, 38, 65, 210
    behavior is "not too bad," 34–35, 40–41
    criticism of, 51, 267, 296
    discusses sex/porn at work, 35–36
    Hill's public stand against, xiii–xv
    sexual harassment by, 2, 33, 42
    See also Clarence Thomas confirmation hearing
Thurmond, Strom, 46
TIME'S UP, 148, 167, 217
Title IX, 21, 274
    colleges comply with, 134–36, 208, 276–78
    lawsuits filed under, 101–4, 121–23, 138, 276–77
    and women's sports, 115–16
Title VII, 21, 28–31, 34, 63–66, 136, 274, 278, 302
Traister, Rebecca, 266, 289
transgenders, 6, 83, 90, 149, 207–8, 239, 243–46, 305

transphobia, 118, 220
Tribal Law and Order Act, 228–29
Trotchie, Jackie, 227
Trump, Donald, 213, 277, 279
    and Access Hollywood, 56, 83, 214, 256, 261–64, 273
    assault/rape charges against, 205–7, 215–16, 219, 273, 285, 296
    condemns accused boys, 238, 242
    fails to tackle sexual assault issue, 206, 214–15
    Kavanaugh hearing and, 49, 56–58, 210, 263
    Matt Lauer's interview of, 166
    misogyny of, 56–57, 168, 206, 214, 261–65, 268, 273, 287
    supporters of, 78, 167, 261–64, 273
    and women protests, 60, 206, 264–66, 287
Trump, Eric, 168
Twitter, 283–84
Tyree, Tia, 237–38

Uber, 151, 155–57
Udall, Morris K., 24
United Nations, 10, 161
United States v. Morrison, 196–99, 210–11, 302
University of California, 134, 245
University of Illinois, 82–83, 279
University of North Carolina, 118
University of Oklahoma, 36, 114–17, 120–21
    College of Law, xiii, 2, 116
University of Texas at Austin, 82–83
University of Utah, 48–49, 53–55
University of Wisconsin, 124–25
Urban Indian Health Institute, 224–25
Ursuline Academy (Montana), 226–28, 252
U.S. Commission on Civil Rights, 64, 297–98
U.S. Congress, 33, 66, 72, 91, 135, 196–97, 210–11, 288, 297, 302
U.S. Constitution, 28, 41, 175, 197–99
U.S. Court of Appeals (D.C.), 27–28
U.S. Department of Defense, 168, 297
U.S. Department of Education, 92–93, 97, 99, 117, 277
U.S. Department of Education's Office for Civil Rights, 87–90, 110, 133–34
U.S. Department of Housing and Urban Development, 300–301
U.S. Department of Justice, 50–51, 92–93, 97, 210, 257–58
U.S. Department of the Treasury, 72
U.S. District Court (D.C.), 27
U.S. federal government, 64, 72, 76, 103, 305
    antidiscrimination claims and, 159
    failed Native American tribes, 228
    and its protection of women, 196–98, 210–11
    mandates reforms in school, 95–96
    collects sexual assault data, 19–20, 214–15, 297–98
    takes up gender violence issue, 279, 298

U.S. House, 61, 175, 206, 248–49
U.S. Merit Systems Protection Board, 19–20
U.S. Olympic Committee, 120
U.S. Senate, 27, 42–43, 46, 50, 56–61, 68–69,
    168–69, 261–64
U.S. Senate Ethics Committee, 269
U.S. Senate Judiciary Committee, 257
    of 1991, 2–4, 33–43, 50–54, 57–62, 66, 69–70,
        75, 180, 231, 233, 267, 269, 280, 287, 294
    of 2018, 45–62, 66, 69–70, 210, 265, 279–81
    disregard for sexual harassment, 69–72, 210,
        278, 296–97
    gender/racial makeup of, 50, 58
U.S. Supreme Court
    defines school responsibility, 101–4
    first sexual harassment case of, 30–31, 195
    guts VAWA's protections, 293
    and mandatory arbitration case, 270–71, 286
    peer-on-peer harassment cases and, 99, 101–4
    and racial discrimination case, 197
    role in addressing gender-based violence,
        59–61
    and social media harassment, 79
    and workplace harassment, 65–66, 196–99
    See also Brett Kavanaugh confirmation hearing;
        Clarence Thomas confirmation hearing;
        specific cases
USA Gymnastics, 119–20

Valizadeh, Daryush, 167
van der Kolk, Bessel, 86, 88, 93
Vance, Maetta, 65–66
Vance v. Ball State University, 65–66, 71, 73, 286, 302
Vassallo, Trae, 152–53
verbal harassment, 7, 23–24, 34, 64–66, 87, 123,
    146, 201. See also homophobic slurs; racial
    slurs
Verdú, Sergio, 137–38
victim-centered solutions, 294, 303–6
victims/survivors, 2–5, 9, 70–71
    burden of proof and, 187, 278
    coping mechanisms of, 38–39, 63, 225
    credibility of, 61–62
    have a right to be heard, 52–53, 57–58
    and memories of assaults, 54, 57, 86
    personal harm/terror of, 68, 70, 202–5
    self-doubt of, 39–40, 51, 69
    and speaking up/out, 246–49, 254, 259–60
    why they don't report abuse, 88, 280–81
Vinson, Mechelle, 30–31
Violence Against Women Act, 168–69, 196–98,
    207, 228–29, 291, 293, 302
Virginia Polytechnic Institute, 210

Wal-Mart Stores Inc. v. Dukes, 286
Walker, Alice, 233–34
Wallace, Michele, 233
Walsh, Debbie, 61
Walsh, Seth, 92–97, 108, 111, 246
Warren, Elizabeth, 68–69
Washington Post, The, 83–85, 269
Watkins, Mel, 233–34
We, As Ourselves, 243
"We Have Her Back" pledge, 167
Weinstein, Harvey, 202–3, 216, 286
Well (blog), 81
"What Men Do to Women on the Job," 18
White House Council on Women and Girls,
    214, 293
White supremacists, 167, 234, 262, 287
Whitmer, Gretchen, 287
Whitney, Ruth, 288
Whittaker, Meredith, 157–58
Wiegand, Shirley, 31
Wilkerson, Brenda Darden, 55
Will, George, 143, 274
Williams, Patricia, xiv–xv
Williams, Spencer, 24–26, 28, 34
Winkler, Jack, 123
woke generation, 79–80
"woman's sphere," 198–99
women of color, 7, 51–52, 208,
        242, 305
    and criminal justice system, 237
    and gender-based violence, 175, 241
    gender pay gap and, 173
    at higher risk of assault, 6, 220–22,
        238, 241
    keep silent about abuse, 250
    overlooked, 148, 172
    as political candidates, 60, 167
women's rights, 60, 200, 264
    movement, 160–61, 169, 176
    suffrage, 160, 167, 173–76, 205, 209
Women's March (2017), 56, 60, 206–7,
        264–65, 290
Wood, Carmita, 21
Woodiwiss, Catherine, 181–82
World Bank, 12
World Conference on Women (1995), 272
World Health Organization, 189
Wynn Resorts, 201

Yale Law School, 121–22
Yale University, 21, 57, 117–18, 121–24, 130, 171,
        276–78
Young, Andrew, xii